Guide
to the
Successful
Thesis and
Dissertation

BOOKS IN LIBRARY AND INFORMATION SCIENCE

A Series of Monographs and Textbooks

ADDITIONAL VOLUMES IN PREPARATION

Guide to the Successful Thesis and Dissertation

A Handbook for Students
and Faculty

Third Edition,
Revised and Expanded

James E. Mauch and Jack W. Birch

University of Pittsburgh
Pittsburgh, Pennsylvania

Marcel Dekker, Inc.   New York•Basel•Hong Kong

Library of Congress Cataloging-in-Publication Data

Mauch, James E.
    Guide to the successful thesis and dissertation: a handbook
for students and faculty / James E. Mauch and Jack W.
Birch. — 3rd ed., rev. and expanded.
    p. cm. — (Books in library and information science; v. 55)
    Includes bibliographical references (p.) and indexes.
    ISBN 0-8247-8972-5 (alk. paper)
    1. Dissertations, Academic — Handbooks, manuals, etc. 2.
Report writing — Handbooks, manuals, etc. 3. Research —
Handbook, manuals, etc. I. Birch, Jack W. II. Title. III. Series.
LB2369.M377 1993
808'.02 — dc20   93-13645
                                                            CIP

The publisher offers discounts on this book when ordered in bulk
quantities. For more information, write to Special Sales/Profes-
sional Marketing at the address below.

This book is printed on acid-free paper.

Marcel Dekker, Inc.
270 Madison Avenue, New York, New York 10016

Current printing (last digit):
10 9 8 7 6 5 4 3 2 1

PRINTED IN THE UNITED STATES OF AMERICA

To our wives, Rebecca and Jane

Preface

This book is designed to inform and advise about the thesis and dissertation process, how to get through it and get the most out of it. The fact that half of the students who complete course requirements do not go on to complete the dissertation (in some schools as high as 70%) makes our objective more urgent (Monaghan, 1989).

This third edition was prompted by suggestions from students, colleagues, and other users of earlier editions. In response to those helpful recommendations and our own observations, we believe that the book is substantially improved in the following ways:

- More attention is given to the use of up-to-date technology, (e.g., computers and software) in the thesis and dissertation process, from initial research to writing the final results.
- New suggestions designed to help foreign students are made, with special emphasis on critical points, such as helpful advice for advisors of foreign students.

- Reorganization, consolidation, and altered sequencing of topics, with an enlarged index, should enhance its use as a reference.
- By including additional suggestions for students and faculty in the academic disciplines, we have tried to balance the second edition's emphasis on the professional disciplines, so the book promises to have broader usefulness.
- The three general forms of dissertation now current in higher education — theoretical syntheses, policy analyses, and empirical studies (see page 93) — are recognized and acknowledged to be different but equally appropriate ways to assemble data and focus on a problem, depending on the nature of the problem to be addressed.
- A very useful table of contents is offered for both the thesis and the dissertation, as models for student researchers.
- A checklist for theses and dissertations is included to help student researchers in critiquing and revising their own first drafts, as well as the work of others.
- More than a dozen operational models have been spelled out for dealing with specific problems in the thesis and dissertation process, from topic selection through evaluating the finished product.
- Attention is given to the honors thesis as an important and rapidly growing category of student research.
- This edition's bibliography is probably the most comprehensive one in print on the thesis and the dissertation.

Perhaps the most unusual quality of this book is that it is addressed to both students and faculty members. Certainly it is aimed primarily at students. Yet we found it necessary to write both to the student and to the thesis or dissertation committee members in order to convey certain concepts like colleagueship and consultation. So one should not be surprised that the student is advised about interactions with committee members at the same time that suggestions are given that committee members might apply in their dealings with students. We hope that our treatment of the subject encourages discussion between and among all who are involved in the enterprise.

One of the surprising weaknesses in the thesis or dissertation process is that there is relatively little scholarly literature and a remarkably small number of empirical investigations about it. This is true not only for the professions but also for the arts and sciences and all aspects of the honors thesis.

A few comparative and descriptive studies of T/D topics do exist. However, the theoretical articles and the data-based studies one might expect to find about the principles and processes of such an important part of academia are few. That is why we report little hard evidence on most of the issues in thesis and dissertation preparation. In fact, we found it necessary to conduct our own investigations to help us arrive at the viewpoints we present in the various chapters.

To broaden our database we interviewed more than 100 faculty members, each of whom had directed more than five dissertations. The insights they shared during structured and informal interviews that averaged considerably more than one hour each afforded us an unparalleled opportunity for learning. The findings from those interviews, supplemented by publications, constituted the raw material from which the various chapters were constructed.

When we spoke to university colleagues about our work during the years we were preparing this book, the most common reaction was a kind of happy surprise. The initial comment was, "Say, that is a great idea! There is nothing written about it and there really should be." The second comment was most often a wistful, "I really needed something like that when I started my own research." The third remark after we had talked a little about the proposed table of contents was, "I really wish I had a book like that right now!"

We are grateful to Professors R. M. Bean, A. Ducanis, J. T. Gibson, A. K. Golin, T. Hsu, R. D. Hummel, L. Pingle, M. C. Reynolds, M. Spring, G. D. Stevens, G. A. Stewart, M. Wang, and

T. Zullo for reading and critiquing the book, for using early drafts of the book in seminars, and for employing it with individual students in graduate research direction and guidance. We appreciate their wise and acute observations on how to improve it. For assistance in building a relevant bibliography we owe thanks to many professors, graduate students, and bibliographers from the University of Pittsburgh and other centers of higher education in the United States and abroad. We would also like to thank Dr. Carol Baker, Director of the Office of Measurement and Evaluation at the University of Pittsburgh, for her help and wise counsel throughout the years with respect to thesis and dissertation research and writing. Special appreciation is acknowledged, also, to the series editor, Allen Kent, for helpful counsel and support throughout.

Whatever merit the book has is owed in good part to the thoughtful help we have had from all who aided and advised us along the way.

We are naturally pleased that the response to our work has been both substantial and warm. We hope that the third edition will prove even more useful than the previous editions to students and faculty.

James E. Mauch
Jack W. Birch

Contents

8. WRITING THE MANUSCRIPT   225

The thesis/dissertation format   An approach to the first
draft   Using advice and technical assistance   The review
of the first draft   When the writing is finished   Summary

9. DEFENSE OF THE THESIS OR DISSERTATION   253

Structure of the oral examination   Preparation for the
examining committee session   Conduct of the oral examination   Decision making regarding the oral defense
Follow-up after approval or disapproval   Summary

10. THE COMPLETED THESIS OR DISSERTATION
AND FUTURE GROWTH   275

After the research is approved   Writing for publication
Improvement of one's professional or academic discipline
Follow-up studies based on T/D research   Reinforcement
for follow-up   Future trends   Summary

List of Figures

1

Getting Started

This book is for:

Students looking for practical help with honors and master's theses and doctoral dissertations

Faculty seeking instructional tools to use in seminars on research and with advisees

THE RIGHT BEGINNING

Two precious commodities dare not be wasted in T/D* work: student time and faculty time. Guidelines in this book emphasize high-quality effort, excellence of product, and minimum loss of time.

The four essentials for a good start are:

1. A clear understanding of the meaning and purpose of graduate student research work.

---

*For convenience T/D means thesis and/or dissertation and other terms used by various colleges and universities to designate the T/D work product. When necessary, distinctions will be drawn.

1

2. Accurate knowledge of what constitutes an acceptable T/D.
3. A detailed plan of action.
4. The technical skill to implement the plan.

These essentials are interrelated. Serious efforts should be devoted to getting all four well in mind right away.

Special Note: If you are unfamiliar with computers, we urge you to immediately take an orientation course in the use of one, preferably through your own department or school. The computer can be of great help in all aspects of T/D study. A number of references are made to computer utilization in each chapter, with indications of the advantages that come from employing that technical resource. Also, you can get an overview of some of the kinds of assistance available if you turn to Appendix A.

MEANING AND PURPOSE OF THESES AND DISSERTATIONS

Clarifying the Meaning and Purpose of the T/D

Students who know the *official* answers to the queries below tend to begin the T/D process with more confidence and a good prospect of success.

1. What are the purposes of the T/D according to (a) your university, (b) your school, and (c) your department?
2. If more than one kind of honors or master's or doctoral degree can be earned in your department, which should you aim for, and why?

Avoid misunderstandings by talking with your academic or research advisor to get full responses to the above two questions. If answers are not available in writing, take notes on what you are told, and by whom. Then write a summary of your notes and give a copy to your advisor for verification.

Keep a copy of the verified notes. If any doubts linger, recheck your notes with the department chairperson. Here and elsewhere in this book we advise keeping verified notes. One key reason is that both faculty members and procedures can change during the period of your study and your verified notes can prevent your progress from being interrupted or delayed by such changes. It helps to use a computer file (see Appendix A) and to maintain a backup.

Distinction Among Honors, Master's, and Doctoral Levels

In the United States, honors programs are typically opted for by outstanding undergraduate students. Honors research normally takes place in the junior and senior years. Common to honors research is the requirement of proof of the student's capacity for independent scholarship, shown by the production, presentation, and defense of a senior thesis. That thesis is held to a standard of quality and depth usually reserved for the graduate level (*University Honors College*, 1992). The U.S. honors programs are substantially different from the British honors system, and students from countries that employ the British system (e.g., India, Pakistan, and some African nations) should not confuse the two.

Master's and doctoral degree research expectations are strikingly similar among schools. These statements, for example, are from an engineering school publication (Stuart, 1979).

The master's thesis must demonstrate the candidate's ability to make use of appropriate research procedures, to organize primary and secondary information into a meaningful whole, and to present the results in acceptable prose. The length of the thesis is not important so long as these ends are fulfilled. (p. 1).

The doctoral dissertation is expected to represent independent and original research in the field of the candidate's graduate study. It must add, in some fashion, to understanding in the candidate's field. Such contribution to knowledge may result either from the critical examination of materials not hitherto dealt with or from the re-examination of traditional materials by means of new techniques or from new points of view. The project undertaken must be of sufficient difficulty and scope to test the candidate's ability to carry on further research

[independently] and it must ensure ... mastering the skills
needed for such research. (p. 1)

These quotations illustrate an overarching concept: the T/D is
done to provide a demonstration of the candidate's ability to carry
out, with substantial independence, a rational investigation that is
significant in the field and to report the results in a sensible and
understandable fashion. There are marked differences among
fields as to what constitutes "independence" and "significant" in
the research process and product. Yet, essentially the same principles apply to thesis and dissertation study in all professions and
academic disciplines [Council of Graduate Schools (CGS), 1990b].

A major higher-education theme is that thesis and dissertation
study is part of learning to identify significant problems, investigate them, analyze the findings, relate them to important concepts
or issues, and convey conclusions and implications to others in
clear, objective prose. In that context, thesis and dissertation study
is a stimulating activity carried on by students in an increasingly
collegial relationship with faculty members. It is a culminating
and synthesizing activity based on prior study, and it should be a
launch pad for future independent investigations. Finally, thesis
and dissertation work should prepare graduates who become faculty members in colleges and universities to guide students
through the same experiences later.

WHAT CONSTITUTES AN ACCEPTABLE T/D?

General statements about the meaning and purpose of T/D work
need to be brought into sharper focus to be helpful in particular
instances. To accomplish that, students should ask their advisors
specific questions.

1. What forms of investigation, if any, are favored by the faculty
    of the department? What forms of investigation, if any, are
    unlikely to be approved?
2. Are any topics discouraged or even out-of-bounds for T/Ds?
    Are any topics of special interest to the faculty?

3. Does the department have a particular orientation (e.g., the family, public policy, geriatrics, or intercultural concerns) that characterizes much of its student and faculty research and other scholarly work?
4. Is there a published list of departmental faculty with notes about their individual or team research interests?
5. Are computer workstations and software packages available for student use in T/D work? Is the library automated and are its holdings accessible online?
6. Is word-processor-generated text approved for submission of the T/D manuscript? Is there a list of approved statistical packages?

In connection with Items 5 and 6, research-related computer terminology is listed and explained in Appendix A.

Inquiries like these six can be used to initiate conversations with one's advisor. Also, it is helpful to talk about such questions with students who have recently completed T/Ds successfully. It is suggested that notes be taken and summaries written after discussions with faculty and students. The more clarification one can obtain at this point, the more likely is one to avoid difficulties in the future.

MAKE A PERSONAL TIME LINE

A realistic Time Line projection is imperative. It helps keep the project on course and it encourages disciplined use of time. Moreover, it is a communication tool with the advisor and committee members. It allows advisors to react to and to be aware of the student's orderly approach. Our stress on the value of using a Time Line is reinforced by Bowen and Rudenstine (1992), who urge the use of Time Lines to help improve the effectiveness and the efficiency of advanced study in general and the dissertation phase in particular.

The T/D Time Line (Fig. 1-1) that follows can be used as it is or adapted. The Action Points may need minor alterations to make them match the specific procedures of a given school, but

Figure 1-1 The thesis/dissertation Time Line.

Student's name:_____ Date initiated:_____		
Step no. **Action points**	**Time estimate**	**Date**
1. Selection of advisor	_____	_____
2. Submit potential topic(s) to advisor	_____	_____
3. Tentative approval of topic by advisor	_____	_____
4. Departmental approval of advisor and topic	_____	_____
5. Selection of other committee members	_____	_____
6. Departmental approval of committee	_____	_____
7. Draft of proposal reviewed by advisor to show committee members	_____	_____
8. Proposal draft cleared by advisor	_____	_____
9. Meetings with individual committee members for comment on proposal	_____	_____
10. Considerations of committee on proposal with advisor	_____	_____
11. Inclusion of committee and advisor suggestions in proposal	_____	_____
12. Approval of proposal document by advisor and institutional human subjects review board	_____	_____
13. Proposal committee meeting	_____	_____
14. **Final approval of proposal**	_____	_____
15. Beginning of thesis/dissertation study	_____	_____
16. Progress reports to advisor and committee	_____	_____
17. Adjustments in study procedure approved by advisor/committee	_____	_____
18. Completion of study	_____	_____
19. First draft of completed thesis/dissertation written	_____	_____
20. First draft of thesis/dissertation typed in correct style and format	_____	_____
21. Review of first draft with advisor for corrections	_____	_____
22. Corrected first draft approved by advisor	_____	_____
23. Corrected first draft submitted to committee members	_____	_____
24. Individual interviews with committee members	_____	_____
25. Discussion with advisor to integrate committee comments	_____	_____
26. Advisor approval of changes	_____	_____
27. Final copy of thesis/dissertation to committee	_____	_____
28. Oral defense meeting	_____	_____
29. Correction as specified by committee	_____	_____
30. **Final approval**	_____	_____

each of the 30 items appears as an essential step somewhere in the process in most schools. It is helpful to put this T/D Time Line on your computer and to update it daily.

Start Now to Use the Time Line

First, define present status by checking off those items that are completed and circling the one or two currently under way. That allows a precise answer to questions like: "How is the investigation going? Where are you now?" *Second,* use the Time Line in planning. Reference to the Time Line encourages thinking ahead, making appointments with committee members, and scheduling one's own time. *Third,* use the Time Line to project one's graduation date. Universities commonly require that final approval (Action 30) be certified by the T/D committee by a specified date that falls some weeks prior to the close of the term in which the student intends to be graduated. Ordinarily the committee-approved final copy of the project must be submitted by that same date. Insert that date at the bottom of the appropriate column and work backward, estimating how many days, weeks, or months it will take to move from one action to the next, until the current status is reached. This vital exercise brings into the open any discrepancies between a student's wishful thinking and the actuality of the calendar. Most students find it helpful to enlist their advisors' aid in making time estimates and in gathering information about special considerations related to timing.

TAKE ADVANTAGE OF TECHNOLOGY

Most students are familiar with the calculator and the word-processing functions of computers because those functions are most helpful in completing assignments in college and university courses. *But very few students have had experience with computer usage and computer-related technology for the independent kind of research called for in theses and dissertations.*

Today's applications of integrated circuits and their linkages allow research to be done more quickly and more accurately.

Investigators can use technological tools profitably in almost every stage of a study, including pinpointing the topic, doing the literature search, selecting the research methodology, collecting, analyzing, and displaying the data, and publishing the results and conclusions.

Probably the computer would come to mind first if one were asked for examples of technological tools rich in research applications. The modern computer certainly has great value in almost every facet of research. And it definitely exemplifies high technology.

But not to be overlooked are a number of other devices of real potential utility, too. Here is a partial list:

Automated address file	Telephone answerer
Calculator	Telephone conference
Fax machine	Typewriter, electric
Photocopier	Typewriter, manual
Smart phone	Word processor
Tape recorder	

Also, many of these devices can be connected to one another at nearby or distant places to bring resources together for the researcher's advantage and to conduct procedures in a matter of seconds that would otherwise take hours or days of the investigator's time. In succeeding chapters, such technological applications will be suggested as they might fit the requirements of a particular stage of research. (See also Appendix A.)

The Terminology of T/D Work Needs to Be Defined

Terminology in higher education is not standardized. The definitions that follow do, however, enjoy common usage.

Thesis: The thesis is the product of a scholarly and professional study at the honors or the master's degree level. It is usually a document in a format and style specified by the particular university. (Sometimes "thesis" is regarded as a synonym for "dissertation." That is acceptable, but we elect to link thesis with

honors or master's degree studies and dissertation with the doctorate.)

Dissertation: The dissertation is the product of student work at the
doctoral level, distinguished from thesis study chiefly by its deeper,
more comprehensive, and more mature professional and scholarly
treatment of the subject.

Proposal: A proposal (synonymous with "overview") is a written
plan for a thesis or for a dissertation developed by a student for
consideration and possible approval by a T/D committee.

T/D Committee: The T/D committee is a group of faculty members, usually at least three for the thesis and four for the dissertation, responsible for assisting the student in planning a proposal,
for determining if it is approvable, for guiding the student in the
conduct of the study and in preparing the T/D, and for examining
the student at the end of the process.

T/D Advisor: The T/D advisor is the faculty member officially
designated to chair the T/D committee and to have chief responsibility for the student's guidance in all matters through the process;
sometimes also called the research advisor; not necessarily the
student's academic advisor.

T/D Chairperson: The chairperson and the T/D advisor may be the
same person or they may be two different persons. In the latter
case, the chairperson has primary responsibility for convening
meetings of the committee, monitoring matters of regulation and
protocol that need to be observed, and assuring that the student's
rights and privileges and those of the faculty members are understood and not abridged. Thus, the research advisor has primary
responsibility for guiding the student in the conduct of the study
and in the preparation of the T/D document.

Graduate Office: The graduate office is the university office with
responsibility for issuing, implementing, and interpreting regulations about the T/D, such as forms to be used, time schedule of
events, and style guides. This office also usually has record maintenance functions. For the honors thesis the above functions are
usually located in the office of the dean of the honors college.

Academic and Professional Disciplines: There will be occasions to refer to substantive bodies of knowledge in the sciences, humanities, and arts such as physiology, history, literature, philosophy, chemistry, and music, as well as reasons to refer to such professional fields as education, law, social work, nursing, and engineering. In many lexicons, these bodies of knowledge are called "disciplines." In order to clarify a distinction that is grounded in a real difference, we will refer separately to the "academic" disciplines and the "professional" disciplines, as in the following illustrations.

Examples of academic disciplines	*Examples of professional disciplines*
Art	Accounting
Chemistry	Architecture
Economics	Clergy
English	Education
Geology	Engineering
History	Journalism
Information science	Law
Linguistics	Library science
Mathematics	Medicine
Music	Military
Philosophy	Pharmacy
Physics	Social work
Psychology	Theater arts

The person trained in an academic discipline is master of a large and involved, but unified, body of knowledge and is primarily interested in adding to that body of content. The person trained in a professional discipline, on the other hand, is master of diversified information and concepts that focus on the efficient and effective conduct of some operation, such as teaching, treating an illness, trying a case in court, or designing or directing plays. So it is reasonable to expect that T/Ds done in the academic disciplines and the professional disciplines would differ.

Characteristic Similarities and Differences Between T/D Research in Professional and Academic Disciplines

Similarities: The same three elements must be present in all acceptable T/D work in both the professional and the academic disciplines: originality, individuality, and rigor. Originality means that the research has not been done before in the same way. It is rare to find a topic that has not been researched before to some extent and by some procedure. So originality does not mean that the research questions or hypotheses are entirely new. Instead, the "originality" criterion is met if the student continues to study an unresolved problem in a way that is substantially different from prior approaches and that has a reasonable prospect of adding to an understanding of the problem. Also, replication of prior research meets the "originality" criterion if features are added to the replication that make it possible to check on the procedures and findings of the earlier study, thus making the replication more meritorious research than was that being replicated.

Individuality means that the study is conceived, conducted, and reported primarily by the student. Topics may often be suggested by others. Also, advisors may help in thinking through the concepts and the procedures to be used. But the chief decisions about whether to study the topic, how to study it, and how to report it must be made, rationalized, and defended by the student. When one applies the "individuality" criterion, it is difficult to accept a T/D that is simply "a piece of" a large research project being carried on by the advisor. If a student's T/D is to be related to the research program of the advisor (and that idea has much to recommend it), special care must be taken to assure real independence for the student in conceptualizing and conducting the study.

The third element common to T/D work in the academic and professional disciplines is rigor. To attain rigor means to be characterized by strict accuracy and scrupulous honesty and to insist on precise distinctions among facts, implications, and suppositions. Rigor is achieved by sticking to demonstrable facts when reporting procedures and results, by building on a foundation of facts when drawing conclusions, by specifying links to facts when inferring implications, by always bringing forward *all* relevant data, and by being both self-critical and logical in reporting and when projecting needed research.

The individuality, originality, and rigor criteria are common requisites for investigations in both the academic and professional disciplines, even though research in the two kinds of disciplines may differ markedly otherwise. And there are real differences both in objectives and in procedures, as elaborated in the next section. Many students and faculty members take up work in professional schools after study and experience in academic disciplines. For them, especially, as well as for T/D students in general, it is valuable to compare and contrast research in the two settings.

Despite overlap in the topics studied, we have found seven points on which there are conceptual or administrative differences (see Table 1-1). To make the differences explicit, read item 1 under *Academic Discipline Research* and then item 1 under *Professional Discipline Research*. Note the contrast. Then do the same through the list of seven pairs of items.

These seven comparisons should help students and faculty members to clarify their thinking as well as to recognize and rationalize the differences listed. It should be evident that there is no special quality in any T/D work that does not have its roots in the social-professional mission it is intended to support and foster. Thus, the better one understands the social role and function of a profession or an academic discipline, the better prepared one is to conduct or direct T/D study within it.

Note also that within a professional discipline there may be distinctions between "applied or practice-oriented" T/D and "theoretical or concept-oriented" T/Ds. *Now is the time* to ascertain whether your school or department values that distinction and what it might mean for you.

Table 1-1 Distinctions Between Research in Academic Disciplines and Professional Disciplines

Area of difference	Academic discipline research[a]
Purpose of the research	1. The chief purpose is to increase knowledge in a particular disciplinary field.
Nature of the problems researched	2. The topics studied are clearly linked to other problems previously studied within the prescribed and academically recognized bounds of the discipline. Thus, a physicist or philosopher might say of a proposed topic, "Interesting, but it isn't physics (or philosophy)," and fully expect that a great majority of colleagues would agree.
Criteria for assessing the worth of the research	3. The worth of a thesis or dissertation is assessed chiefly on the basis of the amount it advances knowledge, clarifies or adds to a theory, or stimulates further investigation.
Reasons for gathering knowledge through research	4. Knowledge is accrued for its own sake.
Position on the relevance of values	5. Matters of value are deliberately eschewed, except as primary data. The objectivity of the academic scholar is most closely tied to dealing with concepts, ideas, animate or inanimate objects, materials, documents, and events.
Methodology of research acceptable	6. Each academic discipline has certain especially respected methods, legitimized by the power they have shown in helping uncover or prove matters of importance to the discipline. Witness the controlled experiment in chemistry or the dig plus analysis and documentation in archaeology or physical anthropology (later polished by hydrocarbon dating).
Who may approve acceptance of a T/D	7. The thesis or dissertation is submitted to judges from within the discipline. The candidate's examination may be relatively public (within the university community), but its approval or disapproval is in the hands of three or four members of the discipline, perhaps with one additional voting examiner from a closely related discipline.

[a]Compare with like-numbered statements under "Professional discipline research" in latter part of table.

Table 1-1 (continued)

Professional discipline research
1. The chief purposes are twofold: to increase knowledge about a matter relevant to the practice of the profession and to reinforce the attitude of using objective and systematic approaches to problem solving. 2. The problems studied may range anywhere in the realm of human concerns so long as they also have demonstrated implications for society's professional enterprises. 3. The worth of the T/D is judged mainly by the potential applications of the results and conclusions in professional practice and knowledge. 4. Knowledge is accrued to validate or to bring into question aspects of professional practice, to create better practices, and, generally, to foster and guide the improvement of the profession and its services. 5. Both matters of substance and of value can be legitimate and necessary topics of inquiry; sometimes values are the essential data subjected to study. 6. Methods of investigation used are invented or adapted to suit the problems that need to be probed. Investigators freely borrow procedures from the academic disciplines or from other professional disciplines if they seem to have promise. 7. The acceptability of the thesis or dissertation is judged by members of the profession who have backgrounds consonant with the topic of the investigation. Also, it is prevailing practice to invite the participation of specialists from academic disciplines or other professional disciplines whose competencies bear especially on the topic. Approval is usually by a majority vote of the four or five examining committee members who are also graduate faculty members of the university.

The next section turns to the following questions: What factors go together to make up a high-quality T/D? How can students make those factors operational in getting started on their own work?

CHARACTERISTICS OF HIGH-QUALITY STUDENT RESEARCH

In a thesis or dissertation it is the integrity and objectivity of the investigator that count most. These criteria prevail regardless of the form of investigation or analysis used. *Integrity* is shown when every component of the study is carried out with scrupulous honesty. The criterion for *objectivity* is met if the investigator recognizes and sets aside any personal interests and desires about outcomes and maintains a steady state of scientific and professional inquiry from the beginning to the end of the project.

For a definitive analysis of these important concepts we recommend three works: *Honor in Science*, (1991), *On Being a Scientist* (National Academy of Sciences, 1989), and "Breaking Faith" (Root-Bernstein, 1989).

What Is High-Quality Dissertation or Thesis Research?

Research cannot take the place of thoughtful reflection and even-handed deliberation. Research can produce facts and ideas which, in turn, can fuel thought. Research can help the investigator to know whether or not all relevant matters are being considered in the study of a problem. But research itself does not produce solutions. Human thought—not research—is the sovereign problem solver. Only when thought is applied to the information unearthed by research is it probable that valid, reliable, and operationally useful outcomes can be expected. Thus, the quality of an investigation is a function both of the research that has been done and of the human cognition that has been applied in the process.

Some consider that the term *research* should be applied only to a very restricted form of controlled, experimental scientific inquiry. But that point of view leaves out many important realities in the professions. Also, the investigations of historians, anthropologists, or sociologists would frequently not qualify for the title *research* under that rule, nor would many of the studies in the arts and in literature. Those who invent new theories, new psychosocial measures, new techniques of instruction, or who design new curricula or do qualitative research would often be excluded, too, despite the fact that they may employ very sophisticated procedures leading to objective evaluations of what they do.

If the term *research* is to be used meaningfully in the context of T/D study, it must encompass not only controlled experimentation, but also many additional forms of planned, thoughtful, investigative activities. The definition should be broadly inclusive, encouraging full use of the ability and the creativity of the student and the advisor. The following definition of research best accommodates these needs. "Diligent and systematic inquiry or investigation into a subject in order to discover or revise facts, theories, applications, etc." (Flexner, 1987, p. 1219). It is only fitting that the specific nature of T/D work, and how "research" is defined, should depend on the kinds of problems that need to be investigated to enhance the particular body of knowledge of concern in each discipline.

No one research approach is inherently better than another. Rather, there are research methods that match some problems well and others poorly. For example, morale factors among supervisors probably can be studied more adequately through polling, critical incidents, or case studies than by other methods. If the question is the effectiveness of a new or modified traffic control system, it is probably best attacked through an evaluation procedure. For decisions about long-range building programs, comparative financial projections and analyses may be important contributing studies. Research about changes in motivation or about improvement in human skills may be best undertaken through applied behavior analysis or other forms of controlled experimentation. Researchers need all forms of investigation, need to respect them equally, and need to attempt to link each problem to the research approach that has the best likelihood of helping to apply human thought to solve it. Such types of research are illustrated in Chapter 4, with examples.

THE THESIS IN AN HONORS PROGRAM

An honors program (sometimes called an honors college) is a distinctive undergraduate course of study that is more than ordinarily demanding academically, that requires consistently high achievement, and that culminates in a senior thesis, through which the student demonstrates a proven capacity for academic initiative and for independent scholarship. The advisor and committee guidance during the thesis preparation and defense is similar to that found in master's degree study.

The Thesis as an Element in the Master's Program

The master's degree is a highly valued degree that has been increasing both in number awarded and in prestige (In brief, 1992). The number awarded grew 48% from 1970 to 1990. Since 1987 about 300,000 have been earned annually, most in the applied sectors like business and nursing. From the above survey, it was learned that master's recipients credited the degree program with helping "sharpen their ability to connect theory and practice, refined their critical ability, and allowed them to see the 'big picture'."

In preparing a master's thesis the graduate student can present evidence of the competencies required to make use of accepted procedures of scholarly inquiry. For instance, the student can combine data from primary and secondary sources into a unified presentation in correct and readable prose. The general objective of the thesis as part of master's degree study has been stated as follows:

It is reasonable to expect that, in a fifth year of academic work of respectable quality, a student will have had an intellectual adventure which can be described in writing. And such description gives an experience which will be obtained in no other way; by it, one is introduced to the methods employed in the acquisition, preparation and the analysis of material. Depending upon the field and the type of degree for which one is a candidate, this exercise may represent a small piece of research, the solution of a complex problem of design, a critical understanding of a sector of knowledge of considerable dimensions, critical appreciation or creative work in literature or one of the arts. (Report of the Committee on Graduate Work of the Association of American Universities, quoted in and adapted from the *Style Manual* of the School of Education, University of Pittsburgh, 1981, p. 88)

This statement did not differentiate between professional school and academic discipline master's projects. Note, too, its similarity in substance to the master's research requirement from an engineering school quoted earlier (Stuart, 1979).

Both the honors and the master's thesis can serve these functions:

1. They can give first-hand experience in conducting investigations and can familiarize the student with the kind of effort and integrity demanded by research. That, in turn, can help to prepare those who aspire to the doctorate.
2. They can make the student expert in at least one aspect of a professional or academic discipline.
3. Either can serve as a capstone for a significant unit of advanced study.

From 1940 to 1960 there was a rapid increase in new forms of master's degrees that do not require a thesis, a project, or a paper that approached the status of a thesis. We have found, we believe, a recent and commendable return to the requirement of theses and comparable papers in master's study. At the same time, honors programs with the senior thesis required have increased in numbers and in stature.

Preferred Practices in Student Research

Students and faculty alike are probably most interested in what characteristics a T/D should have to merit acceptance. That is what the student wants to know when seeking guidance in the selection of a topic and a procedure to use in studying it. That is what the faculty member wants to know when trying to decide whether to encourage a student to move ahead with a proposed investigation, or, later, whether to settle for what the student has produced at the end of a period of study, analysis, and writing.

A landmark national study reported on practices in doctoral study in the more than 100 institutions in the United States that had doctoral programs in the profession of education (Robertson and Sistler, 1971). According to that study, the dissertation "is considered a training instrument in the techniques of scholarly research and of reporting findings; it also represents a contribution to the knowledge of a given field." The Council of Graduate Schools, in 1990, stated that a "Doctor of Philosophy program is designed to prepare a student to discover, integrate, and apply knowledge, as well as to communicate and disseminate it." (CGS, 1990b, p. 1) Thus scholarly investigation and the presentation of findings to others is a pair of characteristics that has an historical association with doctoral research, whether in professional study or in the academic disciplines. Contemporary writing uniformly reports training in scholarly and research procedures and contributions to knowledge as the chief features the graduate student's research should have (Barzun & Graff, 1985; Cortada and Winkler, 1979; CGS, 1991b; Krathwohl, 1988; Martin, 1980; Porter and Wolfle, 1975; Sternberg, 1981).

Another feature reported by Robertson and Sistler (1971) was its service as the subject of a final examination for doctoral students. The last examination of the student by the faculty covered only the research project in 85% of the queried institutions. Three-fourths of the time this examination was oral. No institution used only a final written examination of the student's research. Approximately 10% used both, with the written test at certain schools invoked only if students did not perform satisfactorily in an oral interrogation. Less than 10% of doctoral programs had no final examination. The role of the final oral doctoral examination remains essentially the same today (CGS, 1991b).

THESIS AND DISSERTATION OBJECTIVES

Students may well ask, "What is involved in completing T/D work?" "Why should I do this work?" "What will it have to do with my professional and academic competence?" Faculty members, particularly new ones, can be plagued by related questions. "What am I supposed to be conveying to the students whose investigations I direct or on whose committees I serve? What really are the functions served by this phase of graduate study?" "What has this process to do with the purpose of the university?" A core element common to those questions is "Why?" For an answer we look first at the commonly stated objectives of graduate student research found in institutional publications.

General Objectives

Published objectives, as we said earlier, emphasize evidence of scholarly work, research competence, and contribution to knowledge. These have the validity of academic consensus. Faculties agree that both theses and dissertations should aim at those objectives. Moreover, they agree that those qualities should be easily discerned in acceptable documents submitted by students.

Operational meanings for *scholarly work, research competence,* and *contribution to knowledge* are not easy to specify, however. Criteria for judging those three matters are highly individualistic. They vary from faculty member to faculty member and among the academic and professional disciplines. Our findings from interviews with students, faculty members, and other university institutional representatives, therefore, led us to the decision to group objectives into scholarly work, research competence, and contribution to knowledge as major qualities to be developed or augmented in studies.

Objectives of Students

These include short-range objectives and those which look to the more distant future.

Professional and Academic Standing: Students often find that the qualifications they seek are linked to obtaining the master's or doctoral degree. Thus, the attainment of an advanced degree may be tied to goals like being recommended for qualification as a specialist in teaching, doing research, promotion in rank, supervising, managing, counseling, or a specific realm of practice or administration. Foreign students are often under specific direction from the ministry that provides the scholarship and support, e.g., an expectation that a Ph.D. will be earned rather than another doctorate. Hence, it is appropriate that the T/D be recognized as an essential short-range objective, the outcome of which will be evaluated by others along the student's way to some desired position, certification, or licensure.

Completing Course Work at a High-Quality Level: When the student's aim is doctoral study, the master's degree becomes a short-range objective, one which must be reached at an acceptable level of quality before doctoral study can be undertaken.* Some schools set a limit on the residence time, the number of graduate credits, or the particular graduate courses a student may take before completing the thesis, thus operationally defining the thesis as a short-range objective.

Staying Within the Statute of Limitations: Almost all schools put a time limit on the completion of the dissertation, too. Commonly, a statute of limitations reads like this: "The dissertation must be completed within three years of the time the proposal received initial approval." The number of years allowed may vary from school to school, but some such time constraint is all but universal, though extensions may be granted for cause.

Finding Good Advisors and Models: Students do detective work, trying to find out what faculty members consider an acceptable T/D. This effort to define what might find favor with potential advisors and committee members can be motivated by a sincere desire to do a worthwhile job because of what it means for self-

---

*Some schools permit or encourage students to move from the bachelor's degree directly to the doctorate. Students in those cases, we believe, should be advised to do directed independent study equivalent to master's thesis work along the way to help prepare them for the dissertation experience. Honors thesis students may be at an advantage here.

esteem and in gaining added respect from the faculty. In pursuing this objective students look for models primarily in the recently completed T/Ds of other students.

Foreign students are often especially dependent on their advisors, so for them the choice of an advisor may also involve affective considerations of empathy, learning styles, and personal relationships. Such considerations, while possibly important to all students, seem to be less an issue when cultural differences between students and faculty are small or well understood by both parties (Mallinkrodt and Leong, 1992; Mauch and Spaulding, 1992; Parr et al., 1992).

In short, it is natural for students to form pragmatic objectives in terms of the specific situations in which they find themselves and to react positively to the objectives created by the faculty.

Objectives of the Higher Education Institution

Institutional objectives are stated in broad, sometimes lofty, terms. Hence, it would be unusual to find them phrased in language specific to student research. It can be inferred, however, that the T/D elements of a student's advanced preparation are expected to be consistent with the institution's mission. The three statements below represent how a professional school faculty might phrase institutional objectives.

Providing Leadership: Preparation of leaders for the profession for communities, for state and federal agencies, for colleges and universities, and for other components of the public and private sectors.

Expanding Knowledge: Fostering theory building and conducting studies that create new and better approaches to our profession and encouraging and carrying out demonstrations that illustrate and disseminate information about improved practices developed at the university and elsewhere.

Improving Professional Practice: Development of master practitioners who will bring professional and humanistic advances to the fields in which they apply their skills.

As predicted, these statements say nothing directly about T/D activities. Yet, embedded in those objectives are clues to the kinds of proposals that ought to be well received at this particular institution. (It is suggested that students look for statements of institutional objectives and discuss them with their advisors. Not only will that trigger ideas about possible topics, but also it may help to establish part of the rationale for the selection of whatever topic is chosen.)

Objectives of the Faculty

Major faculty objectives for T/D activity are to enhance scholarship in the sense of looking for truth, to build on the existing body of knowledge, and to create original works. Steggna (1972) speaks of scholarship as an activity inherent in the mission of a university, one that should be exemplified in the work of the faculty. He calls it a faculty duty to search for the truth, add to knowledge, and produce new cultural materials. That role for scholarship is reemphasized, directly or implicitly, in more recent publications (Bowen, 1981; Ziolkowski, 1990). Certainly, the faculty efforts devoted to guiding student investigations should contribute to the discharge of that duty to an appreciable degree.

Yet, here we return to an earlier question: What is scholarship and what is scholarly work? The expressions are often used but seldom defined. This need for definition is more than a matter of intellectual curiosity—more than an academic question. For example, students who are told that their work will have to be "more scholarly" to be accepted really deserve to be given a definition in operational terms, plus examples. Likewise, assistant professors who have, after due process, been refused tenure because their publications were not sufficiently "scholarly" should have illustrations for comparison and criteria for reference. Tenure and promotion committees in universities are hard put also to define "scholarly" in sufficiently specific and objective terms to allow them to develop reasonable standards for the up-or-out decisions they must make. A more behavioral definition is needed. Any one chosen will not be entirely satisfactory. However, the definition below will be useful now and it may lead to a better definition in the future.

Inculcation of Scholarly Standards

Following is a list of seven characteristics which, in our judgment, characterize scholarly written work. Few scholarly works meet all seven criteria, but a work that meets none of them is almost certain to be in trouble with the scholars. Faculty members try to inculcate these seven scholarly qualities during T/D work.

1. A scholarly work is published in a respected, referred journal or in book form.
2. It has been available for a sufficient period of time to be subjected to the criticism of other scholars in the same field, and it has stood up successfully to that criticism.
3. It is based on the expert wisdom and literature of the field. The work indicates that the author is familiar with the conventional wisdom of the field, and if it departs in new directions, it presents a sound and rational defense for its departure.
4. It demonstrates the workings of a thorough, careful, critical, and analytic mind, looking at all sides of any proposition, examining and testing hypotheses, setting up and knocking down arguments, and marshaling in a complete and fair way all the facts in the process of critically analyzing the study's findings. A scholar will, of course, believe and support the findings of a careful investigation, but a scholar is not an advocate or a promoter. The scholar is even-handed and is willing to entertain the possibility that errors can be made by even the most watchful investigator. Scholars should be happy to find error in their own positions when such errors exist, for only in this way can truth be sought. (We suspect, however, that only in the *paragons* of scholarship can such a degree of virtue be found!)
5. It demonstrates to other scholars that the writer is a competent specialist who understands the theories and concepts of

the domain and who has a systematic knowledge of the chosen field rather than a smattering of insights here and there.

6. It is nonpolitical and amoral. It may, of course, be concerned with political and moral judgments and related phenomena as fields of study and specialization, but a scholarly work is not a polemic. It is not selectively cleaned up or toned down or otherwise slanted because it may be popular or unpopular with the contracting agency, the government, the church, the boss, or with professional colleagues. An essential ingredient to scholarship is the assumption that politically, socially, and morally unpopular and even repugnant works may be scholarly, and decisions about whether one should work in these areas and about whether or not they should be published, examined, and debated should be based on the scholarship of the work and not its popular "acceptability." Scholars seem to agree on this, but the point has to be made because everyone at times can find the commitment to free and open scholarship weakening under the various pressures that can be brought to bear so skillfully, subtly, and punitively by defenders of sacred cows (sometimes our own).

7. It must be useful, as indicated by how often others cite the work. This also constitutes an index of scholarship. A well-regarded, innovative, or provocative publication will be referred to frequently by others. Thereby, it demonstrates that it has qualities that are of significant value.

Evidence or Promise of Scholarly Work

As one reviews these seven standards, it becomes evident that student research would need to be on public view for some time before it could receive the in-depth testing implied in several of them. Moreover, it would be too much to expect that T/D work by students should match the productions of seasoned and polished investigators.

Therefore, it is *the indications* of and *the promise* of scholarly work, as characterized by the list, that advisors and committee members look for in the productions of their students. There are occasions when student work is qualitatively equal to the best of that of well-established investigators and theorists. But more often the faculty member is satisfied to lead students *toward* that level of attainment and to judge by comparison and inference whether or not students finally reach a respect for and an understanding of scholarship as a concept, internalize it as a goal, and demonstrate by their own work that they show substantial potential for attaining it.

Preparation for the Advisor's Role

In addition to the faculty's objectives that have to do with the student's attainment of a scholarly point of view and the promise of scholarly productivity, there are others. A major one concerns the student's own possible future role as an advisor or committee member for others. Faculty members who guide graduate students recognize that their own performances are models for their students—perhaps the only such models the students will ever know so close at hand and with such intensity. It is also plain to those faculty members that they will be both judge and jury in determining the extent to which their graduates are ready to help other students as fledging advisors.

Emphasizing Responsibility and Development

Especially important, too, in all disciplines, is balance in assessing graduate research scholarship quality. Earlier we noted the blend of pragmatic technology and pursuit of knowledge for its own sake that needs to be achieved. Alfred North Whitehead (1953, p. 199) said, "There is something between the gross specialized values of the mere practical man and the thin specialized values of the mere scholar. . . . What is wanted is an appreciation of the infinite variety of vivid values achieved by an organism in its proper environment. We want concrete fact with a high light thrown on what is relevant to its preciousness." That can be achieved by guiding students to insist that they be able to demonstrate that their work has relevance for the advancement of their disciplines while, at the same time, to show that it meets the requirements to search out truth, contribute to the sum of knowledge, and produce fresh material for the culture.

SUMMARY

A Time Line is one of the first essentials for a student who wishes to embark on T/D work. It helps to develop a plan of action. It has increased value, too, when linked to an understanding of modern technology, of the meaning and purpose of graduate student research, and to a grasp of the standards for acceptable work.

Students and faculty members, academic and professional, make important contributions through theses and dissertations. There is an historical Time Line, extending back at least to the Middle Ages, which validates such investigations as culminating achievements in advanced study.

In recent years academic disciplines and professional disciplines have moved into separate paths. The professions have matured, while continuing to acknowledge their roots in the arts and sciences. There are palpable differences now between the T/D in the academic disciplines and in the professions. Also, it is possible to specify some of their special characteristics. Purposes differ, depending on whether they are examined from the viewpoint of the student, the institution, or the faculty. Yet they have much in common. T/D study is growing. Both students and faculty need and deserve more objective and specific information about the process than they have had available in the past.

2

The Research Advisor

The research advisor, who typically also chairs the T/D committee, is the starting point for this discussion. Since the more common practice is to give students some voice in research advisor selection, it is valuable to know what that individual is supposed to do and how to make constructive contact with potential research advisors to assess their interests and compatability. We agree with Allen (1973), who said,

> . . . since you may be working with this committee for an extended period of time, you should – if at all possible – attempt to influence the selection of a committee that increases your chances of competing a high-quality research paper in the time you have allotted for the task. (p. 30).

Others have since advised or implied the same notion (Blanton, 1983; Krathwohl, 1988).

LEARNING ABOUT ADVISOR FUNCTIONS

The advisor is the most important person in the scholastic life of the student during T/D work. Moreover, university publications repeatedly stress that much of the initiative for finding a research advisor must come from the student. One reason is that faculty members are reluctant to seem to be "selling" students on their specific interests or their particular view of an area. Another reason is that choosing an advisor tends to be tightly linked to choosing a topic for investigation. That relationship will be noted in this chapter, but the details of topic selection are elaborated in Chapter 3.

Starting to Talk with Potential Advisors

A good place for students to start building a list of potential advisors is with the *faculty background booklet.* Many schools and departments supply students with an annually updated list (under some similar title) of the research interests and other scholarly activities of faculty members. Ordinarily, faculty members are pleased to talk about their interests with students. Such get-acquainted activities should be started by students soon after admission to advanced study.

Before approaching a faculty member, the student should be sure there is something to talk about. That calls for planning a brief agenda. One way to start is by reading one or two of the faculty member's most recent publications. Look for places where the faculty member calls attention to the need for more information or to prior research that did not fully resolve the matter that it attacked. Use those references to open the conversation; ask whether anyone known to the faculty member is doing research to close those knowledge gaps. Suggest that you might try to develop a proposal related to the question or questions, if no one else is already doing so. Be ready, too, with a few written first-draft research questions or hypotheses that you have developed on the subject(s), but recognize that neither the student nor the faculty member expects that they are in final form. The most important point is to show that a serious effort has been made in prepare for the interview and that the student has accepted responsibility for the initiative.

In some instances faculty members may demonstrate strong interests in subjects but have done little or no writing or research on their own. The previously mentioned form of approach is equally applicable with those professors, with one change. Since the faculty member has not reported work that can be studied, the student can seek out two or three recent publications by other specialists in the same field and then proceed in essentially the same way. In that case it is well to let the faculty member know that those particular publications are items the student will wish to discuss.

Still a third effective variation on this approach is to study T/D recently completed under the faculty member's direction. The majority of academic and professional T/Ds contain well-thought-out sections on implications for further research. Equally important, the faculty members who approved them had already tacitly agreed to the relevance and importance of the proposed investigations. Foreign students may seek advisors who have successfully worked with other foreign students or who have conducted or directed studies having a strong international component.

As part of getting underway on the selection of an advisor, we urge the student to do two other things without delay. One is to obtain, carefully study, and follow any policies, statements, or procedure that the local school or department has about research advisor selection. The other is to commit time to a careful reading to the rest of this chapter and to at least skim the rest of the book to identify areas to be studied later. The background and action suggestions the book contains are intended to be useful in making the most of the student's important initial steps.

The Advisor's Role

The research advisor is mainly a teacher but also a guide, mentor, confidant, and senior research colleague. The role definition rests on the premise that the advisor is instructing the student in the final stages of learning to conduct investigations independently. Successful students and advisors often describe their relationships as similar to the roles of parent and mature offspring. The advisor, usually older, wiser, and knowledgeable about the ways of the university world, wields a considerable amount of power. The student, typically plagued with anxieties about the ability to do what is expected, looks up to the advisor as someone who has done it and who can teach or impart the needed knowledge and skill.

A general theory of the student-advisor relationship can be illustrated graphically as shown in Figure 2-1.

In its basic form the theory holds that the relationship at the outset of T/D study is one to one, with the advisor mainly in the role of teacher and the T/D candidate in the role of pupil. Then, as the work progresses, the relationship moves more and more toward that of a junior colleague collaborating with and maturing as a researcher under the influence of a senior colleague. That theory underlies the discussions and the recommendations about student-advisor interactions in the major contemporary reports on the subject (CGS, 1990, 1991b; LaPidus, 1990).

Currently the above theory fits best in fields where the prevailing model is that of the T/D scholar working, for the most part, alone, with no one else sharing the same or very similar research activities and goals. In some disciplines, though, T/D research projects are typically small components of much larger collabora-

Figure 2-1 Progress of student-advisor relationship.

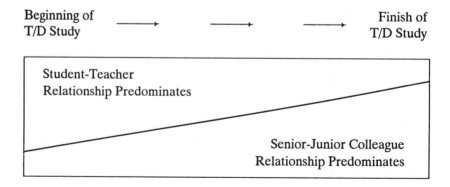

tive studies. In the latter case, the vested interest of the advisor in the research may prove to be paramount from the outset, with the result that the advisor takes a larger hand in managing the student's investigation from the very beginning, thus casting the student in the role of junior colleague and collaborator all the way through the T/D experience.

In a policy statement, the Council of Graduate Schools (1991b) says:

> Because of the inherent status differences of the participants, student/faculty collaboration can present opportunities for abuse; when students work on faculty projects, conflicts of interest can arise over ownership of the data and the research results. How is an equitable division of credit achieved for collaborative research between a doctoral (or master's or honors) student and his or her advisor? (p. 11)

The policy statement goes on to respond:

> Faculty and graduate students alike see a need for some mechanism to identify and evaluate a doctoral (or master's or honors) student's individual contributions to a collaborative research project.... Universities should have clear policies governing collaboration among faculty and students and among students. These policies should insure the integrity of the various functions of doctoral (or master's or honors) research and protect all parties' rights in the research results. (p. 11)

We agree with Myers (1993) who says:

> I have never met a student who did not hope to make a personal imprint on his or her dissertation. Often the research idea comes from the student's own experience. Even when this is not the case, there is a strong desire to implant one's self-concept in the work. Of course, there are examples of a student taking a minor spinoff of a sponsor's programmatic research. This is a very efficient way to do dissertation

research, but it seldom results in feelings of fulfillment for the student. The internal drive to make it one's own is powerful and pervasive. (p. 334)

Truly, there is collaboration, in the broad sense of willing cooperation, between students and faculty members inherent in the T/D process itself. But when collaboration promises to involve the student as one of a number of investigators jointly working on more or less connected aspects of a large research enterprise, the above general theory of student-advisor relationship (Fig. 2-1) needs the protection of clear, written guidelines to assure that the traditional purposes and goals of the T/D process are never unintentionally subverted, with the real loser being the student.

Students often feel absolutely dependent on the advisor to finish. It can be lonely. The camaraderie of classes, groups, and grades is all but gone. Prior learning now has to be synthesized and actively drawn upon in a rigorous fashion to produce something of worth, something that will be open to the critical examination of the advisor and later a committee of learned peers of the advisor.

Although the roles are different, both students and advisors aim for successful completion. Like any good parent, the advisor becomes anxious if the student falters, if there appears to be a waste of time, fumbling, or indecision. Like a real parent, the advisor will chastise, cajole, encourage, reinforce, and perhaps, at times, threaten. All this seems to be tolerated to a remarkable degree when the student respects and trusts the advisor and knows that the advisor is acting out of concern and interest.

The parent-offspring role can become unhealthy. There must be, after all, an academic respect toward the advisee in order that the thesis or dissertation preparation be a growth experience. Too much direction and hand holding can stifle creativity and independence, blind both parties to reality, and weaken the selectivity of the program. No matter how humanistic our concerns, it is difficult to argue that all candidates in an honors, master's, or doctoral program should complete it. The parent who defends a child under any circumstances is understandable, but the advisor who defends an advisee under any circumstance has gone beyond the bounds of appropriate behavior.

A more appropriate role for the advisor is that of advanced instructor. Here the advisor presumes that the student is a mature person, possessing the skills and tools of research appropriate to the topic.

A colleague, C. Baker (personal communication, Dec. 18, 1992), has collected statements made by students to advisors that she labeled "things dissertation advisors hate to hear." These statements were gleaned from years of experience working with graduate students and their advisors:

Things dissertation advisors hate to hear:

"Just tell me what to do and I'll do it!"

"It would be much easier if you gave me a topic to investigate."

"I know it's taken me 6 months to revise my overview, but could you possibly have it read by tomorrow?"

"What rules were in effect when I started the program?"

"You mean that I should have committee members from *my* program?"

"I'll study any topic as long as it doesn't require statistics."

"Don't expect me to know what I'm doing; I've never written a dissertation before."

"You have to sign off on this because I have made arrangements for my family to fly in from across the world for graduation."

"Couldn't you make an exception in my case?"

Advisor advocacy is appropriate, but it has to be accompanied by advisee responsibility with respect to identifying the topic, personally conducting the research, setting reasonable and realistic goals and meeting them, and using clear language in writing. If the student fails in any of these respects, without acceptable cause, it is time for some difficult evaluation and reassessment, with requests for appropriate changes in behavior. The student has the right to know what is expected, to understand and discuss these expectations, and to know the consequences of failing to meet them.

Phases of Faculty-Student Interactions

From experiences related by faculty members it is possible to identify three sequential phases of faculty-student interaction. First is an *exploratory* phase; the student is given encouragement to look for an area of study. Having been contacted by a student, the advisor throws out leads and gives information about where and how to look for problems in need of investigation. But the student is not directed toward specific problems. The advisor supports the search and offers encouragement to continue it. This is an opportune time for advisor and student to discuss how best to use electronic technology to help accomplish the literature explorations — the browsing — and then to carry out the literature searches that are needed. Advisors can help students learn how to use computer-assisted literature searches to examine what has been reported in a particular "problem area" and to move from that activity to the identification of specific potentially researchable topics within the problem areas being explored. In this phase, also, the advisor informs the student of criteria that can be used to help determine whether a topic is one that would lend itself to T/D work. For discussion purposes, criteria can be grouped in three categories: the student's criteria, the advisor's criteria, and the institution's criteria. The latter include university, school, and departmental criteria. Chapter 9 supplies a suggested checklist of criteria.

The second stage in the advisor-student interaction sequence is one of moving toward *problem focus* . The student settles in on two or three problems in a topical area (sometimes more than one topical area). The problems are described and a beginning is made on stating their boundaries. Though specific T/D problems have not yet crystallized, there is movement in that direction. The advisor and student have fairly well-defined problem areas to examine. In this stage literature search is an important activity.

Also, reference back to the criteria discussed in the first stage should prove helpful.

The third stage is *generation of research questions or hypotheses*. The student formulates questions or hypotheses and tries them out on the advisor, on friends, and among the other graduate students, too. Still endeavoring not to be overly directive, advisors tend at this point to critique the students' toward a narrower and more precise problem definition. All of that is done, to the extent possible, in a spirit of cooperative helpfulness. Inadvertent discouragement of students at this stage is all too easy, for the closer the student comes to defining a T/D problem, the more strongly the criticism is felt.

The Advisor* as a Mentor/Tutor

Mentor "refers to a person of competence who volunteers to instruct a student in an area of mutual interest. . . . The person who finds a mentor will be able to prepare for a lifetime career without losing one's own identity. Out of the relationship comes the confidence in one's own ability to suceed by one's own efforts" (Sellin and Birch, 1981, pp. 105 and 108). Such a relationship is especially important to foreign students.

Mentoring is probably the most applicable instructional term for the style of faculty-student interaction in T/D work. Unlike a tutor devoted to subject matter, the mentor tends to become more sharing and confidential. The student is apt to learn in depth what the advisor thinks about topics of mutual interest. The faculty member who is truly a mentor is liable to learn much about the student's motives, plans, and hopes. The searching and reporting by the student often bring new information and insights to the faculty member, who, in turn, enriches the contacts with the student (and with classes) by talking about them.

---

*Some universities use the term *mentor* as the official designation for the T/D advisor. Fordham is an example. Mentor, in Greek mythology, was Odysseus' trusted counselor, in whose disguise Athena became guardian and teacher of Telemachus, Odysseus' son. Other meanings of *mentor* are adviser and wise one.

Both students and faculty remark that they learn from each other during graduate study. But there is little literature bearing directly on the learning experiences accruing from T/D study or advisement (Blanton, 1983; LaPidus, 1990). Hints as to potentially valuable procedures can be found, however, in the extensive literature on the education of the gifted. Most T/D students are in that category, based on conventional definitions (Sellin and Birch, 1980, 1981; Passow, 1979).

There remains however, a constant acknowledgment that the advisor has power that the student does not have and that the student may need to rely on. Krathwohl (1988, p. 262) urges the student to look for an advisor who, among other qualities, is "secure enough to stand up to others in your defense if she thinks you are right. . . ." He suggests asking other graduate students about potential advisors who have that strength and who are respected by fellow-faculty members for it.

The Advisor as a Model

The advisor is probably the only faculty member the student will see in action so closely and in such an intense way. Thus, it can be expected that the student, if later in the position to serve as T/D advisor to others, will be greatly influenced by earlier example. The behavior of the advisor is of signal importance, therefore, because it becomes the model for others.

To summarize, the Council of Graduate Schools characterizes the dissertation advisor in this way, and we believe that the same description should hold for the thesis advisor (CGS, 1990b, pp 7 and 8).

The principal advisor of a dissertation in particular is a mentor in a special position of influence and trust. Inasmuch as dissertation advisors have the most to say about whether the student has done adequate research, and make employment recommendations for positions after the degree has been completed, they have a most serious responsibilty to foster in the student intellectual autonomy, appreciation of the highest academic standards, and a realistic sense of appropriate career options for the particular case.

At all stages, advising is a reciprocal responsibility. Faculty are expected to be diligent in providing counsel and guidance, and to be available for consultation. They should demonstrate flexibility and critical thinking, a willingness to be challenged and to challenge constructively, and the desire to help the student to become better at research and teaching than they are themselves.

Both research and anecdotal evidence testify that advisors (and committee members) have power over students and that the power is sometimes exercised inappropriately (Heinrich, 1991; White, 1991). If a person is sexist, has racial or ethnic biases, enjoys bullying, or has other inappropriate tendencies and attitudes, a "safe" place to show them is where the victim is intimidated and has few, if any, defenses. Many women students, especially, develop a view of themselves as "victims" in the one-to-one advisor–student relationship (Vartuli, 1892). But women are not alone in experiencing the unprofessional behavior of certain advisors. Sexual harassment, for example, can occur in a same-sex advisor–student setting, though it is doubtless more frequent in cross-sex situations. But sexual harassment or harassment of any other kind is reprehensible and not to be tolerated.

Both students and faculty should be made aware that they will be given a fair, objective hearing if there are cases reported of inappropriate advances or insulting or demeaning behavior involving them. For all advisors and committee members, we propose this guiding rule:

I will never exploit my position of power or status to take advantage of a student – academically, professionally, socially, personally, sexually, financially, or otherwise.

Advisors who pledge themselves to this credo have set the foundation for being worthy models.

THE T/D AS A TEACHING DEVICE

Students and faculty both need to remind themselves that the T/D is a teaching device; that is at the heart of its reason for existence. The graduate student research process normally yields more opportunities for faculty and students to interact on a close academic and professional basis than any other institutional situation. Nowhere else in the university is so much individual time devoted to students by faculty, on a one-to-one basis, in examining substantive issues and academic–professional concerns at the edges of current knowledge and practice. The guidance of student research provides the major opportunity for systematic identification and attack on a problem of interest to both faculty advisor and student.

Practicum in Guided Independent Study

Thesis and dissertation study is aimed at increasing the student's ability to work independently on problems and researchable issues, building on existing literature. The ability to work independently on a research problem is one of the qualities that often separate those who finish and those who do not. It is not as easy skill to learn to the proficiency level required by the T/D; it depends very much on one's attitudes toward doing research and toward one's own professional skill. But it can be strengthened by going through earlier, similar processes successfully several times, thus building confidence. Some useful ways universities have to provide this experience are: enrollment for directed study, research papers in courses, and research seminars in specialized fields. These experiences should precede rather than parallel the dissertation if they are to be of maximum help. *

---

*A number of schools use a T/D seminar both as a screen and as an aid to students having difficulty. A typical requirement might read: Upon completion of course work and written comprehensive examination, doctoral candidates will register for the T/D seminar. There they are expected to develop a T/D proposal that will meet the approval of the seminar faculty. Students who do not prepare approved proposals after two semesters of seminar will meet with the student progress committee to determine future directions of study.

Perhaps at no other time in the graduate program is there such opportunity to help students work through questions about the nature of evidence, the nature of scientific investigation, the processes of inductive and deductive reasoning, and the drawing of inferences and generalizing, appropriately or inappropriately, from a body of data (NAS, 1989). Readings, lectures, examination of examples of good investigations, discussions, and hands-on experience in conducting research are all tools that should be common in the work of the advisors and students. At least the opportunity is there if the university provides faculty with the resources and if the faculty is competent to use the resources.

Long-Range Influences of Guided Independent Study

The impact of seminar research reports and of T/D production on future professional work is not known in detail. There is good reason to believe that such investigative activities do have an influence. Lewis Terman (1954, pp. 222-223) reported his own recollection as follows:

> I was a senior in psychology at Indiana University and was asked to prepare two reports for a seminar, one on mental deficiency and one on genius. . . . The reading of those reports opened up a new world to me, the works of Galton, Binet and their contemporaries. . . . Then I entered Clark University where I spent considerable time . . . reading on mental tests and precocious children. . . . By the time I reached my last graduate year I decided to find out for myself how precocious children differ from the mentally backward, and accordingly chose as my doctoral dissertation an experimental study of the intellectual processes of fourteen boys, seven of them picked as the brightest and seven as the dullest in a large city school. . . . The experiment contributed little or nothing to science, but it contributed a lot to my future thinking. . . . My dream was realized in the spring of 1921 when I obtained a generous grant from the Commonwealth Fund of New York City for the purpose of locating a thousand subjects of IQ 140 or higher.

Perhaps not many dissertations presage such monumental contributions as Terman's Stanford-Binet Tests of Intelligence and Genetic Studies of Genius, both active today. Many contemporary leaders in the various professions, however, can identify links between their master's and doctoral investigations and important work they did later.

Teaching Function Involved in All T/Ds

In guiding T/D work, teaching opportunity is constantly available to faculty members, whether in experimental investigations, critical analyses of social problems, health issues, developments in physics or computer technology, analytical study of public policy or practice, or developmental projects such as improving the mathematics curriculum or staff of a school. Studies in the USA and abroad indicate that most students need continued instruction in research skills during the time they are engaged in T/D work (Reynolds, 1987; Zuber-Skerritt and Knight, 1986). It cannot be too often emphasized that T/D activities should teach the candidate to (a) identify and critically examine alternative approaches to any question, (b) systematically marshal facts and data to support choices among alternatives, and (c) test the adequacy of these choices against the reality of the professional workplace and the views of one's academic colleagues.

An Exercise in Synthesis

Finally, the T/D should build on a synthesis of all earlier courses, readings, and professional experience that the candidate brings to the task. It is the major opportunity in the scholastic career in which all past experiences can be brought together in a creative independent work of the student's design. The synthesis is not accomplished without help, but is essentially an independent exercise; as such it is an opportunity for personal/professional integration unequaled elsewhere in higher eduation. The *instructional obligation* of the advisor is to set that goal before students and to help them both internalize it and achieve it.

SCOPE OF ADVISOR RESPONSIBILITIES

Advisors have responsibilities to a number of people and groups: the advisee, other students, the university, the school and department faculty, the fellow members of the student's T/D committee, the members of their academic field or profession, and the registrar and graduate office. While none of these should be ignored, most advisors set as priorities three main responsibilities: to the student, to the other committee members, and to the university.

Responsibilities to the Student

Advisors ought to be deeply committed to the belief that first responsibility is to the student. At no other time is the student so vulnerable and so in need of close identification with one faculty member. The advisor ideally should be as involved and interested as the student, within the restrictions of time and competing responsibilities.

The obligation to the student is expressed in part in a consultant relationship. The student should feel free to ask questions, try out new ideas about procedures or substantive issues, and obtain guidance and direction when it is requested. No other faculty member should be as ready to help in the dissertation process as the advisor, specifically with regard to two matters: the topic the two persons have agreed to pursue and the university, school, and departmental rules and processes applicable.

The help of the advisor in choosing a topic is expected. After all, the advisor too will have to live with the topic. The position of the advisor is delicate, steering a tight course between giving the student a topic and allowing a completely free choice. The risk with the topic chosen by the advisor is, of course, that the student may have little interest in it and may feel inadequate to tackle it. The possibility of conflict of interest arises, too. Will the study become an article or part of a book for the advisor? Is it serfdom —performing work that the advisor is unwilling to do? Such suspicions inhibit work and endanger relationships. If the suspicions are confirmed and the activity is allowed to continue, one wonders what the real purpose of the dissertation is in the eyes of the advisor, the faculty, and even the institution. It is still a learning situation for the student, but the model may persuade the observer that it is appropriate to use the university to act in unethical ways if it serves one's purpose and if one can get away with it.

The problem with allowing the student a free choice is no less difficult. It is a shirking of responsibility, putting it all on the student. It provides the perfect faculty excuse for failure at any point in the process: "Well, you chose the topic completely by yourself." It encourages a minimum commitment on the part of the advisor. It may deny the student the benefit of the experience and the expertise of the research advisor—one of the compelling reasons, presumably, why the university provides this very costly teaching relationship.

It is the research advisor's responsibility to ascertain that the topic is well thought out, that the student can give cogent arguments as to why the specific topic was chosen, and that these arguments cover all the standard questions in the literature, such as feasibility, efficiency, importance of the topic, competence of the student to attempt the specific topic, and a theory base underlying the student's understanding of the topic. (These are explored in depth in the next chapter, along with suggestions for satisfying them.)

The student should come to an acceptable topic with the advisor's sound advice, but not with a dependent or authority-beholden attitude. The student exercises independent judgment within criteria agreed upon, analyzed, and discussed with the advisor. Such a process regards both parties as mature human beings, capable of being self-directed, but capable also of recognizing and accepting suggestions from each other. Each will understand their mutual concerns and commitments to the topic. Each will understand the problems connected with the topic and will be prepared to help resolve the problems. This process can set the tone for interactions throughout the T/D study period and help to weather many storms along the way.

Unsatisfactory Student Progress: The faculty member who regards little or no progress at the T/D stage solely as student failure does not understand the advisor's job. Students' failure to complete graduate research work may ensue mainly from their own errors or failures, but in some ways the advisor, the faculty, and the university may have also failed.

In most university programs the student signs up for a substantial number of credit hours during the development and writing of the overview, the thesis, and the dissertation. The system is designed to reflect in a general way that the student is taking valuable time and that time carries with it costs to be paid and credits to be awarded. In many programs this is a substantial block of time — perhaps one-fourth or more of the total post-master's credits required for the doctorate. Viewed in this way, it becomes clear that the student has the right to reasonable faculty time and advice and has paid for this right. The advisor, especially, has then the responsibility of being available for help, advice, and guidance, and of offering such advice and guidance on the highest professional and academic level. Failure in the context of this system is seldom entirely one-sided.

Ethical Responsibilities: The advisor's professorial responsibility transcends material considerations. Whether the student is contributing directly to the support of the institution or not, one would expect the professional behavior of the advisor to be the same. In fact, this concept is at the heart of the idea of professionalism. Specifically, what are the ethical respnsibilities of the advisors?

First, the advisor does what is best for students in all professional situations. Although the principle is easy to state, it is not always easy to know or determine what is best for the students. Conflicting values make life difficult for those who try to maintain high ethical standards. For example, if a student hands in a paper that is not his or her own, or cheats on an exam, how does the advisor ascertain what is in the best interest of the student? Faculties face many examples of conflicts of values in what is best for the student, and agreement is not always reached. Nevertheless, there must be at least the sincere attempt to put the student first as a fundamental value of advising. An advisor who operates in this way—working as fairly as possible—is usually perceived so by colleagues and students; that action and perception helps to minimize ethical conflicts.

Second, the advisor avoids using the position for personal gain and refuses to accept the offer of such gain. There are instances where faculty admitted being given valuable gifts by an advisee, instances of lavish entertainment provided advisors by advisees, and the provision of other personal and professional favors.

If a foreign student proffers a gift and insists that it is considered an insult in his or her homeland to refuse to take it, the advisor can, gently but firmly, point out that they are not in the student's homeland and that the customs of this land must be applied. The advisor can then explain that here it is considered improper for a student to offer a gift and not approved for an advisor to accept one. It can be suggested by the advisor that the whole matter will be resolved with honor if both the student and the advisor agree to forget the incident entirely and return to their normal relationship.

Sometimes it can be difficult to draw an exact line between ethical and unethical behavior, but that difficulty is no excuse for failing to try to do so. It is the responsibility of the university as well as the profession to publish codes of ethics and to monitor ethical behavior. In our view, accepting any favors (or the promise thereof), awards, gifts, professional grants, and the like from a dissertation advisee creates an improper and unethical situation. It prevents the advisor from being critical or objective in evaluation. It creates conditions of expectation by the student. It is unfair to other students who are unable or unwilling to engage in similar behavior. The situation compromises the integrity of everyone it touches, indeed of the whole institution.

A *third* matter involving professorial ethics is the use of student work as if it were the work of the advisor, so that the advisor gains the credit. If each advisor puts the legitimate work of the student forward, encourages the student to publish, to read papers at professional meetings, to pursue further research, and to do all this under the student's name, there will be little likelihood that the advisor will have to worry about professionalism on this score. Certainly the contributions of the advisor, where real and substantial, should receive due credit. A guide that helps govern such questions is to divide the credits commensurately with the amount of work and time invested by each. If that guideline is followed, it is difficult to imagine how an advisor's name could appear at all as a coauthor, much less a senior author, on a publication arising out of a thesis or a dissertation done by a student unless a very substantial amount of additional analysis, interpretation, discussion, and editing is done by the advisor after the T/D has been approved by the final oral committee.

A *fourth* note on ethical behavior concerns competence. Qualitatively, within the narrow confines of one's own specialty, the self-examination of competence seldom arises. In fact, however, faculty competence varies a good deal; it is indeed the wise and ethical advisor who is aware of faculty limitations.

A reasonable position regarding competence would be something like this: be as parsimonious as possible in the selection of research-advising responsibilities; serve only on T/Ds of other advisors when you are sure you have a needed competence and can make a substantial contribution; be willing to admit that there are many dissertation areas where about the best you can do is learn from the student; and finally, lace the committees of your advisees with the most competent experts you can find. *

Maintain Competency: One of the important responsibilities of advisors is to maintain their academic and professional competencies. Without this, an advisor is not much good, and even may be harmful to the student. A faculty member maintains competency by reading the literature, by keeping up with the latest thought (even though the latest is not always the best), by teaching and keeping in contact with colleagues and students, by taking a

---

*For an example of published university guidelines on academic integrity, see those of your own university or *Guidelines on Academic Integrity*, published by the Office of the Provost, University of Pittsburgh, Pittsburgh, PA 15260.

meaningful part in professional meetings, by listening and discussing, and by speaking and writing. Perhaps no other activity keeps faculty as sharp as rigorous research and writing and the subsequent exposure to the critical analysis of colleagues and other experts. After all, one can say or write what one wants, within the bounds of propriety, before a class of students who will be graded on how well they restate it later; it is quite a different experience to address a group of colleagues and experts.

We do not maintain that the best advisors are those who do the most research and writing. The variables associated with excellence in advisors are too complex for such a conclusion. The point is that a given faculty member will probably be a more competent advisor for having personally done research and writing. We, in fact, feel so strongly about this point that we recommend that one of the criteria for the appointment of doctoral research advisors from among the general faculty be evidence of high-quality research and writing. We do not believe that such evidence would be as difficult to assess by peers as some may suggest.

Responsibilities to Other Committee Members

Traditionally the advisor chairs and sets standards of committee behavior. The research advisor sets the climate of expertise and high standards within the committee. No one else is in a position to have such a positive or negative influence on the committee climate, for no one else can set at so high a level the expectations for committee behavior. Most faculty will tend to conform to the expectations and leadership behavior of the chairperson of the committee. It is unlikely that the committee will rise above it. Indeed, the accepted (though unstated) rules of committee behavior make it very difficult for members not to conform to the pattern set by the chairperson.

Defining Committee Roles: Many advisors hold a preoverview work session with the committee to go over and agree to rules for operation. Sometimes the institution or a professional group has detailed standards for expectations (CGS, 1991b). At many institutions, though, each committee sets its own standards under general rules. Indeed, the frequently vague guides for students or faculty is one of the motivating forces behind the preparation of this book.

Useful rules with respect to committee role start *first* from the notion that the committee should know and agree upon its expectations for itself. These are best discussed openly and explicitly before individual instances come along to test the limits of the principles. *Second*, rules should enjoin the committee to act always in the highest interest of the student, consistent with maintaining high professional, academic, and institutional standards. Of course words like "high" and "highest" have to be operationally defined within the institutional context, but agreeing to the principle is a good place to start. *Third*, operating at a professional level implies that committee members consistently treat the student and one another with respect and maintain a collegial atmosphere. Persons can disagree without being disagreeable.

Encouraging Committee Participation

The research advisor has the job of assuring that the committee members participate throughout the T/D process. The committee is selected for the expertise of each individual and the student has a right to that expertise. Furthermore, if the members have been taking an active part throughout, there should be no surprises at the final defense.

The amount of guidance and time to be expected of committee members falls into proper perspective if it is understood that the research advisor has the primary responsibility for guiding the work of the student. The advisor keeps the committee informed of progress and assures that the student sees the committee members — or attempts to see them — periodically to keep them informed and seek advice. The advisor and student share responsibility to see that committee expertise is used and that committee members are kept involved. Specific ways to seek creative suggestions of members and to follow through on them are spelled out in a later chapter.

If the advisor and student sincerely try to involve the committee, the response is usually quite good. At the very least individual committee members will read the proposal, critique it, be available for consultation when the student asks for consultation, read the document and critique it before a final defense, and attend scheduled overview and defense meetings. Anything more is to be encouraged, desired, and hoped for.

Coordinating Committee Communications: Some faculty want all communication between the student and other committee members to come through the advisor; others think the student should feel completely free to spend as much time and take as much direction as wanted from committee members. These are probably the two extremes; most research advisors fall between them. It is more important that the advisor and the student talk out and agree on the ground rules than to argue about which procedure is best. Probably any reasonable procedure will work if the rules are agreed upon, and if the student understands the consequences of alternative kinds of behavior.

Special attention is advisable with foreign students since cultural differences often mean that the nature and frequency of written communication can create difficulties. A discussion can leads to understandings that forestall such problems.

Faculty experience had indicated certain procedures that are important responsibilities of the advisors. These are more in the nature of good common-sense advice than of laws or dictums. The advisor has the responsibility of negotiating with the committee — all of it — those things which a student cannot negotiate with the committee, such as problems that come up concerning necessary changes in the research during its conduct or personal difficulties of the student. The advisor has to see that the committee is kept informed. Sometimes the advisor does it; other times it is appropriate to make sure that the student sees or at least communicates with every committee member. When committee suggestions are sought on a draft, they must be thoroughly discussed by the student and the advisor, and the student should discuss and understand the risks and positive aspects of whatever action is taken.

The advisor has responsibility to draw a consensus from the committee so that the student does not suffer from faculty disagreements and so that the individual committee members can continue to serve without feeling that their scholarly reputations are in jeopardy.

The only guiding principle that merits support is for the advisor to relate to all committee members with integrity and academic respect. Good communication by the advisor gives all the committee members the information they need to be helpful and to use their expertise in assisting the candidate to successful completion of the T/D. Technology such as E-mail and Bit-Net has made advisor and student written communication easier. The same message can be sent simultaneously to the student and to committee members. Messages can be sent frequently and accurately, with the knowledge that all are getting the same information at the same time.

Administrative Arrangements: The advisor also calls committee meetings for the overview, the final defense, and for other purposes. Another obligation is to see that the student produces the T/D document in required form and has it in the committee's hands in good time before the meeting. The chairperson is also responsible for working with the candidate to ensure that all school and university requirements that call for committee action are met in timely fashion.

Responsibilities to the Institution

Higher-education institutions flourish largely because of the integrity of the individuals who make them up — students, faculty, administration, and staff. Not many other major societal units are so free of externally imposed laws and requirements. And few, if any, organizations are so self-governing. Individual integrity of consistently high order on the part of the members of the university community is an essential quality which has fostered that state of affairs and which must be present if university-based academic and professional preparation and research are to continue.

Maintenance of Standards: The first responsibility of the advisor to the institution is the maintenance of high standards of quality in all T/D and related activities. What constitutes quality is a value judgment, of course, but the judgment is not without guidelines. No other single person in the university has that responsibility or could ever discharge it if it were possessed—not the student, not the committee members individually, not the dean, not the program chairperson—no one but the research advisor.

Relevance of the Student Research: The advisor has the responsibility to assure the relevance of T/D work. It is not a frivolous document. It should relate clearly to the program or department in which the student is doing graduate work, or the question of where the dissertation and the student belong may be raised. If the proposed investigation has an evident and close relation to the expertise of the committee members, one aspect of the question of relevance is well answered. But perhaps the most important aspect of relevance is the advisor's responsibility to assure the relevance of the topic to the student. Does the student see the topic as related to his or her own long-term interests? Does the student have the background to work on the chosen topic? Has the student articulated well the reasons for the choice of topic?

These and other aspects of relevance are dealt with in more detail later, but two need to be named here: useful contributions to the field and usefulness to the growth of the student. Both are essential criteria in weighing the relevance of a topic. Without a rigorous examination of relevance, T/Ds can descend to the level of trivia. Highly relevant, well-conceived, well-executed, and significant T/Ds indicate top-quality professional and academic programs. The T/D is the one product that represents the best of the student, the advisor, the committee, and the quality of prior preparation. It must be carefully reproduced, bound, microfilmed, or otherwise preserved for posterity as the culminating work of long and demanding training. Whatever the student's subsequent career, the signed, bound copy of a relevant and scholarly T/D stands forever in testimony to the relevance and scholarship of the advisor and university.

Academic Interests: Advisor responsibility to the institution includes academic and personal integrity, and integrity finds it severest testing in T/D work, the highest levels of independent study.   The predominantly solitary or one-to-one T/D work leaves both the student and faculty member largely to their own resources.   Individual student behavior cannot be melded into that of the rest of the class.   There is no set course outline and no standard textbook with manual and tests to be interposed between the faculty member and the student.   There are not a specified number and schedule of class meetings.   Colleagues or assistants cannot substitute for the faculty member.   The student cannot find help in another student's notes.   Instead, independent study leading to the T/D is a type of student-faculty member adventure into the academic unknown.   The personal and academic integrity of each becomes a major ingredient in the enterprise.

Research advisors typically have rather hardy self-perceptions, and so do deans and department chairpersons.   Pressure on the advisors can become intense from several different quarters, and of course the advisors have to deal with their own self-concepts and senses of integrity.

Perhaps the best way to deal with possible role conflict related to integrity is to always keep in mind the question "What is the best course to follow in terms of the integrity of the process, the university, and the student?"   That question will not necessarily yield easy answers, but keeping the question foremost in one's thoughts is more likely to yield worthwhile answers than bending with whatever wind blows hardest at any given time.

Where there are no local institutional guidelines, the matter should not be bypassed.   Instead, personal and academic integrity should be discussed in terms of local custom and practice, even though unwritten, and in terms of more general ethical codes of professional associations.   We believe personal and academic integrity are not exactly the same, though we discuss them together.   For example, keeping or not keeping an appointment by a student or faculty member is a matter of personal integrity.   So is inventing a falsehood to explain not completing a task agreed upon, on the part of either. On the other hand, consciously failing to give credit to someone else for a previously stated concept or idea is a matter of academic integrity. So is failure to acknowledge a quotation or disguising it by reproducing it with minor alterations, and without citation.

Differences in Responsibilities at Thesis and Dissertation Levels

The thesis, as has been indicated, is a work of more limited proportions than a dissertation. While an end in itself for some students, it readies others for more comprehensive and complex investigations.

The thesis advisor works with the honors or graduate student (usually during the fourth or fifth year of university study) to produce a useful, well-written work, supported by evidence. Assessment practices differ, but preferred practice includes the overview of a committee. The work should be circulated in the department and published by the university or at least catalogued in the university library and made available for publication or microfilming for a wide audience. The principles of advisor-advisee relationships that apply to the thesis process are the same as those applicable to the dissertation as described in the preceding pages.

The responsibilities of the dissertation advisor contrast mainly in quantitive ways with the responsibilities of the thesis advisor. Academic endeavor, the attributes of scholarliness, use of reputable and replicable investigative procedures and scientific methodology, and a clear and readable manuscript are equally applicable. There is no reason to sacrifice those attributes because the work level may not be as advanced or the nature of the work somewhat different.

SELECTION OF THE RESEARCH ADVISOR

In the search for an advisor, it is best for the student to be armed with some understanding of how advisors operate. In turn, to determine what sort of advisor the student is most likely to need calls for considerable self-knowledge and the inclination to be objective about one's own assets and liabilities as a student.

The essential element we encourage the student to look for in the advisor is the special quality of thinking like a teacher. That is a skilled, articulate, rational, abstract thought process that sorts out the cold, hard academic and professionally relevant facts of the student's situation, ignoring the merely interesting and distracting incidentals. Its aim is to guide the student-advisor relationship toward the most promising topics and toward the most fruitful procedures for attacking the topics.

The student should not be put off because a potential advisor's special way of thinking like a teacher does not manifest itself in a warm and reassuring approach to problems. Sometimes aspiring T/D students are distressed by what they perceive as an icy detachment from their personal trials. These students may truly need reassurance in that part of their lives. Some advisors may indeed be the kinds of persons who tend to supply that reassurance to students. But the student needs to keep in mind the professional objective in the whole process: to obtain the best, most competent, most astute research advice and guidance.

The advisor may turn out to be, incidentally, a good family counselor, financial advisor, lay psychiatrist, and warm friend. But that is not the advisor's job. And in making decisions about the selection of an advisor, decisions that involve both immediate and long-range educational and personal objectives, it is helpful to keep that distinction firmly in mind.

Criteria for Selection of the Research Advisor

The single best criterion the student may use in seeking out an advisor for the dissertation is the track record of the faculty member. Traditionally, research advisors do not advertise. Thus, it is necessary for the student to seek these kinds of relevant data about potential advisors:

1. How do other students who are working with this advisor react to the situation?

2. Is the faculty member one who is or has been productive in theory and research of the kind that interests you?
3. Do students who work with this advisor progress with reasonable dispatch in their investigations?
4. Does the faculty member appear to be regarded highly by colleagues and by others you respect?
5. What has happened to the last four or five students who initiated their work under this research advisor?
6. Does there seem to be a strong element of trust between your potential advisor and his or her students?
7. Has the advisor worked well with foreign students on T/D committees?
8. Is the advisor current with respect to modern technology used in research and scholarly production?

These and related inquiries about past performances can supply data on which to base decisions. In all cases, a personal interview with the potential advisor is a good idea, once the student has some idea of the area of investigation.

A not uncommon situation in a graduate program is the assigning of academic advisors to students upon their acceptance to the program. Thus, the student has nothing to say about the initial assignment. This system may work reasonably well, particularly if it is easy to change advisors without fear of reprisal. However, the choice of a research advisor should be regarded as a separate decision from the academic advisor assignment. That is, the research advisor choice should be regarded by all as a conscious decision that the program expects the student to make, and the student should be completely free to choose to stay with the academic advisor or to go to some other faculty person for research guidance. There ought to be no stigma, difficulty, or discomfort attached to the choice, for the skills one looks for in a research advisor may be quite *different* from those possessed by an academic advisor, not better or lesser skills. Every academic advisor has the responsibility of telling students that they should carefully seek a research advisor, even to the point of suggesting one or two names if appropriate, and that they should not feel that they need to stay with their own academic advisor. This point is especially important for advisors of foreign students, for such students may understandably become dependent on the initial advisor. This is a subject that should be brought up by the faculty member, for it may be awkward for the student to raise it. In a number of cases, the academic advisor may well prove to be the most suitable research advisor.

Support from the Department Chairperson

What we have already said about the responsibilities of the academic advisor ought to be supported in important ways by the department (or program) chairperson. The chairperson needs to support the freedom of the student in this regard, and to protect that important part of academic freedom from the excesses and possessive abuses that occasionally creep into faculty-student relatonships. The chairperson should feel free to suggest research advisors for reasons of appropriateness, time availability, and fields of interest. Of course, such suggestions can in themselves become abused if the students and faculty do not feel free to reject them.

The Graduate Faculty's Role

As a collective body, the graduate faculty is responsible for the quality of graduate work, including the quality of advisement and the quality of the graduate student research that emanate from their domain. It is the responsibility of the graduate faculty to regulate the process to assure high quality. Where the graduate faculty fails to do so, there is no other mechanism for quality control, and the quality issue has no appropriate resolution.

Individual graduate faculty members also have something to say about the choice of advisor. An acceptable arrangement is made only when the student and the faculty member agree to enter into it. It is appropriate for the faculty member to decline to be the student's research advisor when, for example, the research area proposed is outside the field of interest or competence of the faculty member, or when the faculty member is already burdened to such an extent that careful advisement is not possible.

Changes in Research Advisor

A change in research advisor is often a more sensitive matter than the original choice of one. It sometimes does imply a breakdown of relationships or understanding somewhere along the line, and it can be a sticky matter. Fairness to both faculty and students would indicate that the proposal for a change might come from either, and for a variety of legitimate reasons. The faculty member may not have the time that was originally contemplated, or the research may have taken a direction that the faculty member does not welcome. Alternatively, perhaps the new direction involves not so much disagreement as a reevaluation of faculty interest and competence. Either student or faculty may feel that the progress is too slow and come to the understanding that another advisor would be preferable.

In any case, either party should be able to initiate a request for a change, and that request, with reasons, should go to the department chairperson so that an appropriate replacement can be found. In fact, it would be best if a replacement could be found by the student and advisor before they agree to part. That would help to make all persons feel more professional about the process.

The more informal and low-key these procedures can be, the better they are for the student and the faculty, assuming of course that the rights of the individual are respected and that the correct university procedures are followed. It is the primary responsibility of the department chairperson to assure that the transition goes smoothly and that the most vulnerable person in the situation — the student — is fairly treated.

SUMMARY

This chapter concentrates on how to learn about and how to approach prospective advisors and on the responsibilities of the research advisor, as they are commonly seen in professional schools or academic departments in institutions of higher education. Responsibilities to students, other T/D committee members, and the institution are explored. Some suggestions of particular relevance to foreign students are made. From the student point of view, suggestions are given with regard to the selection of the research advisor and possible changes in such selection.

3

Developing the Proposal

QUICK REFERENCE TO ANSWERS TO SPECIFIC QUESTIONS
1. What particular steps should I take to assure that I'm on
   the right track in my consideration of possible topics?   61–70
2. How should my own background influence my
   choice of a topic?   64–65, 70–76
3. How long should my study take to complete?   77
4. How can libraries and librarians facilitate my selection
   of an appropriate topic?   77–82

Between the end of course work and the serious initiation of the thesis or dissertation is a period when most students falter and many drop out. Immediate attention to establishing a personal Time Line, to gaining an understanding of the meaning of T/D work, and to locating and agreeing on a research advisor are key steps that very much improve the chances of completion of the requirements of the degree. That is why the first two chapters emphasize those activities. The title of this chapter indicates the next important step.

The Time Line (Fig. 1-1), in its first 14 steps, covers the schedule for the development of a T/D proposal. The Schematic Diagram of the Proposal Process (Fig. 3-1) can be used to help the student check progress toward proposal completion and approval in a more detailed way. The diagram has been updated and expanded from one presented by Castetter and Heisler (1980), and we acknowledge the source of the idea with appreciation.

Figure 3-1 Schematic diagram of the proposal process.

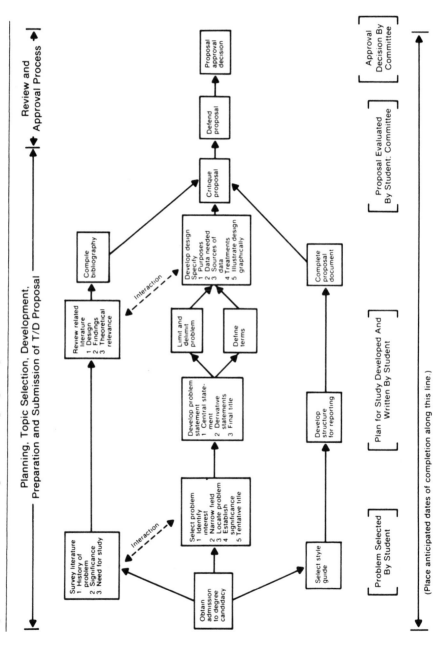

With respect to the Schematic Diagram, this chapter is concerned mainly with the first major segment at the bottom of the figure, namely, selection of the problem by the student. In moving through this and succeeding stages, we again urge students to set target dates realistically and to try hard to meet or exceed them. In this connection, it is the experience of some students that they are helped by making an enlarged photocopy of this diagram and mounting it on the wall behind their computer or typewriter keyboard.

INTERACTIONS OF STUDENT AND ACADEMIC ADVISOR

Many graduate students have rewarding T/D experiences because they find their academic advisors genuinely interested, enthusiastic, and ready and able to help in the next step, that of research advisors. If the academic advisor does not fit this description, the student and the advisor can explore together the possibility of selecting another faculty member to serve. Remember the selection of another faculty member to serve as research advisor has no negative connotation. Assuming it is done for the right reasons, it can be a positive step, a demonstration of honesty and maturity.

If the academic advisor suggests that the student work on the dissertation topic with another faculty member, the referral should be specific. If the statement turns out something like "Go work with someone else," a deeper problem may be involved. The advisor who really wants to be helpful will suggest another eligible faculty member who would be more appropriate to the student's topic, will probably talk with the suggested faculty member, and may well offer to continue to be helpful in such ways as, for example, serving on the overview committee.

DISABLED OR HANDICAPPED STUDENTS

From 1981 to 1991 students with disabilities tripled in number on U.S. campuses. They now make up about 10.5% of all college enrollments (Rothstein, 1991).

Section 504 of the Rehabilitation Act of 1973 of the U.S. Congress prohibits discrimination against "otherwise qualified" handicapped individuals. The Section 504 conditions apply to all educational institutions, whether private or public, that receive federal funds.

The courts, including the U.S. Supreme Court, have held that educational institutions, in making the "otherwise qualified" determination, must provide "reasonable accommodation" to mitigate the handicapping condition.

To avoid problems, misunderstandings, and perhaps costly delays in the T/D process, students with handicaps or disabilities should discuss their special requirements openly and fully with their advisors early, before embarking on a project. Since many faculty members may be unfamiliar with accommodations to such conditions, the student may have to do some "educating" in the preliminary discussions.

But just "talking it over" with the advisor is not enough. The student should keep notes of discussions and of oral agreements. Further, in preparing the written proposal for the T/D, the student should include specifications as to how accommodations are to be made, if anticipated, at each stage of the T/D journey, including the final examination. Thus, when the committee signs off on the proposal, the student has, in writing, the commitment that impediments to progress arising from handicapping or disabling conditions will be minimized.

For up-to-date information on relevant laws and regulations, contact the U.S. Architectural and Transportation Barriers Compliance Board, Suite 1000, 1331 F Street, NW, Washington, D.C. 20004-1111, or call, toll-free, 1-800-USA-ABLE.

CHOOSING THE TOPIC FOR STUDY

Schools and departments differ widely in their acceptance of various substantive content and forms of investigation. For example, one department might reject investigative approaches that do not involve controlled experimentation. Another might disqualify studies incorporating extrasensory perception or astrology. Students, therefore, will save much time in searching out potential topics if they first determine whether they face any restrictions on what types of research or investigative methodology the faculty may approve.

Aids to Thinking About Prospective Topics

Veteran advisors in our interviews seem to agree that students should have little, if any, difficulty in finding suitable topics. The main problem, they contend, is to pick the one best suited to the individual student's interests. New T/D students tend to disagree with veteran advisors on that matter. Many express bewilderment, anxiety, uncertainty, and lack of self-confidence. In short, they do not know how to get underway on a topic search, how to recognize a potentially good topic when they see it, or how to judge the worth of a topic when one is suggested to them. (Bowen and Rudenstine, 1992; Zuber-Skerritt and Knight, 1986)

The gap between these polar perspectives can be bridged. We recommend a two-step procedure that usually works. The first step is to use a checklist to help to collect a list of potential topics. The second step is to use another checklist of questions to assess the feasibility and appropriateness of each potential topic. The next sections describe that two-step procedure and the two checklists.

Collecting a List of Potential Topics

Most of today's students have their own computers and others have ready access to computer workstations. So we suggest that a computer data file named TOPICS be started. If a computer is not available, a notebook called *Possible Topics*, a stack of 3 x 5 cards, or another record-keeping device is essential. If a notebook is used, reserve one full page per topic; if using cards, put only one topic on a card. (If a student is close to settling in on a topic, it is still valuable to take that topic, plus previously discarded ones, through this process to verify that the best choice is being made.)

Early in Chapter 1 suggestions were made about identifying topics that might allow the student to initiate a productive conference with a potential advisor. It was indicated that possible topics would surface from analysis of publications of that faculty member, publications of others writing in the same field, and T/D's recently directed by that faculty member. Those topics, and any others the student has in mind, should be recorded. It is good to state a possible title for the topic first and then to write a sentence or two about what the study might entail. Examples appropriate to various professions and academic disciplines might be:

Title: Emotional and Intellectual Characteristics of Early Readers
Procedure: Children who learn to read before starting kindergarten would be studied to learn their emotional and intellectual similarities and differences from one another and from children who learn to read in the conventional way.
Title: Communication Channels Used in Obtaining Corporate Information
Procedure: People inside and outside corporations need and acquire corporate information.   The formal and informal channels they employ in acquiring needed information would be determined, described, and analyzed.
Title: The Emergence of Artificial Intelligence
Procedure: An analysis will be made of devices that simulate human thought processes, beginning with the earliest known ones. It will be hypothesized that behaviors like memory and computation were simulated first and only later combined to produce more complex phenomena like problem solving, anticipation, and prediction. Primary data will be records of patents and actual devices in museums and collections.
Title: Shunning as a Social Control Mechanism
Procedure: The origin and usage of shunning in Judeo-Christian religious and secular groups will be found by reference to official and other verifiable documents. The employment and the consequences of shunning will be reported and assessed as to its effectiveness in the control of the social behaviors that prompted its use.

Title: The Behavior of Sound Waves in Earth's Upper Atmosphere

Procedure: Upper atmosphere conditions will be simulated in laboratory chambers. Sound will be emitted and recorded. The recordings will be contrasted with recordings of sound made under like conditions on Earth's surface. The laboratory findings will also be compared with the findings predicted by a mathematical model based on theory.

Title: Cause of Pain in Osteoarthritis of the Knee

Procedure: It will be hypothesized that the pain of osteoarthritis arises from cartilage wear rather than inflammation, as is now commonly held. The results of administering acetaminophen, a simple painkiller, will be compared with the results of administering the anti-inflammatory drug ibuprofen. The test population will be male and female volunteers age 65 and above, randomly assigned to treatment groups.

Title: Estimating Need and Demand for Emergency Transportation

Procedure: Three highly probable conditions of emergency will be simulated. Traffic engineers, police traffic control staff, and public transit management personnel will provide need estimates and their rationales for each simulation. These will be analyzed and a formula developed to maximize accuracy of estimate.

Title: Causes of Runaway Behavior in Children

Procedure: A sample of children who have histories of two or more runaway attempts will be studied to determine the antecedent conditions they connect with the decision to run away. Family, social welfare agency, and police recollections and records will be used as corroborative information.

Title: Public Expenditure Patterns in the United States and Canada

Procedure: A comparative analysis will be made of expenditures in the two countries on items that account for major components of national and state and provincial budgets.

Figure 3-2 Checklist of thesis or dissertation topic sources.

1. Have you ascertained if there is a publication on approved types of topics in your school or department?	Yes_____ No_____
If there is, have you secured and studied it?	Yes_____ No_____
2. Have you talked with five or more students who are past the overview stage and learned how they found their topics?	Yes_____ No_____
Did you ask them about other topics related to theirs?	Yes_____ No_____
3. Have you asked for permission to attend T/D defenses at your school for familiarization and topic ideas?	Yes_____ No_____
4. Are there university-affiliated or private research agencies or groups in your region that conduct studies in your field and whose current activities you have explored?	Yes_____ No_____
5. Are you attending local regular meetings or colloquia of professional groups in which you are interested?	Yes_____ No_____
6. Have you examined the T/Ds in your field on file at your school for the past five years?	Yes_____ No_____
Have you talked directly about T/D ideas with the authors of at least five of them in which you have some interest?	Yes_____ No_____
7. Have you compared and contrasted the scholarly and professional interests of your school's faculty with your own?	Yes_____ No_____
8. Have you discussed T/D work in general with a faculty member with whom you feel comfortable and at ease?	Yes_____ No_____
9. Have you reviewed library sources such as Dissertation Abstracts, ERIC, and other database search services to look for research topics of interest to you?	Yes_____ No_____

Figure 3-2 (Continued)

10. Have you browsed through the publications of professional and academic organizations that represent your own major and minor fields of study, looking for research needs suggested by authoritative figures or committees?   Yes_____ No_____

The last of these (10) can often be done at your own computer console, because more and more academic and professional agencies and associations are making available their publications of all kinds through various forms of computer-accessible modalities.

Figure 3-2 is a checklist of additional sources to help identify other potential topics. It can be valuable to use this one or to make a personal one as part of your file. The number of "No's" on the checklist can be an index to the thoroughness and seriousness of a student's search for possible T/D topics. One reason why veteran advisors feel that potential topics abound is because, as professors, they are routinely involved in most of the activities tapped by the checklist.

One illustration is STIS (Science and Technology Information System), the online publishing system of the National Science Foundation (NSF). STIS provides convenient, fast, easy, and free access to NSF publications, which include a broad array of investigative studies, research reports, and policy papers. The only user cost is possible long-distance telephone charges. STIS is available 24 hours a day, except for brief weekly maintenance periods. There are a number of ways to get started on accessing the service, including by E-Mail (Direct, Internet, or BITNET), by WAIS (Wide Area Information Servers), the file transfer method called Anonymous FTP, or by online STIS. The system is described in a flyer, NSF-91-10, a copy of which can be obtained by calling 202-357-7861, the NSF Publications Section, or by using these E-Mail messages: stis-request@nsf.gov (Internet) or stis-req@NSF

(BITNET). By voice telephone information can be requested at 202-357-7555 and for TDD (Telephonic Device for the Deaf) at 202-357-7492.

When one has assembled and recorded a group of likely topics, it is time for another major step. That is a careful examination of each one to determine its relative feasibility and appropriateness in relation to the others. That will be a matter of judgment, of course, but it is possible to channel that judgement by raising a number of questions that highlight significant factors that deserve consideration. That is the purpose of the next section.

Assessing Topic Feasibility and Appropriateness

Using the next checklist (Fig. 3-3) can save time and help narrow down a group of potential topics to a few that merit more thorough consideration. The list starts with general questions and then breaks into six subsections that are applicable to topics that call for different investigative approaches. It pays to read all of the questions in each subsection because the questions themselves sometimes trigger important ideas. (Special Note: One should not be put off or overwhelmed by these questions. Some of them are tough and some may seem at first to pose insurmountable obstacles. But there is help in the rest of the chapter, in following chapters, and from advisors. It is rare that any topic comes through this checklist unscathed entirely, at first. It is in the follow-up repair work and polishing that a topic begins to assume acceptable, workable form.)

The most important thing about the checklist's 42 questions is their power to alert one, to force one to think in specific, detailed ways while considering T/D topics.

PROBLEMS OF FOREIGN STUDENTS

According to the Institute of International Education's *Open Doors* (1990), in 1954-1955 there were 34,000 students from overseas in the United States. They constituted 1.4% of U.S. enroll-

Figure 3-3 Checklist of topic feasibility and appropriateness.*

A. *Questions about the topic in general*
   1. Is there current interest in this topic in your field? In a closely related field?
   2. Is there a gap in knowledge that work on this topic could help to fill? A controversy it might help to resolve?
   3. Is it possible to focus on a small enough segment of the topic to make a manageable T/D project?
   4. Can you envision a way to study the topic that will allow conclusions to be drawn with substantial objectivity? Is the data collection approach (i.e., test, meta analysis, archive study, questionnaire, interview) acceptable in your school?
   5. Is there a body of literature available relevant to the topic? Is it accessible by computer and is a search of it manageable?
   6. Are there large problems (i.e., logistic, attitudinal) to be surmounted in working on this topic? Do you have the means to handle them?
   7. Does the topic relate reasonably well to others done in your school? If not, have you information about its acceptability?
   8. Would financial assistance be required? Is it available?
   9. Are the needed data easily accessible? Will you have control of the data?
   10. Do you have a clear statement of the purpose, scope, objectives, procedures, and limitations of the study? A tentative table of contents for the report? Are any of the skills called on by the study ones that you have yet to acquire?

B. *Questions for topics employing a research question or hypothesis*
   1. Do you have acceptable statements of research questions or hypotheses?
   2. Can you specify how you will answer the questions or test the hypotheses?
   3. Would the T/D be a contribution if the findings do not support the hypothesis or fail to answer the questions?
   4. Have subsidiary questions or hypotheses been identified that deserve study along with the major ones?
   5. Are the alternative questions or hypotheses that might explain the findings anticipated?

C. *Questions for topics requiring interviews for data collection*
   1. What style or type of interview is best suited to the objectives of the study?
   2. Does an interview protocol exist that fits the purposes of the investigation? Has it been pilot-tested?
   3. How will the data be recorded and collated for optimum speed, accuracy, and reliability? Can the computer be used for this?

Figure 3-3 (Continued)

    4. How will matters of confidentiality and permissions be handled?
    5. How will bias in the interviewer and the respondent be minimized or measured?
D. *Questions for topics using a questionnaire approach*
    1. What forms of questionnaire will be most productive for this kind of study? Has it been pretested?
    2. How will questionnaire items relate specifically to the purposes of the investigation?
    3. Why is the questionnaire the tool of choice for data collection? Can it be computerized?
    4. How will it be assured that the questionnaires will be answered?
    5. How will the questionnaire responses be validated? Analyzed?
E. *Questions for topics involving mathematical analysis of data*
    1. What quantitative analyses are planned? What will they produce?
    2. Are the quantitative analyses appropriate to the kinds of data collected?
    3. What level of confidence will be accepted as significant? Why?
    4. Are there computer programs that will save time, energy, and money? Are they available?
    5. What rational and subjective interpretations will need to be given to the statistical findings to make them meaningful?
F. *Questions for topics making use of existing data from other sources*
    1. Are the data relevant? Reliable and valid? Complete?
    2. Are there limitations on the present or future availability or utilization of the data? Can data be accessed by computer?
    3. Why is it better to use these data than to collect one's own afresh?
    4. Will additional data need to be collected? What and why?
    5. What obligations to the other sources go along with publication based on these data? Who will own the data?
G. *Questions for topics involving tests and testing in data gathering*
    1. Are the tests the most valid and reliable obtainable?
    2. Do the tests discriminate against significant groups in the sample?
    3. Do the tests provide direct measures of the key variables in the study?
    4. How will confidentiality be preserved?
    5. What interpretations will be needed to make the test results meaningful in relation to the purpose of the investigation?
    6. Are the tests physically or psychologically invasive?
    7. Can the tests be administered, scored, and results arrayed, tabled, and analyzed by computer?

*We are indebted to Allen (1973, pp. 21-27), for the idea for a checklist of this kind. We have adapted his general format and much longer lists to our purposes.

ment. Thirty-five years later that number had increased more than 10-fold to about 386,851 students from overseas, and the percentage rose to 2.8% of the total enrollment in higher education. Thus foreign students make up not only an important segment of higher education in the United States, but a growing segment as well.

Also, foreign students are of critical importance to some advanced fields, particularly the physical and natural sciences, business administration, engineering, and computer sciences. As the number of U.S. citizens earning science and engineering doctorates has been declining, their places have been taken by foreign students (Atkinson, 1990). Foreign students with temporary visas earned 30% of all physical science Ph.D.'s and 45% of the engineering doctorates in 1988. In some large research universities, foreign students actually outnumber domestic students in doctoral programs such as business and engineering. If the trend continues, it may be that the majority of faculty members in these areas will be foreign nationals or immigrants since future faculty members are prepared in doctoral programs. For example, in 1985, two-thirds of all postdoctorate engineering positions went to non-U.S. citizens (Pool, 1990).

Two difficulties foreign students often encounter are topic relevance and writing. The first arises when students know what problems need solutions in their own countries but find few professors who understand the problems or think them suitable for investigation. The second, writing, appears as a problem if students have not acquired the specialized composition skills called for in phrasing thoughts in the combination of professional and scientific prose common to T/Ds in English-speaking countries (CGS, 1991a).

Our best advice about the topic problem is for the student to persist in the search for an advisor who will listen with sympathy and understanding. The student should look for departments and schools that have "International," "Inter-," or "Cross-Cultural," "Ethnic," "Inter-," or "Pan-American," "Asian," "Middle-Eastern," or similar expressions that smack of interests that cross national boundaries in their names. It is appropriate to seek those out, even though they may be outside the school or department in which the student is enrolled. Very often professors in schools or departments with multinational interests also have appointments in other academic departments or professional schools or know professors there who would be good advisors for foreign students interested in problems that relate to their homelands. Other foreign students and lists of recently completed T/Ds can give clues, too.

With regard to the writing problem, there are three possible solutions. The first is to write in one's native language and to have an advisor and committee members who can read it, or to employ a professional translator for those who cannot. A second solution is to take instruction in English academic scientific and professional writing. Such courses are offered in a number of universities. A third possibility is to engage the services of an editor. Inquiries among professors and students will sometimes reveal that there are faculty members who provide editorial services for students for a fee. This can be a delicate arrangement, but we have seen it work very effectively. The editor must be someone not otherwise connected with the student's course of study and T/D work. Also, the advisor and committee must know of and sanction the use of editorial help, and the assistance must be carefully provided so that it deals only with organization, style, composition, written expression, and the proper use of language, strictly avoiding any substantive or methodological elements.

If editorial service is to be employed or otherwise provided to the student, it is strongly urged that the arrangement be spelled out in writing, with copies to all relevant parties. At least one copy of the agreed-upon arrangement should be initialed or signed by the student, the advisor, the committee members, and the appropriate department chairperson or dean. That copy should be kept on file in the graduate office. Also, it is definitely advisable that the editor employed have a clear knowledge of the terms of the agreement and be acceptable to the advisor and the department chairperson or dean.

PERSONAL CRITERIA FOR STUDENT USE

There are useful criteria to have in mind as possible topics arise. Without these criteria the student is likely to make too many false starts.

The Interest of the Researcher

One's personal interest is very important. But interest is not always maintained easily. The completion of a T/D may well involve some very uninteresting work. For example, if a T/D involves statistical analyses, the tables to display the findings may represent hours of tedious work. Moreover, too high a level of personal interest can engender bias and limit objectivity. Also, students report that a topic that was "just a topic" at first grew in interest as it moved along the T/D path (Isaac et al., 1989).

The Background of the Researcher

To start with an almost entirely unfamiliar topic is a disadvantage. Instead, topics close to one's prior preparation and experience offer better possibilities for successful T/D work.

Students who propose topics outside the scope of their training or experience must spend a great deal of time becoming familiar with a new field. It is unlikely that such a beginning will ever result in the broad background really needed to feel comfortable in doing the study. More likely, there is the danger that lack of a broader understanding of the subject will lead to serious mistakes either in the conduct or in the interpretation of the research.

The Technical Competence of the Researcher

The student should have technical competence related to the topic. For example, the level of competence a student researcher has in statistics should be influential in choosing a topic. Some topics by their nature call for complex statistical analyses. Others may appropriately be completed with basic descriptive statistics. Other examples of technical competencies are the use of archival or library search procedures, use of interview techniques, use of computer programs, and facility with foreign languages. These are research tools characteristic of specific research methodologies. The choice of topic and design should be guided by consideration of the skills possessed versus the skills required.

There are computer packages that offer complete, complex statistical analyses and they can be great time savers. But the use of such a package does not excuse the researcher from responsibility for understanding fully the techniques employed. A guideline recommended by Gay (1992, p. 476) is that one "should not use the computer to perform an analysis that you have never done yourself by hand, or at least studied extensively." The same writer encourages aspiring researchers to become proficient in using some of the more sophisticated hand-held calculators that allow one to enter one or two sets of data and, by using the appropriate keys, to have the results of a desired analysis displayed.

Importance of the Topic

Check your perceptions of topic importance with others you respect, such as colleagues, your advisor, other faculty members, administrators, and other investigators. If most others see the topic as important, it probably is. But use some other tests, also. When you are finished with the T/D, will anyone read it? Could it be published? Does it address an issue of topical interest? How will it affect the academic field or profession? Questions like these lead to answers also useful for the written introduction to your proposal, for they will help to give readers a background and a context with which to judge the worth of the topic (Association of American Universities [AAU], 1990; Bowen and Rudenstine, 1992; Isaac et al., 1989).

One element of importance is generalizability, that is, whether or not it is likely that the findings of the investigation can be applied to other situations. An example of a study that results of which would not generalize would be one done on a population and under conditions so unusual that one could not expect the same results in many other situations (i.e., race drivers' reactions after wrecks).

Appropriate Size and Scope

Topics should be limited to those that are possible and feasible for one person to do within the expected time period. The honors thesis is done during the last one or two years of undergraduate study, along with courses and seminars. A master's thesis is usually thought to be possible, if pursued along with the other requirements for the degree, within three to six months. Ordinarily, one would expect to complete the dissertation in one year to 18 months, if working full time on it.

USING LIBRARIES AND OTHER INFORMATION SOURCES

This is a period of information power. From note taking to literature searching and from data collection to data analysis, automation technology now accelerates research while encouraging both more comprehensiveness and more precision in the T/D enterprise.

Central Role of the Librarian and the Library

Because of technological advances, public and campus libraries have more material available than ever before. A library is still a *place*, to be sure, but it now has the capability to provide the user with the resources of many other libraries in addition to its own. Moreover, the user has access to that vastly enlarged store of material with almost incredible ease and speed (York et al., 1988).

Successful students learn quickly how to use help from librarians and how to use their own computers independently and to operate from distant workstations to make the most of library resources. Here are the most important guidelines:

1. Ask for information and help. Inquire about online or compact disc databases related to the topic(s) of interest to you and find out how you can access them, *independently*, if possible. As an example, find out if FirstSearch can be made available to you, since it has many databases, is adding to them, is relatively inexpensive, is considered to be user-friendly. There are other good ones, too.

2. Become *fully* acquainted with the library and the roles of the various librarians, many of whom are specialists. If you wish, they will assist you in learning to maximize your skill in using catalogs and periodical indexes; they will advise you on search methodology; they will introduce you to the world of computer-assisted literature searching; and they will guide you to special collections. Also, librarians understand disabled student needs and services. These are but a few of the multifaceted capabilities of professional librarians, but they illustrate that they are powerful allies in the research process.

3. Most modern information technology can be utilized from home or office with a five-component microcomputer workstation: computer, keyboard, monitor, printer, and modem. (For explanations of these terms, see Appendix A.) Such a basic station allows one to capture and store the products of a search session for one's own use by downloading to your own disc. Subsequently, the references can be recast into any of the common bibliographic citation forms by using commercially available programs (Rice, 1989). The student who owns or can use a computer ought to acquire and use this approach to literature searches immediately as a research tool.

In summary, recognize each librarian as a highly qualified information specialist as well as a very valuable resource person with respect to the complex and involved operations of academic and professional libraries. Seek the aid of librarians on a one-to-one basis to further your own skills. Remember that it is more important that your library affords you *access* to a source than that your library *owns* the source. And become skilled at accessing your own campus library via computer because that skill can be readily leveraged into access to the other major library holdings of the nation.

Computer Search Services

The university reference librarian is an excellent initial contact. Be ready to say what your purpose is, what field you want to explore, and how you expect to use the information from the data bank. There are excellent computer systems for help in literature searches. Libraries have access to hundreds of databases. And growth and technical improvement are very fast paced in library information storage and retrieval. Therefore, the student ought to stay in close consultation with reference librarians, the on-campus experts in how best to use the current and emerging tools.

First Steps for the Student

In the preceding section on the role of the library and the librarian we have already urged students to acquire key library skills and personal computer competencies. Now those capabilities must be extended and put to practical use (York et al., 1988).

1. To search a database efficiently one must have a topic, or at least a topic area, in mind. To get ready, it is best to examine some current articles bearing on the topic area under consideration. Then try to think of a title for a paper on the subject of your choice. See if you can get all of the main ideas about your topic into the title. An example might be: "Government Policy Development and Implementation Respecting Brazilian Universities in the Past Decade." Since databases are queried by the presence of key words, singly or in combination, the words in the title thus concocted will probably include those you will use when specifying the kinds of documents you wish to retrieve. At this point, or earlier, we recommend seeking advice from a librarian trained in the search language designed for communication with the computer. Since databases can be programmed for retrieval by approaches other than key subject terms, the library specialist may be able to direct you to a more efficient or effective way to call up the information you wish to locate.

2. Research libraries may have access to hundreds of databases. One database collection available in many libraries, for example, is DIALOG. It has more than 100 categories, from Agriculture and Architecture and Art to Veterinary Science and Water and World Patents. The database indexes can be

reviewed in print at the library and, in some cases can be called up on your own computer monitor to scan or, if you wish, to print out for yourself. Companies or institutions sell databases (or access to them), the latter by license or rental. Some of the major sources for databases of the type most useful in T/D research may be known to your librarians or professors. There may be instances in which a student may wish to deal directly with some of those database vendors.

3. Decide how much of each retrieved document you want to receive and keep, either as a printout or in your computer file. For the first trial of the search, you may wish to look only at the bibliographic citations to judge whether or not to change your search terms or to combine them in different ways. Once satisfied that the search is retrieving the kinds of documents you need, you may then want to obtain abstracts of the references you have chosen as probably most relevant to your topic. A next step often is to select, from the abstracts, the documents that seem to be most relevant, ones you would consider primary sources. For those you will need to have the full text.

4. Copies of the full text of books, documents, and articles may be obtained in a variety of ways if they are not shelved and circulated by your own library. Time and ready reference are usually quite important to student researchers. So you may want to own personal copies of the primary source materials you will be studying and quoting and discussing with your committee members. If a book or monograph is in print, your bookstore can usually obtain a copy in less than a week. Back copies of journals are often sold individually by the publisher; a telephone call can ascertain that. Some database services also provide journal articles through the mail or over facsimile machine. The full texts of documents from many sources are available on microfiche and possibly can be read and copied in your own local library. Or if the library or one of your professors has a copy of what you need, you may request permission to photocopy it. This, too, is a matter on which librarians usually have very helpful ideas.

Keep in mind that no computer search will be complete. Many commonly used databases reach back only until the mid-1960s. Also, there may be a lag from publication to insertion into a database. And no matter how well descriptors are selected, significant publications may slip through the net. Moreover, not all journals and other publications are referenced in information banks amenable to computer searches.

Despite these drawbacks, this search approach is a major time saver for what it does do. The routine clerical jobs involved are accomplished rapidly and accurately; it is almost incredibly quicker and more efficient than hand-done card index and journal directory work. We agree with Sternberg (1981), who regards it as "advisable, even mandatory, for literature scanning" (p. 127). Most important, as Martin (1980) says, however,

> . . . a computer search does not eliminate the necessity for substantial library work. This is true because the data presented to the user . . . is [often] only a reference . . . the researcher must read it in the original source. Thus a computer search [sometimes] only helps the user locate important material. (p. 27)

To summarize, your computer can be a very useful tool in carrying out a literature search. But it will do only what you tell it to do and it will not think for you.

Published Suggestions for Research Topics

A number of academic and professional groups publish annual reviews of research. Recently, also, the interest in *direct publication* of books and periodicals via electronic networks has led to testing the practicality of the idea. For example, the journal *Catalyst*, previously sold by subscription in print, is now available free on both Bitnet and Internet. That journal's emphasis is on continuing education through two-year colleges, so researchers with that interest can read or copy the most recent articles in it from their own computer screens. It will pay to inquire of your own library staff about such direct access to books and periodicals relevant to your research topic. These typically contain recommendations about needed studies. Such published suggestions may be of help in selecting research topics. It should be understood, however, that some will be outside the interest and capabilities of the student because they call for special equipment, access to subjects, investigate competence areas, and special staff and funds beyond those the student researcher can provide. Often, however, the student's professor or department chairperson will be able to suggest portions of those topics that need to be researched and that are within the student's reach. Such suggestions are especially valuable because they imply an interest in the topic by the faculty.

Journals are also excellent sources to search. If you are partial to a particular subject, reading the latest issues of journals in that field can stimulate interesting research possibilities. The problem will be to focus on a few feasible topics from among the interesting things one might do.

The process you have underway toward selecting a topic can be illustrated in this sequence of moves:

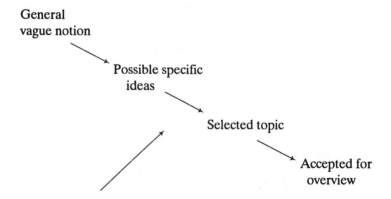

General
vague notion

Possible specific
ideas

Selected topic

Accepted for
overview

And you are here at a very trying transition point. The next chapter calls on the experience of many professors and students to help make the move smoothly and sucessfully.

SUMMARY

Suggestions about the process of selection of research topics are provided, along with checklists to help bring ideas into focus. We offer sample suggestions to illustrate that students will find that each field of study can be reviewed for the research done as well as the research that may need to be done. In some specialized narrow fields one may not find a source entitled "Needed Research in . . ." but the needs of the field can be conceptualized by reviewing the research that has been done and by then identifying logical next steps. Research is never-ending; it usually raises as many questions as it attempts to answer and raises them in the very process of attempting to find answers. That is why almost every report of research contains the seeds of future investigations. Professors who are familiar with the research in their field are, without a doubt, the best sources for ideas about the research that yet needs to be done.

4

Preparation of the Proposal

GETTING STARTED

Write Answers to Questions

Moving the proposal* out of your head and into written form can be done in stages. The very first stage can be quite informal.

One way that works for a lot of students is to write a few short sentences about each of the seven questions below. (Change the order, if you wish, and add other points if you think they are important.) The critical thing is to check where you are on your Time Line and to start to write answers to the following questions no matter how dissatisfying the first draft.

---

*The proposal is sometimes called an overview or a concept paper. Operationally the terms seem to mean the same.

1. What is the tentative title? What do you call what you want to do? What is its name?
2. Why do you want to do it? What will you know or be able to do or say when you are through? (At this stage an involved theoretical justification is unnecessary.)
3. In order to accomplish what you want to do, what steps will you have to take? Can you put the steps in sequential order? What facilities will you need? Why?
4. What kinds of help do you think you will need in order to do what you want to do? When? How might you get that help?
5. Will the project involve people other than yourself? How? To do what? For how long? Will you need any special permissions?
6. What actually goes on if you start to do what you propose? How would it start? What would a typical day be like at the beginning? When you are partway through? At the end?
7. How do you think you could show whether you accomplish what you set out to do? How could you prove it to someone else?

After writing "first draft" answers to these questions, put the document aside for a day or two in your "Proposal Notes" file. Then come back and reread it. Make whatever amendments you think it needs for increased clarity.

Make a Clear, Typed Copy

This step can be a very important one. Take the time to type and save on your word processor or computer what you have in mind, even though it may be a rough draft. Be sure spelling and punctuation are correct. Learn to use spelling checks and grammatical helps from computer software. An outline program, such as WordPerfect's, helps one to think in orderly and deductive sequence. Double space, with wide margins. Set the word-processing program to put your name and date on each sheet. Make at least three copies: one for your file, one to hand to your advisor, and one for you to use while talking with your advisor. Save your work in a computer file.

Why so much detailed emphasis on this point? It is essential to set the stage so there is nothing to distract the advisor's attention from the content of what you have written. A business-like beginning by the student encourages any advisor to try very hard to be helpful. Of course, it is the advisor's obligation to assist the student in any event. But a cleanly typed and error-free statement, even one that needs much more substantive work, will help the advisor to feel that guidance will be taken seriously by the student.

Moreover, this is often the crucial first step in the student's own filing and record keeping. It should set a model for a continuing pattern of neatness and orderliness. Many students have told us that partway through the T/D process they discovered that sloppy note taking and careless storage made information retrieval an all but impossible task. Early attention to details will sharply reduce the chances of mournful losses and misplacements. Thus, the first stage in writing the proposal is one that can be quite informal as to style. But it is one that should be very deliberately organized to introduce a businesslike tone into both the initial conference with the advisor and the records of the student. Develop a regular system to save and file all work on the word processor or computer in a T/D directory, always properly cited in the form to be used eventually in the final document, e.g., APA, MLA. Endnotes, footnotes, and citation systems can immeasurably help store and later find notes and their citations.

Back up important files on a regular schedule by making a separate copy of each file or by adding it to an already existing backup disc. If the original file is lost or becomes flawed or is accidentally erased, the backup copy is then available.

What makes a file "important" enough to back up with a copy? Two factors: First, is its content really needed for producing or defending the T/D? Second, if missing, how much time and energy would be required to replace it? It is more sensible to err on the side of caution, in either case.

Use University Guidelines and Regulations

Even though we encourage informality in first drafts, we also suggest that familiarity with formal guides and requirements for the T/D will pay dividends for the student. Problems are less likely to occur if guidelines on procedural and editorial matters are studied at the outset by the student and the advisor together. Such joint study ought to be done in a spirit of understanding. Clarifying the rationale for each of the guidelines and determining how they can be most helpful to the student, while they also serve the broader purposes of improving communication among the professions and other scholarly groups, is the goal.

Table 4-1 contains an alphabetized list of topics about which universities often have specific regulations pertaining to T/D procedures and format. We urge students to use Table 4-1 as a checklist while developing the T/D first draft and, as needed, later. If, for instance, you think you may need to include a drawing in your manuscript, of if you may need to preserve the confidentiality of certain data, or if you have questions about any other of the 85 items in the table, it is best to ascertain the facts early. Your advisor, your department chairperson or executive officer, your dean's office, and the graduate office of your university are the places to go for details about any of the checklist items.

Many professors believe a useful approach is for the student to become familiar with the contents of the university procedural guide at the same time that the T/D problem is being conceptualized. Following that, frequent reference to the university manual can help the student organize notes and rough drafts so that minimal time is lost in moving toward an acceptable final manuscript.

Use of Style Manuals

Faculty members and students need style manuals. The former use them to quickly refresh their memories about questions, to look up recommendations about new problems in writing as they arise, and to monitor, generally, the consistency of their own writ-

Table 4-1 Administrative and Technical Matters Included in Thesis and Dissertation Regulations

Abbreviations, symbols, and nomenclature
Abstract
Acknowledgments
Ann Arbor, Michigan, services and depository
Appeal procedure for variation from regulations
Appendices
Artwork mounting

Binding

Changes and corrections
Checklist of final clearance requirements
Citation systems
Classified materials
Committee size and composition
Computer printout sheets
Computer programs appropriate to the T/D
Confidential documents and other material
Copies required
Copyright
Copyrighted material; quotations and other uses

Database searches
Dean's responsibility
Definitions of terms
Department chairperson's responsibility
Differentiation of university, school, and department requirements

Editorial consultation or assistance
Endnotes
Enrollment at time of T/D defense
Exceptions to the written T/D

Faculty responsibility
Final copy (deposit copy)
Footnotes

Table 4-1 Continued

Foreign language use
Format consistency
Forms requiring signatures

Grades for T/D

Illustration captions
Illustrations (including foldouts)
Instructions for nonfilmable material and color

Line drawings
Local style regulations

Major divisions of T/D
Manuscript reproduction or duplication
Margins
Microfiche
Microfilming
Model overviews (proposals, prospectuses)
Multiple authorship
Music scores

Optional forms of T/D report to university
Order of contents
Overview, submission and approval of
Ownership of T/D (literary rights)

Paper specifications
Personal copies
Photographs
Placement of nontext materials
Previously circulated, published, or publishable material
Proofreading responsibilities
Publication rights

References and bibliographies
Residency requirements

ing. Frequently, faculty members write for more than one colleague audience; the accepted styles of the two may vary. For
instance, the American Educational Research Association, the
American Institute of Physics, the American Psychological Association, and the Social Work Yearbook all have somewhat different
styles prescribed. That means the faculty member's desk drawer
may well contain several well-thumbed style guides. In the case of

students, style manuals should be used in preparing papers from the time of admission to graduate preparation.

The most commonly used style manuals are listed in this book's reference list and can be identified by (*) preceding the entry. Each faculty member and student should inquire about the school's style requirements and abide by them. Foreign students, still developing skill in scientific and professional English writing, often need to be extra attentive to the characteristics of T/D prose.

Style manuals do not necessarily help one to improve writing skills or to be logical and clear in one's thinking and writing. There are books published to do this, and some are quite readable and useful (Evans and Evans, 1957; Fowler, 1965; Newman, 1974; Perrin, 1972; Strunk & White, 1979; van Leunen, 1979). Once adequate general writing skill is attained, however, the style manual, if used thoughtfully, can be a material aid to producing high-quality prose in a form acceptable for professional publications.

OUTLINING THE PROPOSAL

Format of the Presentation

Some advisors recommend that the student prepare only a two- or three-page prospectus to take to the committee for approval. Others go much further, requiring not only a detailed research plan but also a summary of preliminary research results. Many schools and departments have, in recent years, printed information on proposal requirements in a *Bulletin on Master's and Doctoral Study* or something similar. Also, ask your advisor to let you read two or three recent proposals that were considered of good quality to help you plan yours.

At this stage writing must become more formal. It will save time if drafts approximate the form and style of an actual proposal as it will appear when completed. Then each draft will be a closer approximation of the end goal. You will find this step-by-step development helps you to reach closure on what, at the beginning, might appear as an overwhelming task. Use of a modern word-processing program can greatly facilitate the preparation of each approximation and reduce the task to more manageable proportions.

In T/Ds often a substantial amount of first-hand, observable data is gathered and analyzed. Yet many other T/Ds take the form of a policy conceptualization analysis and interpretation or of a theory-based, critial examination and synthesis of a specific body of knowledge on a particular issue or topic.

Every T/D, of course, relies on the assembling of systematic evidence to focus on the problem at hand. The sources of evidence and the nature of data are quite variable, though, and so are the methods of acquiring and analyzing material. *Theoretical syntheses* ordinarily depend quite heavily on both primary and secondary sources. Much of the material studied will be more qualitative than quantitative. It is in the uniformity, the consistency, and the systematic approach to such data that the theoretical synthesis displays its objectivity and its openness to replication. *Policy analyses* tend to rely largely on library sources such as articles, books, documents, essays, informants, official transcriptions, special surveys, and reports. The arraying and ordering of pertinent information from such sources for analytical assessment is a major challenge to the investigator, and the skill, clarity, and sophistication with which that is done is a prime consideration in judging the merits of the work. *Empirical studies* emphasize control, in the sense that the investigator sets up the conditions of the investigation and specifies detailed questions that will be answered or hypotheses that will be tested. The application and observation of a treatment effect is a common part of such studies, as is the statistical analysis of data.

Each of these three T/D forms—empirical study, policy analysis, and theoretical synthesis—is probably best presented by following a somewhat different structure or outline. In this chapter the Table of Contents of the most frequent form of proposal, the empirical study, is highlighted (Fig. 4-1). Appendix B offers expanded outlines that might be helpful for all three T/D types.

Figure 4-1 Table of Contents for a proposal.

Table of Contents

I. Introduction

II. The problem
 A. Rationale, significance, or need for the study
 B. Theoretical framework for the proposed study
 C. Statement of the problem
 D. Elements, hypotheses, theories, or research questions to be investigated
 E. Delimitations and limitations of the study
 F. Definition of terms
 G. Summary

III. Review of the literature
 A. Historical overview of the theory and research literature
 B. The theory and research literature specific to the T/D topic
 C. Research in cognate areas relevant to the T/D topic
 D. Critique of the validity of appropriate theory and research literature
 E. Summary of what is known and unknown about the T/D topic
 F. The contribution this study will make to the literature

IV. Research procedures
 A. Research methodology
 B. Specific procedures
 C. Research population or sample
 D. Instrumentation
 E. Pilot study
 F. Data collection
 G. Treatment of the data
 H. Summary

Appendices
 Appendix A, B, . . . (as needed)

Bibliography

They are suggested guides; prescriptions cannot be written because no two projects will be exactly alike. The most recent statement of the Council of Graduate Schools (1991b, p. 13) on options for the form of the dissertation points out:

Whether the form of the dissertation is a monograph, a series of articles, or a set of essays is determined by the research expectations and accepted forms of publication in the discipline, as well as by custom in the discipline and the student's program. In the humanities and some of the social sciences, the dissertation ... reflects the individual scholar's approach to research and can ultimately form the basis for a monograph published by a university press. Several article length essays ... may be the heart of the dissertation in economics at a number of universities. In engineering and the physical and biological sciences, which are increasingly team disciplines with large groups of investigators working on common problems, dissertations often present, in varied formats, the results of several independent but related experiments.

The Council goes on (p. 14) to make a very important point: "How a discipline normally conducts its work is distinctly related to that discipline's expectations for the Ph.D. dissertation."

Thus it is vital that the student knows, or ascertains, the norms and expectations for dissertations (and theses as well) in the student's program and discipline. If in doubt, ask the advisor. Also, review several dissertations or theses recently completed in the department; note the name of the research advisor and the format, content, theoretical basis, and the methodology employed in the examples reviewed.

Although no format is common to all institutions of higher education, Figure 4-1 encompasses the topics ordinarily included. View this outline as a general guide rather than a prescription. Adapt it as necessary or as required by the advisor or university. The material that follows is keyed in sequence to the items in the Table of Contents shown in Figure 4-1.

FILLING IN THE OUTLNE

Introduction

Use this to acquaint the reader with the topic. It should be short—only a page or two—but a number of things can be done to make it useful. First, tell the reader what the study will be about and why it is important and even timely. Arouse the reader's interest; build a desire to read on and find out more. Set the stage for what comes after, putting important parts of the topic area in their proper perspective.

Second, be direct, not tedious. Make the Introduction a tasty tidbit, a sample of the good things to come. Aim it at an intelligent, well-informed person, but *one who is not deeply involved* in the particular problem you are addressing.

It has been noted that individuals turn to using diagrams to explain ideas or concepts that seem too difficult to put into simple sentences. Most languages are unidimensional and sequential, so it is truly not possible to verbalize several things at the same time. But a diagram, like a picture, can readily accomplish what mere words cannot. The same is true of graphs and charts. Therefore, we urge that the excellent capabilities of the computer be used to create and insert illustrations at all stages in the body of the T/D. This is important to the ability of the reader, as well as the researcher, to visualize complex relationships or interactive processes. And it can by especially important in making this and other sections of the proposal both concise and clear. Tufte (1983, 1990) supplies superior examples of illustrations made by computer.

After reading the Introduction, one should be able to guess accurately what the problem is. Everything in the Introduction culminates in the statement of the problem as the next logical step.

The Problem

Rationale, Significance, or Need for the Study: Since this heading begins a new chapter of the T/D proposal, it is appropriate to link it to the prior chapter by first summarizing what appeared in the

Introduction. That ought to take no more than two or three sentences. What appears in this section in addition should serve to sharpen and make more precise the purpose of the study. Remember, the committee rightfully expects the student to be able to state, convincingly, the chief reason(s) for doing the study, the potential value(s) that could flow from doing the study, and the urgency to do this particular study at this time. This section need not be long. One can point out that what is presented here will be elaborated later in the T/D document, if that is necessary. However, this *is* the place to present, succinctly, the rationale, significance, or need for the investigation.

Theoretical Framework for the Proposed Study: Many important research topics do not have a clear relationship to a theory. One example is a study that established the most appropriate type size for reading materials to be used by persons with severe vision impairments. It was an important study, but one that was essentially pragmatic, meaning that it pertained to or primarily was concerned with practical results or outcomes. In the case of the type-size study, the problem was to ascertain a size of print that would allow as many visually impaired persons as possible to have access to reading materials while at the same time keeping the size and the bulk and the cost of the printed materials within reason. On the other hand, some T/D proposals are eclectic in their frames of reference, meaning that they select from a variety of theories or systems of thinking rather than building on or testing some part of one theory. Examples can be found in the literature on methods of rehabilitating criminals, where a variety of parts of theories of criminal justice, social learning, punishment, and morality may be interactive. Finally, there are many studies that aim specifically at challenging or attempting to validate individual theories or at testing the accuracy of predictions made from specific theories. Individual theories are, or course, numerous, ranging across all academic and professional disciplines.

Two essential points ought to be included in this section of every proposal. First, it should be made clear whether the framework of the investigation is pragmatic, eclectic, or focused on a single theory, with a brief explanation of why and how. Second, the framework, whichever it is (or in whatever combination), should be stated, with appropriate references to the primary sources where full information on the applicable theories or systems of thought may be found.

Statement of the Problem

This is a short section, but perhaps the most important in the proposal. It lays down a guide to follow in all that comes after, and at the same time it is a serious agreement between the proposer and the faculty. Some institutions even refer to it as having contract-like characteristics. In any case, the statement of the problem in any high-quality university or professional school will be carefully scrutinized by the faculty and, once accepted, will not be changed without faculty permission and agreement. Once accepted, the statement of the problem will be the problem for the student researcher, and that individual will live with it until the mission is completed or aborted.

Sometimes it helps to think about writing the purpose of the study or research as a way to state your concept of the problem in clear prose. In fact, some advisors look for a paragraph right after the problem and immediately before the statement of the problem, identified as the purpose of the study. We think that is a good idea if it seems functional to the student. Alternatively, the "purpose" paragraph could be the initial paragraph of the statement of the problem. The purpose paragraph would be brief and would build on the introduction to provide information concerning the reasons why the study is proposed, what it would accomplish, and the anticipated outcomes of the study as proposed.

After the purpose is given, a paragraph or two ought to suffice for the remaining statement of the problem. Choose words very carefully. Do not promise more than is necessary to do a high-quality study in a reasonable time. The problem statement has to follow logically the purpose statement. It may be expressed as a question or a statement, preference depending on the individual researcher, the faculty member guiding the research, and the nature of the topic. The statement gives direction to the study, gives succinct information about the scope of the study, and suggests, without giving details, how the study will be carried out. Everything one reads in the literature about the statement of the problem says, in one way or the other, that the statement must be clear, concise, and unambiguous. All technical writing should be characterized by those adjectives, but the one place to make doubly sure that they apply is in the statement of the problem. It is easy to say and hard to do.

Elements of the Problem

Elements are stated in studies that do not require hypotheses.[*] Sometimes elements in T/D proposals are called research questions or have similar titles. Essentially, by whatever name, they are a list of specific parts of the problem that will be studied as opposed to other parts, usually unnamed, that will not be studied. Thus, the elements help define and make more specific the problem statement.

Hypotheses, Theories, and Research Questions

The hypothesis is stated as a suggested solution to a problem or as the relationship of specified variables. It retains the character of a guess until facts are found to confirm or discredit it. One or more hypotheses may be generated by a thorough analysis of the theoretical and factual background of the research problem. Without formulating hypotheses, a researcher often wastes time in directionless investigation.

As one might expect from the spelling, the word comes from the Greek *hypothesis*, meaning groundwork, foundation, supposition. The plural of the word is hypotheses. It has come to have a meaning similar to one of the Greek meanings—supposition. It could be called a supposition, proposition, or unproved theory tentatively advanced to explain observed facts or phenomena.

---

[*]Some complex investigations may contain both elements and hypotheses.

Actually people often go beyond giving tentative explanations for what they seem to see—they often use these explanations as a foundation or base for further investigation to determine, if possible, whether or not the tentative explanations seem to be accurate as a description of what is happening, and even whether the explanation is accurate enough to predict what will happen if certain conditions obtain. There we find the relationship between hypotheses and research, for researchers usually want to find an explanation for a phenomenon (i.e., Why is there so much more divorce than ever before in the United States?). If they have reviewed the research and the literature done by others, they usually can develop some likely hypotheses (alienation from earlier mores, breakdown in family life, increased mobility, societal changes, loss of influence of religious groups, and so on) with which to formulate a problem (study) that may more accurately ascertain what is contributing to the rise of the divorce rate.

Investigators often develop hypotheses that help give direction to their work. The engineer who scans mountain terrain preparatory to directing a mining operation or laying out a roadway makes inferences based on facts and observed conditions in coming to a decision. The engineer *hypothesizes*, that is, expresses an informed opinion as to the correct approach to the problem. The child development specialist notices that boys seem to take to science and mathematics more readily than do girls. The specialist guesses, that is, *hypothesizes*, that the difference arises because young boys and girls are differentially exposed to science and mathematics and differentially rewarded for showing interest in them.

Hypotheses are not confined to the experimental research mode. In fact, it is the rare study in any research mode that does not involve hypotheses, either explicitly or implicitly. An hypothesis is a shrewd guess, an assumption, an opinion, a hunch, an informed judgment, or an inference that is provisionally put forward to explain facts or conditions or to guide how one starts to attack a problem. It helps in determining the investigative methods to be used.

Most students have working hypotheses when they start to consider investigations. These are provisional conjectures formed to guide the initial stages of any inquiry.

A student can hypothesize (state a hypothesis) about almost anything because the term simply refers, as we have said, to a more or less educated guess. It is a little more difficult, though, to make a testable hypothesis because that means phrasing the educated guess in such a way that you can determine how correct the guess is. Sometimes one can state the hypothesis in a way that makes it absolutely testable. But most of the time it is possibly only to obtain a qualified test, not an absolute one.

If hypotheses are to be used, they should be well chosen. Keep each one simple and straightforward in language and ascertain that it meets recognized criteria such as the following.

1. Are there good reasons, practical experiences, theories, or previous research findings that tend to support it? If so, it can be said to have construct validity.

2. Is it possible to collect and analyze data in such a way as to show whether or not the hypothesis stands up? If so, it is testable.

3. Does the hypothesis focus on the problem being studied? To be *relevant* an hypothesis must answer part or all of the matter being investigated.

Another important and conceptually related Greek-derived word is *theory*. Perhaps the most misleading notion is that a theory is high-level academic and impractical explanation or idea, something that sounds great but will not work, or even if it does work in some sense, it is so far above the common person that it is not practical or useful. In sharp contrast is the comment by John Gardner, who said a theory is one of the most practical tools of the modern world. He gave the example of the plumber who knows and daily uses theory and scientific laws, even though he or she might not express them in those terms, in order to practice the trade in an expert and professional manner. The plumber who uses inflammable plastic pipes in the walls of a new house or expects water to drain uphill does not know much about either theory or plumbing (Gardner, 1978).

Webster's Ninth New Collegiate Dictionary (1985, p. 1223) defines theory, for our purposes, as "a plausible or scientifically acceptable general principle or body of principles offered to explain phenomena." In comparing hypothesis with theory and scientific law, the same dictionary (p. 594) makes a useful distinction in that

> ... law means a formula derived by inference from scientific data that explains a principle operating in nature. Law implies a statement of order and relation in nature that has been found to be invariable under the same conditions. Hypothesis implies insufficient evidence to provide more than a tentative explanation. Theory implies a greater range of evidence and greater likelihood of truth than hypothesis [but much less certainty than law].

Theory explains the relations among facts, though not completely. For example, theory attempts to explain the relationship between economic conditions and buyer preferences, or between home conditions and child-abuse behavior. Theory can provide a framework to generate hypotheses or questions or problem element statements. In turn, they guide research procedures, objectives, and data collection. For example, if we want to propose and study the effects of a new prison discipline code, we should be able to say why (in theory) we think it will be better. In this general sense, every T/D proposal should be based on theory.

If the investigator is seeking direct answers to certain questions, it is not necessary to state hypotheses formally and design the study to test them. If it is believed, however, that coincidental relationships may exist and should be revealed, or if it appears that one factor may be the cause or the result of another, a hypothesis may be the best way to state what the investigator is setting out to uncover. We encourage students to take the the initiative with their advisors to discuss whether a given topic might better be approached through setting up hypotheses, by posing questions, or by enumerating the problem elements. Significant parts of the study design will be influenced by that decision, notably the data collection, data analysis, and presentation and interpretation of the results.

Delimitations and Limitations of the Study

These two words will be discussed together because they are often confused. A *limitation* is a factor that may or will affect the study in an important way, but *is not under control* of the researcher; a *delimitation* differs, principally, in that it *is controlled* by the researcher. In psychology it is common to use a questionnaire to ascertain the status of something, for example, the job specifications of clinical, school, or counseling psychologists who are employed by public agencies. In such studies, a very common *limitation* is the willingness and ability of individuals to respond at all, to respond in a timely fashion, and to respond accurately. These are limitations on the study; that is, they are important possible effects on the outcomes of the study and they are not controlled by the researcher.

In such studies, also, it is common to have a *delimitation* as to size or nature of the group questioned, for some important and appropriate reason. In the example used, the size might be limited to those in one state, those working in urban regions, or those in certain types of agencies. Also, the size might be limited to 10 or 20% of known psychologists in such employment in order to keep it to a manageable number.

Limitations and delimitations are seldom discretionary in their use by someone preparing a proposal. They should appear only when they are imposed by the nature of the problem being studied. Limitations typically surface as variables that cannot be controlled by the researcher but may limit or affect the outcome of the study. To ignore such factors would be unscientific and one of the gravest moral/ethical errors a researcher could make. Research is useless if it is not honest. One important ingredient in research honesty is that every important limitation be spelled out for the reader and the committee. In our experience, limitations become problems to students when they are not specified, not when they are honestly and openly laid out for all to examine. Every study has its limitations; it is best to call the committee's attention to them. If the limitations are critically damaging to the study, the best time to find that out is when the proposal is in the thinking and planning stage, not later.

In a similar way, plainly stated delimitations help everyone involved to think through the design of the study. Delimitations are integral parts of the design because they set parameters, tell the reader what will be included, what will be left out, and why. A good statement of the problem will itself be somewhat limiting and delimiting, of course. However, in this section one should find detailed strictures recognized by the researcher but not apparent in the brief problem statement.

Definition of Terms

There are two major reasons for defining one's terms in doing research. *First,* define each expression that is being used in a special, very precise sense in the proposal. Unfortunately, unless it is defined, there is not always agreement on the meaning you intend for a word or group of words. A fairly common word, sometimes used by a professional in a specific and precise way, is a prime candidate for this section of the proposal.

Second, the proposed research may depend on an operational definition of a term. "Operational" means that the expression used must be definable in terms of observable, identifiable, and repeatable operations. For example, the expression "functional literacy" is, in itself, open to many interpretations. But if it is specified as a 5.0 or higher-grade equivalent score in reading speed and comprehension on a particular nationally standardized test, then "functional literacy" becomes defined by those operations used to identify it, and its meaning is unambiguous because of the "operational" definition. For another example, two common terms in education are "school quality" and "achievement." Neither one of these concepts means very much unless the user defines operationally what is meant. For example, "achievement" may be defined as the level of test scores from x test, y form, given at z time throughout the school system. "School quality" may be defined operationally by a number of variables, such as expenditure per child, educational level of teachers, years of teaching experience, and pupil test scores on specific tests. Thus, an operational definition is one that specifies the operations that will define the word. Operational definitions not only allow one to say precisely what is meant by terms used, but these definitions also establish a basis for objective tests for the outcomes of the proposed study.

Four general dictionaries we have found useful in defining terms are the *Oxford English Dictionary* (13 vol.) by J. A. H. Murray, the *Random House Dictionary of the English Language, Unabridged*, the *Webster's New World Dictionary of the American Language, College Edition*, and the *Webster's Ninth New Collegiate Dictionary*. Many professional fields have well-recognized specialized dictionaries (e.g., education, medicine, psychology). Librarians are excellent consultants on this and related matters.

Terms that are current or changing in concept may be best defined by their usage in professional and scholarly writing. Eminent persons in the field of inquiry you have chosen will define precisely the difficult terms in their work in order to be clearly understood. The student researcher is on safe ground to cite and use those definitions if they are needed in the proposed research.

Another variation is to review the definitions used by the top scholars in the field and critique them in terms of their appropriateness to the proposed research. There is nothing wrong with a review of definitions found in the literature that ends up with your own new definition, based on that review, provided it is demonstrably more useful and appropriate for the study.

Review of the Literature

In the proposal at least four sources of literature should be searched, namely: journals, major books on the subject, monographs, and dissertations. Today, much of the identification of relevant material in those four classes of publication can be done via computer access to biblographic databases.

By this time you should also have ascertained the bibliographic citation form required for your T/D. You should take pains to record, from every reference you use, the exact information you will need if you decide to cite it in the future. It is much better to err on the side of recording too many references now than to have to return a few weeks or months hence and spend hours trying to relocate some document.

If you are using a word processor or a computer with that capability, we recommend strongly that you store the data for bibliographic citations. Much drudgery can be avoided, too, by using a computer program to structure your bibliography as you build it. Such a datafile stores all types of references and can generate citations in more than 200 publishing styles, plus write footnotes in a variety of styles.

The term literature is employed to include anything appropriate to the topic, such as theories, letters, documents, historical records, government reports, newspaper accounts, empirical studies, and so forth. Some of these, like letters or reports, are called "fugitive materials" because, while such items may actually be of key importance to your topic, the originals may be quite difficult to locate. This is another point at which a professional librarian can prove to be a great help.

Figure 4-1 contains six subheadings under "Review of the Literature." In all these six subheadings, if theory and research are each treated in chronological order in the writing, usually a coherent picture of the topic's background emerges. The key is appropriateness.

A review of the literature is necessary for every T/D, but there is disagreement about the detail and depth of the review at the proposal stage as compared with the final stage. Some advisors recommend a short review, hitting the high spots of the literature, and anticipating the more complete review that will be in the final document. Others insist that the review be essentially complete in the proposal. Those who take the former position feel that the whole proposal, as a matter of principle, ought to be brief (up to 10 to 15 pages) and ought to concentrate on a statement of what the researcher wants to do and why and how, plus how it will add to what has already been done. This, it is argued, permits a maximum of student independence and freedom from committee constraints and reviews during the study.

Those who take the essentially complete review position feel that the student researcher will have a better proposal, clearer procedure, and better final product if the review is very thoroughly done before embarking on the study. Further, they say, the review has to be done anyway, so it is not lost effort. A full analysis of the literature beforehand provides opportunities to educate both the student and the committee to some of the pitfalls ahead.

We lean toward the latter view, but rather than take an inflexible position, which would not do much good anyway, we prefer to focus on what the student researcher should try to get out of the review at the proposal stage. Whatever the depth and detail of the written requirement of this section of the proposal, we encourage students to read widely in the literature, take careful notes, and maintain an organized file and record.

The most important benefit to be gained from a review of the literature at the proposal stage is a good knowledge of the field of inquiry—what the facts are, who the eminent scholars are, where the parameters of the field are, and which ideas, theories, questions, and hypotheses seem most important. The reviewer at this stage ought to be able to carry on an informed, intelligent discussion about the field with an expert, using references and citing authors and concepts important or critical to the field.

Another benefit from the review at this stage is a knowledge of the methodologies common to the field and a feeling for their usefulness and appropriateness in various settings. The reviewer can get ideas of what methodologies are most often used, methodologies appropriate for the proposed research, and when and how these ideas have been successfully used in the field. A careful look at the prevalent methodologies may also convince a student either to alter the topic of inquiry because skills are lacking to do that kind of research, or to keep the topic and acquire the needed skills.

A third potential benefit is reinforcement for an earlier hope that the proposed research is really needed. Even if similar research has been published, the literature review often turns up statements such as "It would be interesting to know if Clark's work could be replicated in other places or with different groups." Or, "It would be very useful to know if Clark's pioneering work is still relevant today." These are clues that an important study needs to be replicated, essential information to know before the proposal is drafted (Lindvall, 1959).

One vexing problem researchers have faced for years is how best to maintain objectivity when reviewing prior research. That is especially difficult when there are many published studies reporting conflicting results. Some researchers have attempted to build tables or charts of the various study results to aid in "eyeballing" the prior reports and to estimate which might be considered more credible.

An impressive breakthrough in weighing the evidence from earlier research (Asher, 1990; Glass, 1977; Hodges, 1986) is now available. Called meta-analysis, the procedure allows one to add substantial objectivity to research reviews. We recommend its use not only to minimize reviewer bias, but also to help one to determine the nature of the hypotheses or questions and the directions they might take. Moreover, meta-analysis can be classed as a research methodology in its own right, and a widely useful one. There is more on this point on p. 118.

Fourth, a literature review at this stage also often helps to narrow a problem. Nothing overwhelms one like getting into the literature of a field of study. There seems no end to the information and to the interesting offshoots that might be pursued with profit. Some get so overwhelmed with the flood of literature that severe frustration sets in. Where does one draw the line? Where and how does one narrow a topic to make it feasible, yet not cut out the important details that impinge on it and make it more understandable and researchable? This is a common problem, shared by almost all beginning researchers. We recommend parsimony based on criteria agreed to with the advisor.

Narrowing the scope of the review has been achieved by some students who employ a three-step sequence that may have to be repeated a number of times. Initially, read widely and voraciously in the proposed field of interest. Then, think and analyze, attempting always to narrow down and weed out. After that, arrange to spend some review time with an experienced, intelligent, sensitive researcher in the proposed field of study and carefully talk through the problems encountered. If your advisor fits all the requirements of a good listener in this case, you are fortunate; use the advisor. If you still have trouble getting the ideas to add up to a proposal, go back to step one again. Each time the sequence is repeated, it will go more quickly. Vary the use of persons as sounding boards. At some point a light will flash in the mind and a good review for the proposal will come into focus.

A fifth value we urge students to wring out of the review is the generation of hypotheses or questions for further studies. The more one knows about a subject, the more questions come to mind. To a researcher, there is always a reason why something (person, group, organization, body, material) operates (behaves, works, acts) the way it does, but that reason (or complex of reasons) is simply not known. It may not have been researched enough, the data may be inadequate, or the theoretical constructs may not yet be available to guide and direct further research. Out of the questioning, searching mind comes a multitude of ideas and hypotheses for further research, based on the work that has already been done. Nothing is as helpful as a review of the literature in relating the research proposed to that which has already been accomplished.

Keep a list of the questions and hypotheses that come to your mind or that are mentioned in what you read. (In the latter case, be sure that you also record *where* you found them so that you can properly cite their sources later, if you wish.) A list developed from your reading will prove useful when you are writing the literature review and when you are writing the section of the final chapter of your T/D in which you discuss the implications of your own findings and the additional research directions your work supports or suggests.

Sixth, the topic being researched now could turn out to be the start of a long-term interest. A current literature review will be useful during all that time, particularly if it is frequently updated and maintained with a consistent citation system in a computer file. It would then be easily available for further articles and follow-up investigations.

In searching the literature it is well, also, to develop a list of subject headings that relate to themes of interest. We recommend that one work back from the new to the old, and work from the general to the specific. Thus, a researcher might start with current reference sources and recent texts and research reviews concerning, for example, nuclear energy applications, dental hygiene in old age, public policy on the rights of victims of crime, adoption practices, or the education of gifted handicapped children. Then working back through the earlier research will provide a depth context and understanding of current problems. Starting with the general topic will provide leads to specific areas of interest and help develop an understanding for the interrelationships of research. For example, the relationship between education of gifted children, handicapped children, mental tests, public policy, equal educational opportunity, separation, and mainstreaming would be cases of interrelationships currently topical in the public affairs, legal, psychological, social work, and education professions.

For those in the stage of reviewing literature, recent journal issues often provide leads to content that should be in the review. The parameters of academic or professional areas, the current thinking in the field, the investigators who are writing in the field, the ideas being discussed, and the references that are most cited and respected in the field are all displayed in recent issues of important journals. At an early stage of preparing the review, hours spent with journals identified as central to the topic may be very cost-effective.

One word of advice about journals: there is wide variation in quality. Some journals are very careful about what they publish; others are not. Some are refereed by top experts; others are hungry for any manuscript that turns up in the mail. Some are read by outstanding scholars; others would have difficulty finding their way into a scholar's wastebasket. How does one tell the difference? Ask professors, colleagues who know the field, and librarians who specialize in the field and look through journals. Read a copy of the journal, look at its format, its publisher, its board of editors, examine the qualifications of writers, and review the procedures for determining what gets published in the journal.

A similar comment could be made about the library's book collection and the library's databases that give access to the collections of other libraries. As a researcher putting together a review of the literature, you do not have to agree with the major contributors to the field, but you do have to know their work and cite it. Often this work exists in books. The seminal work in almost any field is likely to be in the university library book collection, and that is an appropriate place to spend a good deal of time in doing a review of the literature or research. There is no substitute for the hours one must spend browsing the bookshelves and bibliographics of the library and reviewing the major works in the selected field of inquiry.

In short, this part of the proposal should present information about the evolvement and present state of theory and research on the topic proposed for investigation. The review should conclude by showing how the proposed study will add to the subject's knowledge base. The review should make unmistakably clear to the reader that there are some missing pieces to the body of research, what those pieces are, and that the proposed study is directly aimed at filling in one or more of those missing pieces.

RESEARCH DESIGN

As we use the term, research design is a total plan for carrying out an investigation. A completed research design shows the step-by-step sequence of actions in carrying out a scientific investigation essential to obtaining objective, reliable, and valid information. The completed design also indicates how the resultant objective information is to be used to determine conclusions about the accuracy of an hypothesis or the correct answer to a question.

Advanced study in the United States is tremendous in scope and complexity. Also, it is growing and changing. Probably no other sector of higher education generates so many exciting and difficult questions. The varied nature of the questions calls, in turn, for the application of many different forms of research.

In order to assist students from a variety of academic and professional disciplines to envision the overall concept of "research design," we have included Figure 4-2, General Model for Research Designs. The model, it is hoped, wll supply an additional conceptual structure for students to suplement the outlines in Appendix B. The General Model does not parallel, exactly, the chapter or the topic development of this book, but all the items in the boxes in the figure are treated. If referred to in discussions with advisor and other committee members or consultants, the model can be useful in maintaining the focus of a conference on specific problem areas and in working out solutions to them.

RESEARCH METHODOLOGY

This part of the proposal should identify for the reader the one or more research methods the student plans to use, i.e., opinion polling, case study, experimental, or other. The student's objective should be to give the reader a capsule statement about the contemplated research methodology, while indicating that details are to be found in succeeding portions of the proposal.

After the research questions and/or hypotheses have been decided upon, the single most important choice to be made by the investigator is what research methodology to employ. The research methodology, or type, or general method (all meaning the same thing), once selected, tends to govern, or at least limit the range of, other choices, such as how the data will be collected,

Figure 4-2 General model for research designs.

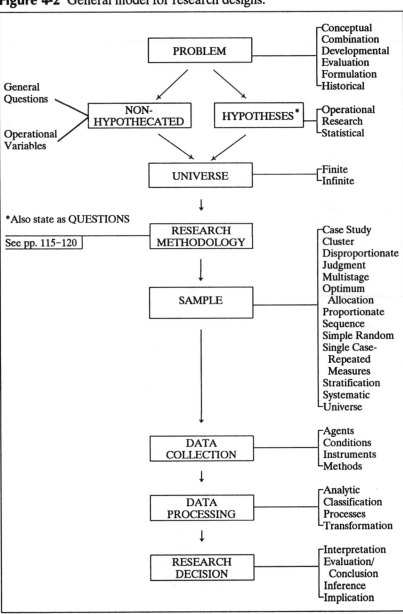

how it will be analyzed, how results will be reported, and even the nature of the conclusions that may reasonably be drawn from the results.

We found no generally accepted classification of types of research. For example, two texts (Gay, 1992; Slavin, 1992) each list five research types, but they agreed on only three of them. Moreover, one text considers qualitative or ethnographic research a distinct and major classification while the other subsumes qualitative investigations under another general category of research. Yet they both agree that qualitative research developed primarily in anthropology and was borrowed as a methodology by other fields. They also agree in defining qualitative research as describing a situation as it exists, without involving formal hypotheses, but focusing upon explaining social processes in great detail.

Because there does not seem to be anything comparable to a taxonomy in the classification of research types, we chose instead to simply list and briefly illustrate a variety of frequently utilized approaches to research.

For more specific aid to the student we have interrupted our orderly development of the outline in Figure 4-1 to insert the section below headed "Types of Methodology." Fifteen types (or methods) are named and illustrated under that heading. One or more of the types may prove an appropriate name or definition for inclusion by the student in what is written under the "research methodology" heading.

Types of Methodology

Student research methodology may legitimately embrace a wide variety of forms.

In fact, there are many actions that can assist in discovering knowledge, and humanity learned much about human nature long before there was [formal recognition of] science and scientific method. Any actions that lead to accurate statements about nature must be considered as having some methodological legitimacy; the characterizations of contrasting methods are simply arguments that some scientific actions are more effective than others at producing statements of good generality. (Johnston and Pennypacker, 1980, pp. 412–413)

In the list that follows, we have briefly identified by name and given examples of 15 fairly common types of research. Each is a valuable method when linked to appropriate problems.

There is, as yet, no standardization in research methodology terminology across academic and professional fields. The terminology used here, therefore, should be reviewed with the advisor before being included in a proposal. The same methodology may be known by a different name in another field.

1. Type: *Analytical:* Classes of data are collected and studies are conducted to discern and explicate principles that might guide action. Special subtypes under this heading include micro-, macro-, and policy analysis.

    Examples: State court interpretations of permissive legislation on nonschool use of school property

    Criteria for accepting applicants in housing cooperatives

    Management of extremes of human behavior in hospital emergency rooms

    Employment of handicapped high-school graduates in an economically depressed region

2. Type: *Case study*: The background, development, current conditions, and environmental interactions of one or more individuals, groups, communities, businesses, or institutions are observed, recorded, and analyzed for stages or patterns in relation to internal and external influences.

    Examples: A case study of open admissions in an American junior college

    The development of cognitive functions in three autistic children: case records analyses

    Establishment and growth of the American Association of Retired Persons

    The National Association of Manufacturers' labor policy; a case study of development

3. Type: *Comparative*: Two or more existing situations are studied in order to determine and explicate their likenesses and differences.
   Examples: Concepts taught in secondary school chemistry in Canada, Great Britain, New Zealand, and the Unites States
   Self-control of children and adults during cardiac diagnostic procedures
   Bid specification procedures for public playground and recreation supply and equipment purchases in New York, Pennsylvania, Illinois, and California

4. Type: *Correlational-predictive*: Statistically significant correlation coefficients between and among relevant phenomena are sought and interpreted; this type includes the determination of the extent to which variations in one or more factors correspond with variations in one or more other factors and the use of such findings in making predictions.
   Examples: Interaction of gasoline prices and automobile travel for business and vacation purposes
   Relationships between nature of crime and amount of recidivism
   Relations among size of family, age, and use of home health agencies
   Relationships between teacher backgrounds and their attitudes toward international cooperation

5. Type: *Design and demonstration*: New operationally related business systems, personnel training curricula, professional education programs, instructional materials, disease control plans, and the like are constructed and described; this type is often called action research and includes, at least, formative evaluation.
   Examples: A literacy program for the Sudan
   Feasibility of a lighter-than-air freight transport system for Africa
   A curriculum in motor development for the birth-to-three-year age period
   A cytotoxicity test for insoluble dusts

Design and establishment of a comprehensive health information system for Western Australia

6. Type: *Evaluation*: A program or a project is expected to be
carried out in a certain way and expected to produce a certain
result; research is intended to determine whether the anticipated procedure and the outcome are realized; evaluation
research that focuses on the procedure is called formative and
that which attends particularly to the outcome is called summative.
Examples: Effectiveness of mental health programs that service hearing-impaired children
Evaluation of a regional family planning program
Impact of county drug and alcohol programs
Evaluation of a rural marketing plan for fire insurance
Effectiveness of rehabilitation counseling: an evaluation

7. Type: *Developmental*: The changes over time in one or more
observable factors, patterns, or sequences of growth or decline
may be traced or charted and reported.
Examples: Growth of child care centers in American business
and industry
Emergence and spread of credit card utilization
The written language development of children
The computer and the knowledge explosion: a developmental
study

8. Type: *Experimental*: One or more variables may be deliberately manipulated and the results analyzed and rationalized —
"true" experiments requiring tight controls and subject randomization.
Examples: Reduction of separation anxiety through use of
mental imagery
Use of programmed instruction to correct errors in the written
language of deaf adolescents
The effects of listening training on salesperson effectiveness
Effects of a parental intervention strategy on reading skill
development

Effects of different options for continued employment on retirement decisions

9. Type: *Historical*: Individuals or activities are studied to reconstruct the past accurately and without bias in order to ascertain, document, and interpret their influences or to check the tenability of an hypothesis.

Examples: The relevance of the thought of Albert Camus for education

Sources of individual differences in solutions to management problems

Historical landmarks in the management of environmental noise

The search for the perpetual motion machine: its contribution to engineering

Origins and status of the Montessori movement in the United States

10. Type: *Meta-analysis*: A procedure for combining results of research across scientific areas in which measurement systems cannot be precise by adding together sources of variance to get a population value of the standard deviation as the basis for establishing effect sizes. Used both in assembling meaningful literature reviews and in testing hypotheses.

Examples: How "real" is the gender gap in aptitude test results?

What is the evidence that air pollution is associated with human illnesses?

Are large automobiles safer?

The effectiveness of hypnosis in curing addiction.

11. Type: *Opinion polling*: The behavior, beliefs, or intentions of specified groups of persons are determined, reported, and interpreted.

Examples: Food perferences of hospitalized individuals by age and geographical region in Canada

Opinions of students and alumni regarding the graduate program in counseling psychology

Political and social beliefs or experienced engineers

Citizen views on a volunteer system of armed forces

Attitudes of Sunday school teachers toward religious and secular educational objectives

12. Type: *Status*: A representative or selected sample of one or more phenomena may be isolated and examined in order to ascertain the characteristics of the object(s) of study.

Examples: Freemasonry in New Zealand: contemporary status

The mail order catalog business in America

The training, background, duties, activities, and job perceptions of public health officers

Employment among minorities in large U.S. cities

The yearbook in public high schools

13. Type: *Theoretical*: Inclusive and parsimonious explanatory principles for phenomena or data are developed, proposed, and described.

Examples: A conceptual analysis of creativity

A theory of compensatory education

An explanatory model for mass appraisal: extension of Rosen's theory of implicit markets to urban housing

A psychological theory to explain faith healing

A theory of intellectual evolution

14. Type: *Trend analysis*: Phenomena that are or have been in the process of change are examined in order to identify and report the directions of trends and to make interpretations and forecasts.

Examples: Trends in the teaching of parenting in American secondary schools

The use of public transportation in Mexico: a trend analysis

Dow-Jones average changes during selected periods of federal monetary policy

Trends in availability and cost of dental health insurance

Trends in public tax support for private colleges and universities

15. Type: *Quasi-experimental*: Experimental rigor so far as manipulation, control, or randomization is not feasible but the

comparison of treatment versus nontreatment conditions is approximated and the compromises and limitations are stated, understood, and taken into account in all conclusions and interpretations.

Examples: All of the examples under item 8 (Experimental) would be applicable here if they were carried out under conditions in which only partial control was possible of variables, treatments, populations, or other important conditions—the case in many real-life situations where field and operational studies are the only feasible kinds if professional and ethical codes are to be properly upheld.

These forms of research do not exhaust all that could be listed. Also, as noted earlier, our category names may differ from those that others would use. The most significant point is to recognize and employ the method most appropriate for the problem, whatever the approach may be called.

Two other points should be noted. First, so far as can be determined, each of the several listed research approaches has resulted in significant, new contributions to knowledge. No one is necessarily to be more highly regarded than another. Second, all students should learn about all of the research approaches. Naturally, a student will tend to become much more familiar with the approaches used in that student's T/D. However, it should be an essential requirement that all students become familiar enough with all the listed approaches to know when and how to use them, and to know when an approach is not appropriate to an investigation.

There are, of course, other ways to classify methods of research (Borg and Gall, 1983; Cooley and Bickel, 1986; Cronbach, 1982; Glass, 1977; Isaac and Michaels, 1971; Kerlinger, 1986; Travers, 1978). Other books on conducting research have a good deal to say about the forms or methods of research, and we have listed a number of such works in the reference list. However, many of the works emphasize mainly the statistical aspects of research and may therefore be limiting. Others of these works simply recapitulate the group of research methods identified by

Campbell and Stanley (1963). They are useful, but we believe the broader view we have urged should encompass those designs and more.

The proposal should clearly name and briefly describe the research method. In the description, citations from authorities may be used to clarify and support the selection of the methodology, although the appropriateness of the methodology selected is a responsibility of the researcher. The criterion measure of appropriateness is whether or not the methodology is expected to yield useful evidence with which to answer the statement of the problem. Thus, the choice is always directly related to the problem statement. Ask yourself: Does the relationship seem appropriate? Will the method yield the data needed to make an intelligent and useful response to the problem statement? These are questions to raise with one's self, one's advisor, and others who read the proposal and critique it.

Specific Procedures

Here one tells the reader how the investigator is going to research the problem stated for the T/D. Clarity is a virtue.

The researcher tells the reader, step by step, what will be done in the conduct of the study. This may include correspondence, the design of questionnaires, pilot studies to be mounted before the complete study, the application of some treatment, the conduct of interviews, the distribution of inquiry forms or other instruments designed to gather appropriate data, obtaining permissions, the use of consultation, or other actions. Leave out only those matters to be dealt with under other, subsequent headings.

Start with a chronologically ordered list of the procedures to be used, and elaborate each item in enough detail to let the committee know what will be done. In a proposal, "enough detail" may vary from a paragraph on one item to a full page on another. If you go too far beyond a page, you may ask yourself if the writing is as parsimonious and succinct as it should be. Surplus words are likely to obfuscate the problem, annoy the committee, and raise the question of how sure you are about what you intend to do.

Research Population or Sample

In this section in the proposal, a few essential points are to be covered. First, what is the population to be studied? Is it a type of flora? Is it a group of research reports on which you will conduct a meta-analysis? Is it a form of virus? Is it a group of people? What are its characteristics? Will the universe (everyone or everything in the population group) be studied, or will there be a sample? If a sample, how will it be selected from the whole? What is the justification for selecting the sample? Is it possible to determine the representativeness of the sample? If not, does that fact constitute a prohibition or just a limitation? How does one gain access to the sample population, and how difficult a problem is that expected to be?

One reminder here—the research population and the sample, if any, should tie in very clearly with the statement of the problem. If the problem indicates a dependence on perceptions of urban residents or workers, for example, one might expect such individuals to be in any research population designated. Similarly, if one wants to be able to generalize to nursery-grown trees in the United States, the sample must be constructed with that goal in mind.

Instrumentation

In this designated section, detailed data should be presented about the instrumentation (tests, apparatus, interview protocols, questionnaires, and the like) proposed for the study. The clear purpose of any instrument should be to help produce or gather data to answer questions raised in the problem statement.

At this point students are encouraged to review the potentialities in contemporary technology for ways to enhance the speed, the accuracy, and the reliability of instrumentation. For example, there are computer programs for administering questionnaires, for displaying stimulus material of a variety of kinds, for administering tests, and a number of other uses requiring an interface with a subject. Such material is coming onto the market in a steady stream, as researchers are recognizing its value in minimizing the human error factor in a number of aspects of research. Not to be overlooked in this connection, also, are other widely available pieces of technology such as the Fax, the tape recorder, the calculator, the photocopier, the telephone with answering capability, and the video recorder.

Keep in mind that, if technological instrumentation is employed, it must be cited, giving its name and where to locate it. As with any other reference or citation, the basic purpose is to allow a reader to access the material directly in order to verify that it was represented accurately by the author.

Careful advisors tend to want to see any instrument before it is applied to a research population. At least the specifications for any instrument should accompany the proposal, and it is much better if the entire instrument does, if feasible.

Pilot Study

If a pilot study is proposed, this part of the proposal should describe when, where, and how it will be carrried out. A pilot study, by definition, takes place before the actual study in order to determine feasibility and to work out bugs. It is important, then, that the pilot have a provision for soliciting and gathering formative evaluation from the pilot study population. This pilot population, in other words, ought to have built into it a systematically designed opportunity for the student to learn the points of view of respondents, including the problems.

It is also necessary to tell the reader if and how the pilot population differs from the proposed study population, and how that difference will effect the study, if it will have an effect. Be completely honest. A difference will not necessarily be a threat to the validity of the study if it is recognized and accounted for beforehand.

After the pilot study is completed, the researcher usually decides whether or not the proposed procedures need to be revised. The proposal must tell the reader what the researcher intends to do after the pilot study is completed, and how it is to be done.

Data Collection

Usually this is a description of the nature of the data, how the data will be collected, including, for example, the mailing of questionnaires, the gathering of specimens, the scheduling of interviews, the search for documents in libraries in specified locations, or the recording of differences between two groups of subjects. A statement of provisions for follow-up is expected. Whatever type of research is proposed, the committee will want evidence that the researcher has thought about the possibility that data may not come easily and has made plans for the eventuality. Also, if human subjects are involved, the protection of their rights and how they will be debriefed should be indicated.

The process of collecting data must be appropriate to the research problem and the specific nature of the data. For example, interviews are very inefficient ways to collect large-scale survey information, although they may be used to supplement or to ascertain validity and reliability of such data. Other examples of inappropriate data collection procedures—which may spoil otherwise excellent research studies—are those that unacceptably invade the privacy of respondents or put human subjects at risk.

Advances in computer technology now make feasible the first-hand collection and analysis of many kinds of data involving events and behavior. A laptop computer may be used to collect and store data and then to generate a variety of tables and reports, including answering many different questions about probability relationships between and among events.

Treatment of the Data

After the proposed data are collected, what will be done with all the information? Will tables and charts be constructed, and if so, what will they display? If the data demand careful analysis, can that analysis be described in the proposal? Will the analysis be done in concert with some theoretical construct, and if so, can that be described? These are the kinds of questions the committee will expect to find answered in the proposal.

Usually the hypotheses or research questions guide the researcher in sifting through a mass of data. They focus the search and provide implicit criteria for the evidence search. Perhaps a simple analogy might be made to archaeologists at a dig. There is a mountain of stuff to sift through, and perhaps all of it is interesting, but without hypotheses guiding the search, it is possible that some important artifacts will be glossed over and some critical relationships missed.

Here, too, computer software can make substantial contributions to the research process. Many colleges and universities maintain centers that furnish consultation to students and faculty on the selection and use of the most appropriate statistical procedures for answering questions or testing hypotheses from a given set of data. Such centers are much like the libraries in the way the operate, being there for use as needed. In some instances they will store data for the researcher and run analyses as requested.

Doing such work on one's own is made easier, too, by statistical software packages on the market. For example, one source for a large variety of statistical and graphic analysis packages for both IBM and Macintosh is Softstat.

The T/D student must remember, though, that use of a statistical procedure carries with it the responsibility of understanding and being able to explain the reasons that the procedure is appropriate. That is part of the prevailing ethics of research in academic and professional circles. If you are the author, you accept responsibility for everything in the manuscript.

Appendices

An appendix may be needed to present drafts of letters to be sent, briefs of related research, as well as drafts of questionnaires and/or interview schedules, tests, rating forms. This is also an appropriate place to put an appendix that shows a Time Line or flowchart of how the research will proceed. That could be adapted from Figures 1-1 and 3-1. In general, an appendix contains documentation or evidence of important points made in the body of the proposal and referred to in the proposal. An appendix is the place for important tables, displays, or other items too long and detailed to be in the proposal's main body. For the proposal itself and its appendices, we recommend parsimony. If in doubt, leave it out. After all, items can always be added if that is the wish of the committee or the advisor.

Bibliography

A thorough, focused, succinct bibliography is mandatory. List only the materials cited in the proposal. This is not the place to list everything you can find on the subject in the library. Remember that the bibliography helps to indicate the authority of the work by the quality of sources cited, not the quantity.

A major purpose of the bibliography is to enable the reader to use the works cited. Therefore, each entry must be complete, so the work cited can be found. If you might use documents that others cannot get, tell the reader in a footnote what they are and why they are important to your study. It will not help the reader if you simply cite such works in the bibliography.

When specifying a reference always seek to cite the *actual* source. If an article you are reading contains a pertinent quotation from another source, there is a temptation sometimes to use the quotation in your own manuscript as though you had found it yourself in the original source. First, that would be dishonest. It would not give due credit to the author of the article where you really found it. And it would give the impression, falsely, that you had read the original source and discovered the pertinent quotation yourself. Second, to appropriate material in that way exposes one to dangers of two kinds. Some studies have shown (Adler, 1991) that citations are likely, often, to have been incorrectly referenced in even otherwise well-edited books and journals. Further, if you pretend to have quoted from an original source, you risk embarrassment if one of your committee members knows the original source well and begins to quiz you about what else it contains. Moreover, even if you have been motivated to locate and study the original source of the pertinent quote, it is a professional and academic point of courtesy to acknowledge the author who led you to do so.

MAKE SOFTWARE YOUR SERVANT

Almost every aspect of T/D work can be enhanced in appearance, done more efficiently, completed more quickly, or made more accurate through using readily available software. That applies from the moment one begins to think about possible topics until the T/D is completed and being readied for journal or book publication.

Where can you find the software you need? Ask the librarian to direct you to Database Descriptions, Files 237 and 278, Buyer's Guide to Micro Software (Soft), and Microcomputer Software Guide, respectively. Their DIALINDEX categories are PCINFO and SOFTWARE, for both. These databases can help researchers locate suitable packages compatible with specified hardware without sorting through the more than 35,000 records now on file. Evaluations are included and each file receives a monthly update.

Consider *keeping records* for a fine illustration of how truly helpful software can be. Make a habit of entering, daily, one's thoughts, musings, ideas, questions, and discoveries in a computer's memory, in the form of one or more *files*. Such files then become your own stockpiles of raw material to which you will probably return again and again as you find new uses for what was originally stored there. Moreover, you will find yourself elaborating on the items already in storage and adding new items.

A key point about filing notes is the value—even the necessity —of keeping track of the sources of your notes, especially those that came from reading books or journals or listening to lectures or participating in discussions. That need emphasizes the importance of being able, later, to *cite* precisely from whence the information came. The need for complete and accurate knowledge about where one got an idea or a quote points up the urgency of starting immediately to construct and maintain a *bibliography*.

A number of students have found it valuable to put the headings in this chapter into outline form right in their own computers, so they can then insert relevant material as they learn about it or conceptualize it. Appropriate software will not only allow that, but will make it possible to arrange and rearrange and edit to help you to clarify your vision of what you want to do, and could lead you toward ways to make your writing, itself, both grammatically correct and compelling.

SUMMARY

This chapter helps the reader prepare the proposal by discussing the most relevant criteria for the process. A suggested format for the overview is presented, with recommendations about how to deal with each section of the proposal. An outline in the form of a Table of Contents is presented as illustrative material. Sections explaining, for example, the problem statement, the review of the literature, and the research design are major parts of the chapter. A list of different kinds of research methodology, with a brief explanation and some examples of each, is included, as are suggestions about maximizing the help available from contemporary technology.

5

The Thesis or Dissertation Committee

It is the norm among reputable institutions of higher education to require that graduate and honors student research be guided and monitored by a committee. The committee typically consists of the chairperson (usually the student's advisor) and an additional number of faculty. Commonly, the thesis committee has three members and the dissertation committee between three and five, depending on the institution regulations. Sometimes there is a requirement that one committee member be from another department or even from another institution.

The committee normally serves through the proposal stage on to the satisfactory completion of the project. Occasional exceptions require two quite separate committees, with separate functions appropriate to the differences between an overview and a final defense.

FUNCTIONS OF THE COMMITTEE

The committee provides both guidance and evaluation. It is the most important guardian of the quality of honors and graduate

129

study, since completion of the T/D culminates in an advanced or honors degree. The process that the committee oversees challenges the student to operate effectively at high levels of independence in investigating concepts of considerable sophistication. The holder of the degree is assumed to be competent to practice as an expert in a professional or academic field. The committee must ascertain that the student has in fact reached the high levels indicated by the awarding of advanced or honors degrees. Additional evidence of this expectation is that the final oral examination may include questions not only on the investigation, but also in the substantive area of academic study or the profession. Thus, the committee functions to assure the quality of the T/D as well as the quality of the student's knowledge and understandings in the appropriate discipline. The list that follows includes the main functions.

1. The committee provides advice and consultation to the candidate throughout the process of the research.
2. It approves or in some other way acts on the proposal of the candidate.
3. It makes qualitative judgements about the candidate's written work, including substance, format, style, grammar, design, methodology, procedures, and conclusions.
4. It sets the direction of the study by approving the proposal and assists the chairperson in providing direction for the study.
5. It approves the style manual to be used by the candidate, with particular attention to any proposed deviation from a standard style manual.
6. It approves, when constituted as a final defense committee, the final draft.
7. It assures that the rights of human subjects are protected.

Figure 5-1 displays an evaluation form that has been used by a number of experienced advisors. We recommend it for students and faculty members at this point because it shows what committees look for in proposals and final documents. Being aware of that early can help in the preparation process.

Figure 5-1 Thesis/dissertation evaluation form. It may be used for either the proposal or the final document. When used for the proposal, omit the asterisked (*) items.

Name of evaluator and date:_____
Title of dissertation or thesis:_____
Name of student:_____

Characteristics being evaluated	Poor	Mediocre	Good	Excellent	Not Applicable	Evaluators' notes on items rated
1. Title is clear and concise						
2. Problem is significant and clearly stated						
3. Limitations and delimitations of the study are stated						
4. Delimitations are well defined and appropriate to solutions of the problem						
5. Assumptions are clearly stated						
6. Assumptions are tenable						
7. The research projected by the proposal does not violate human rights or confidence						
8. Important terms are well defined						
9. Specific questions to be studied are clearly stated						
10. Hypotheses, elements, or research questions are clearly stated						
11. Hypotheses, elements, or research questions are testable, discoverable or answerable						

Figure 5-1 Continued

Characteristics being evaluated	Poor	Mediocre	Good	Excellent	Not Applicable	Evaluators' notes on items rated
12. Hypotheses, elements, or research questions derive from the review of the literature						
13. Relationship of study to previous research is clear						
14. Review of literature is efficiently summarized						
15. Procedures are described in detail						
16. Procedures are appropriate for the solution of problem						
17. Population and sample are clearly described						
18. Method of sampling is appropriate						
19. Variables have been controlled						
20. Data-gathering methods are described						
21. Data-gathering methods are appropriate to solution of the problem						
22. Validity and reliability of data gathered are explained						
23. Appropriate methods are used to analyze data						
24. Sentence structure and punctuation are correct						
25. Minimum of typographical errors						
26. Spelling and grammar are correct						

Characteristics being evaluated	Poor	Mediocre	Good	Excellent	Not Applicable	Evaluators' notes on items rated
27. Material is clearly written						
28. Tone is unbiased and impartial						
29. Overall rating of creativity and significance of the problem						
*30. Tables and figures are used effectively						
*31. Results of analysis are presented clearly						
*32. Major findings are discussed clearly and related to previous research						
*33. Importance of the findings is explained						
*34. The relationship between the research and the findings is demonstrated with tight, logical reasoning						
*35. Conclusions are clearly stated						
*36. Conclusions are based on the results						
*37. Generalizations are confirmed						
*38. Limitations and weaknesses of study are discussed						
*39. Implications of findings for the field are discussed						
*40. Suggestions for further research are cited						
*41. Overall rating of the conduct of the study and the final document						

General comments:_____

_____

_____

_____

STUDENT/COMMITTEE NEGOTIATIONS

Sternberg (1981) correctly points out that candidates face two sets of negotiations: "1. Those with the committee/department as a whole; 2. those with individual members of [the] committee" (p. 138). He recommends as "absolutely essential" that the candidate show each chapter, as it is written, to each committee member for approval. We consider that to be a matter to be determined in consultation with the advisor. But we agree fully when he also points out that "some of one's lines of communication can be sustained/supplemented by progress letters, notes or phone calls" (p. 139). Many advisors we interviewed felt the same way.

In our judgment the regular progress report, in memorandum form, is the single most effective way to stay in touch in a constructive way with each committee member. We suggest that memos be sent *on a regular schedule* every two or three weeks and that a computer file or file folder be used save copies. Such reports are common practice in major research institutes, so it is good to learn to use them. The memo should be written, reviewed with the advisor, and, with advisor approval, duplicated and sent to all committee members. The key to good communication is to keep the memo short and factual.

A useful format for the progress report memorandum is shown in Figure 5-2.

The Activities, Problems, and Other headings cover the substance of the progress report. They are linked in terms of time to the calendar Period Covered, that is, from some date to some later date.

Activities completed might, for instance, be a series of interviews started during the period of the prior report. Activities continued might be a literature search or certain data processing. Activities initiated might be the start of a pilot study. The kind of material reported obviously depends on the nature of the project and what actually occurred during the two or three weeks of time covered. If something is both started and finished during that period, report it under Activities Completed.

Figure 5-2 Progress report memorandum.

Project title: _____
From: _____ To: _____
Date: _____ _____
Period covered: _____ _____
Investigator's telephone: _____
Activities completed: _____
Activities continued: _____
Activities initiated: _____
Problems: _____
Other: _____
_____

The Problems section should be used for unresolved problems only. State the problem briefly and tell what you are doing to try to solve it. Indicate if you are working with a particular committee member or another consultant on the problem, or if you intend to do so. The Other section covers situations like delays because of illness, unanticipated developments in the investigation that are significant but are not problems, and similar matters. If there is something (i.e., a reprint) you wish all committee members to have, mention it under this heading and attach it.

Committee members who receive periodic, short, factual progress reports written in clear English with complete sentences know that the student is taking the research work seriously. In that case, the committee members are inclined to be more serious in their interactions with the student. Also, the student who makes regular reports is unlikely to face confrontations later, with faculty comments like: "Well, you never gave me a chance to help you, and I thought your approach was wrong from the start!" The fact that your telephone number is on every report makes it easy for a committee member to contact you if there is reason to do so.

In addition to the written progress report, which can be mailed or Faxed, or sent by E-Mail or Bit-Net, we recommend that a telephone contact be made with each committee member at least every month or six weeks. Even if there is no pressing reason, use an approach like checking to see that the progress reports have been arriving and that they are clear. Ask if there is any particular part of the investigation on which the committee member wishes more information. In this and other ways, keep communication channels open.

As to whether or not to provide members with chapters or other segments of the document as it is being written, we are less adamant about that than Sternberg (1981). Some dissertations do almost require that approach. A critique or a theory development about social policy or monetary policy might profit very much from step-by-step committee input. A poll, a case study, or an experiment, though, might more usefully be reviewed by committee members in a first draft of a full report. We recommend discussing this matter fully with the advisor and then, if appropriate, with individual committee members. Try to accommodate to the advice of the advisor and to the individual style preferences of committee members. It is appropriate to ask the advisor to clear the arrangement with the other members on the committee if it appears you might be caught in a conflict of views where you have responsibility but no authority.

SELECTING THE COMMITTEE MEMBERS

Preferred practice calls for committee members to be named with care. Competence, interest, and current workload should be the chief criteria. Deans, chairpersons, or graduate study directors who act arbitrarily in naming committee members and who do not involve students in that determination deny them a potentially rich experience in decision making. Also, anyone who assigns faculty to committees without prior consultation with them comes dangerously close to infringing on academic freedom.

Earlier, a number of suggestions were made to help students exercise intelligently their share in the choice of a chairperson. The same considerations can be reviewed while thinking about other committee members. Some added ones are these.

Can you identify faculty members who, when put together as a committee, provide good resource coverage for all the proposed project's parts?

Do you have a particular weakness in one aspect of the projected work? If so, have you located a committee member who has recognized strength in that area?

Are you going to propose the use of a procedure or of a tool that is very specialized or so new that many faculty members would be unfamiliar with it? If so, have you found at least one prospective committee member who is acknowledged by the rest of the faculty to be a responsible authority or specialist with that procedure or tool?

Do you know enough about the possible committee members to feel confident that there are no personal or professional animosities among those you are planning to propose? Are you reasonably compatible with each?

Selection Criteria

Universities have formal criteria for the selection of committee members, but the criteria tend to be concerned with bureaucratic rules rather than with the more value-laden qualitative judgments significant for students. For example, a common requirement is that the majority of the committee be members of the graduate faculty. Another example: usually at least one member of the committee must be a member of a department or school other than the candidate's, for professional schools.

For the student and the advisor, qualitative criteria ought to determine the membership of a committee. They should look for faculty known for integrity, scholarship, expertise in the candidate's field of study, high standards in writing, and both T/D guidance and personal research experience. The bureaucratic criteria are important, for they generally guard the institution from abuses and improprieties, but the more qualitative criteria are essential to a high standard of scholarship.

Procedure

Students should find out and follow the published or unwritten local rules that govern the selection process. Usually the rules involve both the advisor and the student. The school or department faculty ordinarily reserves the right to approve the selection of the advisor and the committee members. This right may be latent, it may be clearly authorized but unused, or it may be used in a pro forma way, but it is usually there to be exercised. This approval process may also extend to chairpersons and deans in addition to faculty recommendation or approval. The advisor is responsible for whatever needs to be done to satisfy this matter.

Student Role: The extraordinary importance of the committee strongly suggests that students take special care about their part in the selection. How does one use good judgment in this matter? Review the criteria recommended previously for committee members. Are they reasonable for the selection of your committee members? Try to assess prospective committee members in some of the ways described in previous chapters; consult your advisor, fellow students, graduates of the department's program; talk to a number of faculty about your proposed statement of problem to see if they are interested in or knowledgeable about it. Ask for advice and suggestions from those with whom you talk. Carefully weigh the reception, the consultation, the expressions of interest, and the quality and direction of advice you receive. Work carefully but try to move quickly, too. The early selection of appropriate committee members can save a great deal of time, effort, and frustration later and will certainly enhance the quality of the final product.

Advisor Role: The advisor has the most important faculty role in the committee selection process. The research advisor is normally the person who, with the student's help and concurrence, makes the selection of faculty members to serve on the committee — such persons meeting both the formal rules of the university and the qualitative criteria applicable to the proposed research topic.

It is common, as noted earlier, for the advisor to submit the proposed committee to some person or body which has the right of approval, but that approval is usually expected. The nature of the university and the research process makes it difficult and often dysfunctional to disapprove a proposed committee, except in extreme cases and on very good grounds, unless the committee does not meet the formally stated requirements of the university.

The most certain way to continue to assure high quality in committee selection (and, indeed, committee action) is by assuring that the process is open to systematic and continual peer checks and review. Such overt and systematic review might include, for example, the posting of defense times well in advance, distribution of notices of receipt of proposals and final drafts far enough in advance to permit faculty review, and the holding of final defense meetings in such a way as to encourage the attendance and participation of any faculty or students having an interest in the research topic. The advisor's role in committee selection includes taking leadership in assuring that characteristics like these distinguished the process.

Departmental Chairperson Role: This role is one of assuring quality and equity. The interests of the student, the faculty, and the institution have to be protected, to the end that the purpose of graduate research is fulfilled with excellence. That is expected of the chairperson by all significant others who take part in the process. The chairperson may have formal authority to deal with some matters directly, such as the power of appointing or approving the advisor or the committee. Sometimes, though, chairpersons have to work in less formal ways by suggesting, encouraging, and rewarding. The integrity the chairperson can maintain is related to the strength and academic vigor of the administrative leadership of the school or university. Both faculty and students need to be vigilant to assure proper emphasis on the two essential attributes—high quality and equity for everyone.

A Committee Selection Model

We found much variation in committee selection and assignment practices. Of all the models, the one with the features in the list that follows seems to have most to recommend it. *

1. The dean or department chairperson's office distributes annually to all honors and graduate students a list of faculty members that contains three items.
    a. The titles of *completed* T/Ds the faculty member chaired in the previous three academic years.
    b. The titles of *completed* T/Ds on which the faculty member served as committee member in the previous three academic years.
    c. A list of the one, two, or three special-interest and competency areas of each faculty member, as prepared by themselves, such as law, social psychology, anthropology, welfare policy, transportation, rehabilitation, early childhood, finance, microbiology, astrophysics, computer science, research methodology, human stress, supervision, counseling, speech pathology, program evaluation, instructional theory, or others.

2. Students are advised in writing by the dean that they are encouraged to discuss prospective T/D topics with *any* faculty members.

3. Faculty members refer students to one another with the primary objective of helping the students learn for themselves what others think of their ideas in the early formative stages.

---

*We urge students to try to dig out the kind of information in this model on their own if it is not supplied routinely by their school or department administration.

4. Each advisor maintains gentle but steady pressure on advisees to formulate proposals in writing and to discuss them.
5. There is a published departmental deadline by which time the student must have a proposal approved by a committee, or the student will not be permitted to enroll for more courses.
6. The advisor offers assistance to the student in identifying a research advisor and committee members.
7. Students are made aware from the outset that it is their responsibility to make the nominations of chairperson and committee members to the department chairperson.
8. Once nominations are received, the department chairperson is obliged to first check two items.
   a. Do the student's nominees already have full loads with respect to these tasks?
   b. If not, are they willing to work with this student?
9. If conditions (a) and (b) are acceptable, the department chairperson notifies the student, the student's advisor, and the nominated committee members of the appointments.

This model for committee selection and assignment has the virtues of openness and orderliness. Misunderstandings are minimized. The interests and the workloads of faculty members are taken into account; the student is supplied with useful leads and clear guidelines. Within the school and departmental contexts, the process and its outcomes are public and can be maintained on a professional plane. The model does presume that the matter of faculty workload, as it relates to advisorship and committee membership which we discuss later, has been settled.

Size of Committee

We recommend committees of four and five for the thesis and dissertation, respectively. That is larger, by one, than the usual requirement. Usually there is no prohibition against having a committee larger than that specified in regulations. Often, the final defense committee is encouraged to add members for the purpose of enlarging its scope as an examining group.

Large committees take large amounts of time; that may be one reason for the prevalence of very small ones. While a small committee—some schools require only three faculty members for the dissertation committee—may be reasonable, a larger number can enhance quality and equity. Five is not too many, particularly in light of the variety of expertise that usually needs to be gathered. We also recommend that in case of emergency the committee be fully authorized to operate with one less than the required number, that is, with three and four for the thesis and the dissertation, respectively. Thus, if one member retires, moves, becomes ill, or goes on a sabbatical leave, as is not unlikely in a committee constituted over a number of years, it is less likely to hold up progress and penalize the student. Finally, a very subjective comment: Our experience suggests that larger committees tend to be run in a more open and above-board fashion and that they tend to focus more on the quality and relevance of the work than on the worker.

COMMITTEE MEMBER ROLES

The role of a committee member is somewhat like the research advisor's role, but there are important differences. A committee member's does not carry as much responsibility. Also, the depth of the role is greater for the chairperson. Such differences allow committee members to exercise more flexibility and creativity in role definition and to make the relationship one of positive growth and maturation for the student.

Foster Creativity

Faculty members come to the T/D committee task with varied perceptions of its nature and the opportunities it offers. Students, too, are not sure what to expect. The T/D committee membership is not well defined in professional literature or by easily observed modeling of role incumbents. The lack of overt, consistent definition means the job is open to a good deal of professional judgment, independence, and self-direction. It also means that there are opportunities for both the student and faculty to be creative in determining how a committee member works on a given study.

For the faculty member, much of the joy of working with students on creative projects is present without all the responsibility of the chairperson.

Seeman (1973) offered a theory-based point of view on supervising student research. He emphasized the creative aspect of what the student is to produce, namely, a contribution to knowledge, defined as a novel product. Then he drew heavily on published research on creative persons, leading to the conclusion that "an optimum learning climate (in which to foster creativity) would involve considerable latitude for the student to go off into unconventional cognitive byways, along with a support system that provides them with occasions for doing so."

In a pamphlet called *Research Student and Supervisor* (LaPidus, 1990), the Council of Graduate Schools offers its viewpoints on that relationship and suggests ideas relevant to disciplines that prepare students for the Ph.D. Some key observations from that publication are:

> A peculiarly close relationship exists between the research student and supervisor. They start as master and pupil and ideally end up as colleagues. Obviously, under the circumstances, it is desirable that the student and supervisor should be carefully matched.
>
> There are two aspects to supervision. The first and most important has to do with creativity and involves the ability to select problems, to stimulate and enthuse students, and to provide a steady stream of ideas. The second aspect is concerned with the mechanics of ensuring that the student makes good progress. (p. 1)

Note the similar emphasis on creativity in Seeman (1973) and LaPidus (1990), almost 20 years later. Moreover, the Council of Graduate Schools (CGS, 1990b) also urges that originality on the part of the student should be fostered as a central concern in the T/D process. And originality is another word for creativity.

However, Seeman argues that what really happens is almost the opposite: a climate of conformity prevails, produced and sustained by the research guidance given the student. He blames this, in psychology, on the discipline's homage to the conventions and procedures of "science." He says:

> For students, the phenomena of scientific ritual and scientific respectability appear in the form of rapid and insistent preoccupation with questions about sample size, controls, instrumentation, statistical procedures, and other formal questions about the structure of their inquiry. I am saying that a too-early concern for these structures puts the accent on formal rather than substantive issues, deflects the students' energies from their original questions, and, most crucially, emphasizes an external locus-of-control attitude that may dilute the sense of ownership and responsibility which the students feel for their problems. (p. 901)

Going on to suggest a connection between student behavior and the perceptions conveyed to students by the learning atmosphere in which they start to think about research, Seeman says:

> It is small wonder that many students experience the development of a research problem in terms of finding some pre-existing question "out there." They search the literature, read other student's theses, seek ideas from professors, and in general disregard the possibility that a research problem might come from some question of their own. (p. 901.)

As to the role of the system in generating that kind of student behavior, and as to the function of the faculty in keeping the focus of the student's attention narrowly on the formal aspects of T/D work, Seeman reasons that a restrictive. limiting, learning climate is the inevitable result, not an optimum learning climate. He puts it this way.

> What I am suggesting here is that science has become a quasi-legal system, and that deviance is just as much punished in this domain as in any other domain where people make laws. Seen thus, the task as experienced by the student is to go about his/her proper business while at the same time making sure to

obey the law. In this context, professors are part helpers and part social control agents of a very powerful kind. They become advisers-policemen who assist the student, but who also make sure that the student obeys the law with respect to scientific procedures.

In short, the psychological climate for the student is one in which the helping process and the evaluative process become thoroughly entangled. The most likely consequence is interference with learning. (p. 901)

If Seeman's analysis is correct, it raises serious questions that seem applicable to many of the conventional forms and processes in graduate and honors student investigations. Research procedures and designs used in a number of professions have been drawn from psychology, long recognized as an undergirding discipline with major applications in professional human services work.

Seeman (1973) does not report data drawn systematically from students or from faculty members to verify his analysis or his conclusions about the climate of learning and about the behavior of students and advisors. Neither do LaPidus (1990) or CGS (1990b). Seeman finds analogs in studies of other situations, mainly those that involve counseling and psychotherapy, and argues from those presumed parallel instances. It would certainly be valuable if his provocative and insightful ideas were put to a more direct test.

We have drawn a number of implications for the professor-student relationship from the Seeman analysis and our own observations. They are potentially helpful guides to action for students and faculty.

1. Foster a secure relationship in which the student has confidence in the support of the professor. (The professor says, honestly, "I believe in you and in your ability and integrity. You can count on my guidance and I will give it freely and in a helping spirit.")
2. Recognize and encourage independence in the student. (The professor praises students for taking actions on their own. The

professor says, "You can expect me to encourage you to make decisions for yourself, whether or not I agree with them. This will be, all the way, *your* project. I will enjoy helping you to make it that. At the same time, I will try to teach you how to judge the adequacy of what you do.")

3. Teach the student to understand how the professor views personal and professional accountability. (The professor lets the student know that both their professional reputations are on the line, afresh, with each decision they make about the investigation. The professor says, and means it: "It will be important to me to help both of us to avoid conflict with each other and with our associates. At the same time, if either of us believes in the rightness of what we propose to do, even though it appears to be leading to a confrontation, we should not hesitate to initiate a discussion about it. We should speak our minds, try to work out the differences, and if that fails, separate with full respect and regard for each other.")

Seeman believes that the experience of autonomy can be used to make explicit the nature and kinds of responsibilities the student and the faculty member each will accept. He says:

> I have started to take this route by making explicit contracts with my students. For my part, I accept two kinds of responsibility. . . . I take responsibility for certification of a student's performance; that is, I accept as a social responsibility the evaluation of professional competency. My second responsibility is to make available to the student the professional resources and skills that I have. On the students' part, their enrollment in a program signifies that they have committed themselves to developing competence. . . .

> I see the concept of a contract as a powerful tool for developing responsible interpersonal relationships.(p. 905)

Aside from anecdotal pieces (Krathwohl, 1988; Mecklenburger, 1972; Merrill, 1992; Pulling, 1992; Sternberg, 1981), there seems to be little established information about the student as such in the T/D process. Yet a profession's most able students, as they do graduate and honors research, and afterward, would seem to be most logically and most appropriately the best sources of information and insights about how to make the most of the major commitment colleges and universities have to that advanced work. MacKinnon (1962) remarks that

> ... creative students will not always be to our liking. This will be due not only to their independence in situations in which nonconformity may be seriously disruptive of the work of others, but because ... they will be experiencing large quantities of tension produced in them by the richness of their experience and the strong opposites of their nature.

He was describing the behavior of creative architects when they were students. He went on to report that

> ... clearly, many of them were not easy to take. One of the most rebellious, but, as it turned out, one of the most creative, was advised by the Dean of his school to quit because he had no talent; and another, having been failed in his design dissertation which attacked the stylism of the faculty, took his degree in the art department. (p. 495)

Other professions, too, attract individuals who combine the ingredients that make up creativity. The academic and professional nurture of such men and women can be a stormy experience. The long-range outcomes, however, enrich the student, the advisor and committee members, the institution, and the professions. Data about how to best encourage such positive outcomes are needed.

One of the opportunities to foster creativity is to brainstorm — to explore problems, hypotheses, and conjectures without being too evaluative at the early stages. It is important in this context for students to be encouraged to *see* and to *understand* side issues, offshoots, parallels, and branches of their topics and to acquire the discipline to stay on the main track, nonetheless. It is a chance to explore with the student the relationship of the emerging T/D to the development of personal effectiveness and personal goals such as autonomy and professional and academic maturity. Faculty-student interaction around the graduate or honors research project provides many opportunities to help the student grow as an autonomous, self-directed person at a time in life when that help is perhaps needed most. The honors or graduate student experience up to that stage has often been directed by others; the T/D stage is a transition from dependence to autonomy.

Committee members also have excellent opportunities to enhance both the student's and their own research competence. Committee members can help the student-writer on a one-to-one basis to examine the associative relationships that are projected in the study. It is a time to help the candidate to look for possible cause-and-effect relationships in variables identified or phenomona to be observed. It is a time to examine theory and engage in some preliminary efforts at building new theoretical constructs. Opportunities to teach the value of suspending early judgment, to teach by example some aspects of critical thinking and deductive reasoning, are available to the committee member throughout the advisement process. These opportunities are especially valuable because they come at a time, with respect to an interest in a commonly shared subject, when the openness to learn and to share ideas is strongest.

Encourage Clear Writing

Not all committee members have the same interests or expertness, but everyone should care deeply about the student's ability to express ideas about complex matters in clear and direct prose. Many investigations deal with complicated subjects; students often feel that their writing has to be equally complicated. Committee members can help students see that there is an artificiality about complex and overly complicated sentences and paragraphs full of long words which obfuscate rather than foster understanding. Further, such writing all too often is a facade hiding a student's lack of clear comprehension. There is no subject that cannot be made clear in simple words to the average intelligent adult, if the explainer knows the subject well enough and has good facility with written language. Committee members who help students express themselves in clear, concise, and direct language perform an invaluable service. The student gains not only with respect to the immediate task, but in future writing and publishing.

Foster Growth Through Writing

Committee members can set examples for students by participating in professional meetings and engaging in scholarship. Also, committee members often have the contacts and information that permit them to encourage student participation in professional and scholarly meetings. Some of the most valuable experiences have come to students who were encouraged to write, publish, and read papers at such meetings during their advanced study years. Often these activities were related to T/D work—perhaps literature reviews, descriptions of pilot studies, or the findings of the T/D research itself. Numerous examples, out of our own experience, can be cited regarding the encouragement of students to write, to publish, and to prepare papers for professional and academic meetings. There are, for example, citations in this work that refer to important contributions made by students on whose committees the authors served, or who worked with the authors in some similar way. Papers can be written and presented jointly. Panels and reactors can be chosen to include a student researcher.

If money is a problem, often ways can be worked out to help the student researcher attend meetings and present papers through the use of awards, travel with faculty colleagues who may drive, and the payment of modest honoraria for services performed at the meeting. We have seen examples of colleagues helping to pay expenses of students. None of this is a part of the formal responsibility of the committee members, perhaps, but it all could be a part of the mentoring role which faculty members define for themselves. Sometimes just words of encouragement and the offer to help are enough to set the student off in the proper direction, with self-motivation taking over the progress toward final autonomy and participation.

The role of the committee member must always be seen as fostering the autonomy and professional and academic maturity of the student researcher. This does not assume that the student is immature or dependent, but the behavior typically encouraged or enforced all too often turns out to be toward dependence and following directions. For that very reason the obligation is there, in the research stages of study especially, to encourage the emergence or reassertion of autonomy and self-direction.

Serve as a Model

Advisors and committee members themselves acquire role behavior through observing models. New faculty members watch committee members and chairpersons in action while in the process of doing honors, master's, or doctoral work and later imitate them. Committee members' behavior also impresses the student and tends to be remembered and copied if, later, the student assumes the committee role. Therefore, the behavior of senior committee persons is of great significance. It becomes the model for others.

Modeling is also one very good way students learn to become advanced researchers. This has implications for the role of the committee member who works closely with the candidate on a research problem, or who thinks through the formulation of a research problem with the student researcher.

Students and colleagues respect the committee members who insist on excellence and fairness. It is the responsibility of each committee member to provide serious and consistent help to the student, with the aim of assuring the high-quality work of which most students are capable, and to work toward making the whole process as rigorous and fair as humanly possible. Every vote counts on the committee, and every vote cast, in some instances, could be the vote that makes the difference between outstanding scholarship and just sliding through.

Allen (1973), Sternberg (1981), and Krathwohl (1988) all picture the student as tightrope walking. The choice may sometimes seem to be between alienating the committee, on the one hand, by sticking to a point of view on what should be in the T/D, and becoming completely confused and prey to every shift in committee thinking, on the other. We believe, as they do, that the advisor and the student should figuratively link arms in such a case, and together they should stand for what they believe. When that happens, committees tend to work around to accepting the candidate's way of dealing with the matter so long as there is confidence in the integrity of the individual and confidence that the knowledge base is sound. This is especially likely to be the outcome if, as Sternberg suggests, the candidate "persists in a dignified and firm manner."

SUMMARY

Universities normally require a research project supervised by a faculty committee as the culminating work of honors or graduate study for a degree. Committees of faculty are appointed to work with the candidate on the project from the proposal stage through to the final defense. The committee functions as a guide and help to the student through the process, and it also evaluates the work as it progresses to the final defense. A form for use in T/D evaluation is included. The committee is so important at most institutions that great care is taken in the selection of members, and there are various roles played in the selection process. The obligations of committee members to one another, the student, the advisor, and the institution are specified and discussed.

6

Approval of the Study Plan

The study plan document takes its form from the nature of the problem to be investigated. Earlier (p. 6) we suggested a format that covers essential proposal elements. Terminology differs from place to place, but the most common names given to the document that makes up the study plan are *proposal* or *overview.*

The goal of the student at this point is to gain the approval of the committee to embark on the conduct of the proposed project. That approval, if given, is certified by an actual vote of the committee. The committee members affix their signatures to a form that specifies salient information about the meeting.

The committee's collective judgment is reached by the end of the overview meeting. Each member has earlier read the proposal itself. During the overview meeting members raise questions, engage in discussions with the student and each other, and offer suggestions about the proposal.

Each committee member should have assisted with the proposal idea earlier in conference with the student, and each committee member should have seen earlier drafts of the proposal.

However, the overview meeting may be the first discussion regarding a document that the student now believes is ready for the entire committee's stamp of approval.

The committee's goal at this point is to determine whether both the student and the written plan are ready to move into the operational stage of the T/D activity. The overriding question is: "Has a state of adequate preparedness been reached by the student, and has satisfactory preparation been demonstrated in the written project proposal?" A crucial part of the proposal is the section that sets forth how the investigation is to be conducted. That section, sometimes called procedure, includes the steps the student expects to take from the moment the plan is approved to the time the analysis of findings is completed.

Actually, of course, when the study plan is considered for approval, we recommend that the section that details the procedure be embedded in a larger document, the T/D proposal. Also, the proposal should be a coherent document, in that each part is linked meaningfully to each other part. But while other parts of the document may be in less than final form (i.e., the literature review), that cannot be true of the procedure section. If the overview committee is to approve the study plan without imperiling the future of both the project and the student, procedures should be complete and detailed.

CHARACTERISTICS OF A SOUND OVERVIEW

Students will find that advisors and committee members vary in their views as to what are the necessary components for an appropriate overview. Our recommendation is to try to satisfy three criteria, as follow.* *First*, include consideration of at least these elements.

A brief title that describes the investigation.
A face sheet with appropriate identifying information.

---

*For more details about organization and structure of the proposal, review Chapter 3 and pay particular attention to the T/D evaluation on p. 131.

A table of contents.

An introductory statement of the problem to be studied.

A specific problem statement couched in terms of questions to be answered by the study's results, or hypotheses to be tested, or definitive information to be supplied, or a product to be developed, or some combination of these. This is a good place to define terms, if necessary. Here the investigation types on pp. 115–120 and the General model for research designs. (Fig. 4–2) may be helpful. They may also stimulate thinking about the next elements in this list.

A list of classes of literature (i.e., theoretical, research, philosophical, and so on) germane to the problem with a critical and analytical review of that literature which supports the need to conduct the proposed study.

A step-by-step procedure section that includes specific information about which data will be collected, from which sources data will be obtained, how the validity and reliability of the information will be assessed, and how the data will be analyzed to respond to specific problem statements.

A brief summary of the proposed investigation as previously outlined plus any other matters that should be part of the record (i.e., human subject concerns, threats to the study).

A sample of each data collection form or test or similar material to be used in the study.

A bibliography of the references in the overview document.

Second, try to assure that the ambiguities and anticipated problems are openly discussed. For example, suppose some of the data to be collected depend on responses to inquiries mailed to parents. Suppose, also, that there has been a history of very low response rate to similar inquiries to parents in similar circumstances. This should be brought out in the overview document, with a clear statement of what measures are to be taken to encourage a satisfactory return, and with a contingency plan, should the return be insufficient for analysis.

Third, we recommend the inclusion in the proposal document of a systematic planning procedure that spells out the anticipated time line of the investigation. That may well be an appendix. Help in setting forth the entire procedure and time sequence may be found by studying Figure 3–1.

Even though there is variation among advisors' and committee members' views regarding what constitutes an approvable overview, the elements suggested include what many professors expect. The three key elements are a full and detailed proposal, clarification of potential ambiguities, and a rational time sequence.

PURPOSES OF THE PROPOSAL OVERVIEW MEETING

This section is concerned with the proposal overview meeting's purposes. University in-house publications tend to specify administrative details, such as that a proposal be in typed form, how many committee votes are required to approve it, and where the approved document must be filed. In some cases certain of the purposes can be inferred from university publications. In addition, we list purposes drawn from an analysis of interviews with experienced faculty members. The committee should, according to them, also ascertain that:

1. The topic of the investigation is suitable.
2. The student is competent to undertake the study.
3. The program (or department) in which the study is undertaken is appropriate for the topic.
4. The study would constitute a valuable contribution to the literature.
5. The topic is manageable in relation to the student's time.
6. The study would be a relevant learning experience for the student.
7. The student has access to the needed human and material resources.
8. The student is able to be objective about the study.
9. The student and committee members understand the agreements resulting from overview approval.
10. The student understands any alterations needed in the proposal.

Each of the 10 items is important; each deserves amplification and discussion. The student, the chairperson, and each committee member might well use the 10 items as a checklist to make sure that they are adequately covered in the course of the overview examination or before it.

Suitability of the Topic

This is an important characteristic of a sound overview proposal. It means that the topic is suitable in terms of the scholarly and research interests of the academic discipline, profession, or field of study. Demonstration of the relevance and suitability of the topic to the discipline is the proposer's responsibility.

Another aspect of suitability might have to do with the utilization of human subjects. Some investigations could require that human subjects be deprived for a time of food, educational stimulation, or affection, compensation, or rights that other subjects receive. Such studies would be unsuitable unless acceptable compensatory arrangements could be made and higher-level approvals received. The question of suitability arises, too, when the investigation proposed has so many unique qualities that little possibility of generalization can be anticipated.

Suitability ought not be taken for granted. The student should deliberately ask each committee member, so the student's log and notes, by the time the overview meeting is convened, will show that suitability is not in question.

Student Competency to Undertake the Study

Three main factors are looked at here: the student's substantive academic and professional background, the student's investigative skills, and the complexity and difficulty of the proposed study in relation to the first two.

For the first, let us suppose that the proposed topic is *"Design of a Graduate Curriculum Model for Training Community Planners in Brazil."* The operative expressions in the title are in italics. The student proposer needs knowledge of design procedures and principles, knowledge of graduate professional curricula, appreciation of the personal and professional characteristics and job requirements associated with community planning, a sound conceptual base regarding Brazilian higher education, and in-depth understanding of the history, present status, and the goals of community development in Brazil. Certainly it would not be necessary that the student have *all* of the background at the outset, but it would be questionable if the committee should allow the study to begin without ascertaining that it was feasible for the student to fill in any gaps quickly and thoroughly.

As to the investigative skills, the student should know how to unearth already existing information about the operative expressions in the title. That would call both for knowing sources and for how to search international literature. Reading knowledge of Portuguese seems essential. Also, it might be necessary to plan and to conduct interviews.

The judgment of expert faculty members or other consultants would be essential to assess the complexity and difficulty of this study. They could determine whether the country's educational and political climates would be supportive. They could judge how much time, if any, would need to be spent in Brazil. They could help judge whether substantial ground preparation would need to be done or if the foundations were ready and waiting for such a study. And they could ascertain whether the proposed study might be overambitious, and suggest how to reduce its scope, if that is the case.

Appropriateness of the Topic for the Department

In this instance, let us assume that the student proposes a study called "Career Preparation of the Private Black College Graduate Relative to National Manpower Needs and Trends." If the student is enrolled in a department of elementary education and is specializing in early childhood education, it would probably be far-fetched to consider the topic appropriate to the department. It would be unusual to find faculty members in elementary education who have and maintain sophistication about the broad field of college career preparation.

Occasionally students do put forward ideas that appear, on the surface, quite out of harmony with the departments in which they are matriculated. It is well to discuss them rather than to dismiss them out of hand. Sometimes such apparently divergent proposals are signs that students' interests or goals are changing, and those possibilities deserve thoughtful attention from the advisor. Actually, at the time of the overview meeting it should be very unusual to see topics proposed that are patently outside the scope of the particular department in which the major part of the study is to be done. More often the questions are more subtle.

For example, if a study is to deal with interactions among school of business faculty members, business education faculty members, and the local business community, should its home base be in the school of business, the school of education, the department of sociology, or elsewhere? If there is any question at all about such a matter, and if the question does not surface until the actual time of the overview meeting, the guiding principles for resolution ought to include these:

The student should not be delayed or otherwise inhibited from pursuing the study simply because of interdepartmental or interschool disagreement.

The department or school in which the student is enrolled should continue to have responsibility for administering the T/D process of the student.

Members of other departments and schools should be added to the committee to the extent necessary to assure that the necessary faculty competencies are represented.

Contribution to the Literature

Most discussions of the essential requirements of the T/D include the statement that the product be a "contribution to the literature." Yet few phrases have been so ill-defined. In the absence of helpful guidelines, students (and sometimes faculty) erroneously conclude that to make a contribution one must discover a hoard of new information, demonstrate a new truth, devise a new instrument, or at least construct and validate an original theory. Actually, graduate research studies that did any of those things would certainly be welcome, and they would be hailed as contributions. But they would be extraordinary T/Ds. There can be quite valuable contributions of lesser magnitude. Most are in the latter class.

Students often worry about getting negative results or about "finding nothing" at the end of a heavy investment of time and effort in an investigation. Rumors abound regarding the flat rejection of theses or dissertations that wind up with either equivocal findings or with no solid basis for supporting the original hypothesis.

Krathwohl (1988) has this to say about the absence of positive results:

> Must the dissertation have positive results to be acceptable? A proposal ought to have a reasonable chance of showing positive results. But if it doesn't work out as expected, must you start over? ... I know of no instance where this has been required. Instead, students are asked to explain as best they can why negative results appeared and what can be learned from the apparent blind alley.

Earlier, Sternberg (1981) made much the same observation about negative outcomes. A Council of Graduate Schools publication, (LaPidus, 1990), offers an additional cogent comment, namely, "One must, however, remember that we are talking about original research where, by definition, things do not necessarily go as intended" (p. 6). In short, it is certainly a helpful contribution to identify and demonstrate that a research approach that appeared to have promise is actually not fruitful and to delineate the reasons why.

The committee, at the overview meeting and before it, will keep in mind that the *process* of T/D work needs to be given somewhat more attention than the *product*. The student's knowledge and application of investigatory processes, including intelligent reporting of what transpired and what was found, is what is being demonstrated. The topic certainly must be shown by the student to be both relevant and significant to the literature. But it is enough to ask simply that the potential results of the study be judged capable of adding to or helping to clarify a matter that needs investigation, and that the findings will probably have some generalizability.

In thinking about these criteria, both student and faculty should note that one of the most obvious needs in many fields is to redo studies that have already been reported. Exact replication is seldom needed; we mean repetition with new or enhanced populations and with strengthened design and improved controls. Frequently, also, creative reanalysis of previously reported data opens the way to clearer interpretations. Studies that help us to understand better an already reported phenomenon or principle, studies that make our knowledge more reliable or more generalizable, as well as studies whose findings are suggestive of further exploration or which tell us that a given course of investigation is probably not profitable can all be contributions to the literature in the sense that the term should be applied by the overview committee.

Manageability of the Topic in Relation to Time

T/D work has specified time constraints. A six-year time span, for instance, is usually allowed between permission to begin the doctoral dissertation and its completion. The period is less for the master's thesis. The honors thesis is ordinarily done during the last two years of undergraduate study. In some cases students are admitted to study for the doctorate after achieving the baccalaureate, but are required to complete a master's thesis along the way. In that instance the student may not be permitted to take courses after a certain number of credits have been earned or after a certain elapsed time unless the thesis is finished and approved. There are temporal factors, too, such as sabbatical leaves, the period the data or the study populations will be available, and the decay of data relevance over time. All things considered, the overview committee needs to help the student reach a rational decision about what anticipated completion date to place on the overview approval document.

The Study as a Learning Experience

Many doctoral students already have a substantial amount of academic or professional experience. Some of the experience may have included involvement in or responsibility for research. The advisor and committee members should be familiar enough with the student's background to assure that a proposed study is not simply a rerun of competencies that had been demonstrated at an earlier time. Naturally, the use of already confirmed capabilities is appropriate if the T/D tasks build on them and exert them significantly beyond any prior work.

From another direction, too, the committee has to satisfy itself that the student will be assured fruitful learning opportunities. Sometimes a chairperson is so caught up in the T/D itself that the student has little or no opportunity to work out problems or procedures independently. At such times the student may be led by the advisor so closely and meticulously that questions are answered before they are fully asked and there are no opportunities to make mistakes and acquire understanding by working out how to recover from them. Finally, on this point, the atmosphere of the overview meeting itself may be viewed quite differently by each advisor and committee member. Some of the variations in the tone and attitude of faculty toward student during the meeting are shown in Figure 6-1. They are arrayed from desirable to undesirable.

As in a class or seminar, individual research students are entitled to the best instructional efforts their faculty advisors can muster. To be sure, the instructional style is different. It is closer to the one-to-one tutorial sometimes; at other times it takes on the interactive fashion that characterizes peer consultation, or the approach of partners in seeking the solution to a problem of mutual interest. That student entitlement to top-flight instruction holds, too, not only for the overview meeting, but for the entire length of T/D activity. It is particularly important, though, to

Figure 6-1 Faculty tone and attitude during overview committee meetings.

Undesirable	*Desirable*
	• Collegial
	• Instructional
	• Consultative
• Advocate	
• Maternal/paternalistic	
• Nondirective	
• Laissez-faire	
• Adversarial	
• Dictatorial	
• Punitive	

highlight it for the overview meeting, for if that standard is not upheld, the overview meeting can degenerate into something it should not be, an examination,* or even worse, an inquisition.

Access to Needed Resources

What needed resources come immediately to mind if one is to attack this topic: "A History of Changes in U.S. Public Policy Toward Migrants and Their Children"? This one: "Predicting Reading Achievement of High-School Students with Measures of Intelligence, Listening, and Informative Writing Ability"? This one: "Reactions of Married Persons to a Geographic Move Resulting from Spouse's Job Transfer"? This one: "The Influ-

---

*In a certain sense the overview meeting is an examination and the proposal is or is not passed. The focus is less on the student's achievements in doing research, however, and much more on helping the student to produce a proposal that will get a whole-hearted positive response from the faculty. It is an examination much in the sense that a diagnosis is an examination; the purpose is to find the difficulties and improve the prognosis.

ence of Unionization on Equal Employment Opportunity Practices"? Or this one: "Organizational Behavior in Time of Crisis"?

The student's advisor would ordinarily encourage the adoption of some orderly method for keeping track of resource needs as they appear in the process of developing the proposal and would assist the student, if necessary, in gaining access to them. The culmination of that aspect of planning should be exemplified in the proposal document. If there is any question about whether the needed resources (a) have been identified and (b) access to them assured, the question should be satisfied before approval of the study plan.

Student Objectivity About the Study

A student designed a portable floor mat on which was imprinted a hopscotchlike game of numbered spaces. It was expected that children with number-related learning disabilities could be helped to overcome them by individualized exercises that employed the mat. A well-controlled, carefully planned study was proposed for a dissertation by the student to determine whether or not the expectation could be substantiated.

In the meantime, the student's device was manufactured and widely marketed, commercially. The student received substantial royalties. Anecdotal information, based on uncontrolled observations and individual case records, suggested that children did improve their number skills as a result of prescribed exercises. That information was also distributed to prospective buyers.

The dissertation study proposal was approved. The investigation was conducted. The results indicated that individualized exercises on the floor mat had no appreciably different effect on the number skills of children with learning disabilities than did ordinary number instruction.

The student, after completing the dissertation, could not accept the results. An entire additional year was taken up in fruitless tinkering with the data, attempting to find a way to make the findings say something else. In all, more than a year of that student's life was spent in a turmoil before the matter was resolved. In the end, the student did complete an approvable dissertation, but the personal and professional costs are still being paid, by student and faculty members alike.

Wise instructors caution to practice objectivity from the beginning of professional study. Yet a number of students each year take the hazardous course of proposing topics about which they have strong personal beliefs rather than strong scientific curiosity. If the proposal itself needs improvement, a very subjective attitude on the student's part might well deter the committee from suggesting ways to make it approvable. Even if the student's proposal is sound, the committee should move cautiously if the student's anticipation of confirming conclusions prejudices the proper conduct of the investigation or threatens the student's own welfare.

First, it is advisable to make the student aware of the committee's concern. That can be done directly in the meeting, and it can be confirmed by attaching a memorandum to the approval document and mentioning it in the letter that informs the student of the official approval.

Second, the committee can insist that data collection and analysis procedures be made explicit in the overview proposal, including the provision that the collection and analysis be done or closely observed by a disinterested third party. This is not to be thought of as suggesting that the committee distrusts the student. Rather, it is an examplar of how any professional person should behave when faced with the task of investigating a matter in which there is known to be a strong enough personal involvement to be potentially biasing.

Third, the committee should give more than ordinarily close attention to the student's literature review. Particular committee attention may focus on assuring that the review does not overlook publications inimical to the student's viewpoint and that all publications are given even-handed treatment. None of this should suggest that T/D work ought to be completely unemotional. There is a noticeable excitement and an evident spirit of zestful probing in students and in faculty during much of the enterprise. That should be encouraged. Rather, it is the possible limiting and even destructive effects of overcommitment on a highly personalized level that the committee is enjoined to help students avoid.

The Quasicontractual Relationship

Some speak of the approved proposal document as a contract between the higher education institution and the student. Lawyer-sociologist Sternberg (1981) found that both Washington University (St. Louis) and Columbia University had, within the previous 20 years, been in court over charges that explicit or implicit conditions of dissertation preparation had been violated. So far as the proposal itself is concerned, he concludes "that a contemporary candidate is warranted in proceeding *as if* a dissertation proposal contract is in force once his committee approves his proposal" (p. 75). If the proposal and the circumstances around it fall inside the purview of American contract law—even in a limited and qualified way—the fact gives some welcome reassurance to the student. As Sternberg comments, "in the generally zero-sum model of power and authority in which he [the student] finds himself in relation to dissertation-supervising professors, the contract element is perhaps the only 'guarantee' of some substance upon which he can rely" (p. 75).

Certainly the approval of the proposal does signal an agreement by the committee on behalf of the faculty that an acceptable plan has been submitted and that the student is judged ready to move ahead with the study. In addition, the approval sets certain limits, directly or by implication. For example:

The anticipated time of completion is indicated.
The voting members of the final oral committee are specified, since they are the same as the voting overview committee members, unless otherwise provided in university regulations publicly available to students.
The work to be required of the student is that which is projected in the proposal as approved.

These limitations have a protective effect for the student. No one can justifiably press for earlier completion than the anticipated date specified on the approval form. While other faculty members may take part in the final oral examination, they have no votes. Capricious changes in expectations about what will be included in the T/D study are obviated.

The limitations previously enumerated tend to be more binding on the faculty than on the student. If more time seems to be needed, for instance, the student is free to open discussions with the committee about it. Negotiations about other matters, also, are usually started on the student's initiative. Tradition has it that the committee does all it can to adapt, support, and encourage the student. All things considered, it may be overstating the case to refer to the approved proposal as a contract. It is, however, evidence of a legitimate set of professional and academic understandings and agreements that students have every reason to expect to be honored. It carries with it, also, all of the same responsibilities that are present between a faculty member and students in a course, seminar, and guided or independent study.

Advisement About Final Alterations

An overview meeting that results in approval is not completed until all required changes in the proposal are communicated to the student. It is common practice that when the signed approval document is forwarded to the school or university office that houses such records, it is to be accompanied by a copy of the proposal as approved by the committee. The student is expected to amend it so it will in fact reflect what the committee did approve. The actual procedures that can be employed in assembling and monitoring the proper inclusion of amendments will be discussed later.

In addition to the items already discussed, an overview session may have other, longer-range impacts. For one, the meeting is an example of group consultation. It may very well be a precursor of similar meetings in which the student will take part after graduation and employment at a university faculty member or as a staff member or consultant for a company, a government, a school system, or another agency. For inexperienced faculty members on the committee, the overview meeting and the behavior displayed by the chairperson and other experienced members may become models to emulate. These should be recognized effects and their potential importance acknowledged.

CONSULTATION WITH COMMITTEE MEMBERS

Students who complete T/Ds satisfactorily agree that they remember three peaks of progress along the way. Faculty members experienced in research advisement tend to name the same three. They are:

The actual selection of the problem to be attacked
The approval of the proposal document
The completion of the final oral examination

All concur that effective consultation with committee members is of fundamental importance in reaching those peaks. Consultation is more than a casual conversation; it is a complex set of interactions. Also, it is work. Like most complicated and strenuous undertakings, planning makes it go better.

T/D problem selection, in its early stages, is usually a consequence of informal consultation with a faculty member. Often, something referred to in a class triggers student interest. At other times, it is a follow-up of a paper or seminar presentation by the student. Increasingly, students are required to take seminars that survey the significant research in their discipline for the dual purposes of learning about the state of the art and of stimulating their interest in contemporary problems that need investigation. Also, departments or prestigious individual professors engage in programmatic study that provides a multitude of possible research topics. In addition, some universities house research and development institutes that, while independent of the "teaching" schools, have overlapping faculty who carry on investigations and other creative activities that include an abundance of opportunities for students in search of suitable topics. Contact with any of these can spark initial interest. The next move, though, is up to the student. For best results, it should be a planned move toward faculty consultation.

Consultation Regarding Problem Selection

A sensible first move is to confer with the advisor. But what to talk about? How to talk about it? What expectations to hold about the results? Actually, those questions themselves and others like them are quite legitimate ones to start with; we addressed them briefly in a previous chapter. Now we go into more detail.

It is reasonable for the advisor to expect that the student will have made at least a minimum level of preparation for the initial consultation regarding problem selection. If the preparation includes these elements, the probability of a successful consultation will be enhanced.

Makes an appointment with the advisor. Clear the meeting for at least 45 minutes of the advisor's time.

Clear personal time for about 30 minutes before the appointment and for an hour afterward, if at all possible. The time prior to the consultation is to assure being on time and to allow opportunity to review notes and other preparations for the session. The time following has the function of allowing the interview to go on longer if the advisor wishes it and has time. Second, it gives the student a period for collecting thought, to make notes and summaries of the items discussed.

Some students send a copy of each conference summary to the advisor and to anyone else being used as a consultant. That helps to reduce or correct misunderstandings at the same time that it guarantees a record of the meeting in the student's log and in the consultant's folder. As noted earlier, modern information technology makes such communication and record keeping convenient and practical.

The choice of a faculty member to direct the study: If the student knows that a topic is well within the range of the advisor's professional specialization, it is appropriate that the student ask the advisor to chair the committee. If that seems inappropriate because of existing commitments or other reasons, the advisor should recommend other faculty members who might be appropriate chairpersons.

The choice of members to serve on the committee: The advisor leads the student to identify the kinds of special help that might be needed in planning and conducting the study being discussed. Then the advisor helps the student match those identified problem areas with faculty members who have particular potential to help with them.

Students who plan carefully, as we have said, will already have in mind persons who would be suitable committee members. Students will often pick persons they have had as teachers and with whom they have established cordial relationships. The advisor often knows about the strengths of colleagues with whom the student has had little contact. Between them they can build a tentative list. As one result, the student broadens an already existing base of acquaintanceship with faculty personages.

The T/D problem selection process has no clear beginning and no definite time limits. Students usually make one or more false starts before a firm choice emerges. During this period it is essential to employ advisor and faculty consultations, as already suggested. It is also essential during this exploratory period to avoid final commitments to a chairperson or to committee members. However, once the student and an advisor reach agreement that a certain topic is feasible and is to be pursued, the committee should be formalized.

Consultation Regarding Preparation of the Proposal

This is a period of intensive consultation. It is very demanding of time and energy for student and faculty members alike. From the student's point of view, the most serious potential hazard arises from failure to keep all committee members up to date through periodic contacts. Use of our recommendation about regular written or computer-mediated reports can ward off that danger.

Advisors should inform themselves about the frequency and the manner in which their students are in contact with other committee members. While it is not essential in all cases, a number of advisors make direct and frequent contacts themselves with other committee members. Some call brief, informal meetings so committee members can update each other. In highly complex projects and in those which run over a long period of time, the latter is certainly preferred practice.

COORDINATION ROLE OF THE ADVISOR

When a student gets input from individual committee members, what should be done with it? Particularly, what should be done when the recommendations of some committee members conflict with or diverge from the recommendations of others? Resolution of those problems makes up a major part of the advisor's coordination role. That necessitates, of course, that both advisor and student keep close track of the views of all committee members and understand the reasons for their views.

A number of advisors are quite directive to their students in this connection. They say, in effect, "Listen carefully to each committee member's criticism and suggestions. Probe, if necessary, to be sure you understand. But *do not argue*. Also, *do not agree* immediately to make the changes that compliance with the criticisms or suggestions implies. Respect the consultation you are receiving. Indicate, politely, that you will give it serious thought. Ask about any matters that you want to be clarified. Then bring the matter to me for discussion."

Whether the research director's style is as forthright as that or not, the essence of that message must be conveyed to the student. Otherwise chaos is probable. Unless the director defines and takes on the coordinator role, neither members nor students have anywhere else to turn for the ajudication and reconciliation called for by strong, disparate viewpoints. Thus, students ought to be able to look to the chairperson for assistance in making optimum use of consultation from other committee members. Like the fabled course of true love, the course of proposal preparation may not run smooth. The skill and diplomacy of the advisor should then serve as a shock absorber, all the while maintaining high professional and academic standards. That exemplifies the preferred approach to meeting the responsibilities of coordination.

From time to time, advisors take quite another course. Like steamrollers, they attempt to smooth the way for their students by crushing and overriding any viewpoints but their own. That action defeats one of the purposes of research consultation, for it prevents the student from experiencing the thrust and parry of ideas in a setting where the best ideas should survive. Also, it sets a poor example, displaying a model of undesirable, irresponsible behavior in the delicate role of chairperson and teacher.

Setting the Stage for the Overview Meeting

Scheduling the time for the meeting about the proposal is simple enough once there is agreement that the student and the document are ready. The best criteria for the latter are these.

The characteristics of a sound proposal document given in earlier chapters have been achieved.

The comments and suggestions of other committee members have been analyzed and, where feasible and appropriate, worked into the study plan.

The student understands the purposes of the meeting and expresses readiness to take part in it.

It is the advisor's responsibility to set a date acceptable to the committee and the student. School regulations sometimes require more lead time than this, but the proposal should be in the committee's hands at least two weeks before the meeting. (The document should be clean, fresh copy, and complete.)

Helping to set the date by contacting the other committee members is a worthwhile organizing experience for the student. Also it supplies another occasion to talk with committee members to obtain any last-minute suggestions they might volunteer. A quiet, uncluttered room should be scheduled. It is advantageous to seat the committee and the student around a table, since there may be considerable paper shuffling and note taking. Usually two to three hours is sufficient time for an overview. To be on the safe side it is best to schedule at least two and one-half hours.

The date, time, location, and subject of the overview meeting are best circulated from the chairperson's office by a memorandum to committee members, the student, and other interested persons or offices. The official notice ought to reach its recipient at least two weeks prior to the meeting date, and it should request a confirmation of attendance. If it has not been distributed earlier, the proposal can accompany the notice of the meeting. Thus, the confirmation of attendance can be taken as assurance that the document came to the committee member in time for careful study.

The advisor and the student researcher should ascertain that all materials necessary for the meeting will be on hand. Some presentations may call for slides or charts for certain parts. Others require the use of chalkboard or models or drawings. Whatever is essential for an effective presentation should be on hand in the room where the meeting will be held. The student should have an opportunity to rehearse the presentation there, if that seems advisable.

Importance of Organizational Arrangements

Students and faculty members both deserve, as a *first* priority, setting and conditions conducive to excellent work. That includes matters of space, noise level, accessibility, and well-managed procedures.

Second, student research work on the university campus ought to be, in all of its aspects, a realistic introduction to participation in scientific investigation as a career expectation. To help accomplish that, the mechanical and administrative procedures ought to parallel the best operational principles and details found in highly respected public and private enterprise, in state or local governmental agencies, on university campuses, and elsewhere.

Third, the student engaged in faculty-guided investigative activities ought to find it stimulating and intellectually worthy. The experience should encourage a lifetime commitment to respect and to use research and development findings. The likelihood of that outcome is enhanced when the student observes evidence that the university administration and faculty attend meticulously to the physical and administrative conditions in which proposed research work is reviewed and its conduct approved. In short, the way T/D work arrangements are staged by the school tells, bluntly and vividly, how the significance of that work is evaluated by the faculty and the administration.

The Conduct of the Overview Meeting

If students know anything about overviews, it is usually what they pick up from other students. Some of that is useful; much, though, may be unrepresentative anecdotal material. Students are grateful when advisors explain ahead of time the general scenario of an overview meeting. The appreciation grows when the explanation is accompanied with tips on survival skills. We recommend that the following role descriptions be discussed in detail with the student well before the meeting.

Chairperson's Role: As *presiding officer*, the chairperson conducts the meeting. An agenda like the following represents preferred practice.

1. The chairperson and the student arrive at the meeting room in enough time to check whether it is adequately prepared.
2. The chairperson arranges for the student to wait in a comfortable place near the meeting room.
3. When a majority of the committee is present and the appointed time is reached, the meeting is officially convened.
4. The chairperson ascertains that the committee is ready to meet the student, there being no valid objections on the part of any member.
5. The student is asked to join the meeting. The chairperson requests a brief summary of (a) the student's education and

professional experience and (b) the proposal being offered for the committee's approval.

6. Questioning and commenting about the proposal begins; the chairperson makes sure each committee member has a chance to participate.

7. The questions and the related discussion and suggestions continue until the chairperson senses that the committee members may be ready to conclude the meeting. The chairperson then asks if anyone wishes to continue the session. If so, it goes on until all members finally signal willingness to stop.

8. Then the chairperson asks the student to return to the waiting area while the committee deliberates.

9. The chairperson puts the main question to the committee; namely, is the student's proposal to be (a) rejected, (b) approved with conditions, or (c) approved unconditionally?

10. The committee reaches its decision and signs the form provided by the chairperson to make the decision a matter of official record.

11. The chairperson recalls the student and, in the presence of the committee, reports the decision. The student may be asked to summarize the decisions and conditions, as an affirmation of the mutual understanding of the student and the committee, and to make sure that the results of the meeting are clear to all.

12. The chairperson and the student have a conference in which the decision of the committee is interpreted and in which any conditions placed by the committee on its decisions are discussed with the student.

This 12-point outline is a skeleton summation of the role of the chairperson as presiding officer. Some may feel that it appears too formal, not suited to the easy relationship that should characterize student-faculty and faculty-faculty interactions. To that objection it should be said that the process outlined (or, for that matter, any other procedure recommended in this book) can be carried out with whatever degree of formality or informality is most comfortable to the participants.

Our concern here is not so much personal style as it is obligation and orderliness. It is imperative that all parties acknowledge and carry out their responsibilities. For instance, it is not a matter of style when a committee member lounges into a meeting one-half hour late and announces, while flipping through the pages of the proposal, "This is too long! I haven't had time to read it." That shows plain disrespect for colleagues who did their homework, and it shows disregard for the worth and dignity of the student and of the review process itself. The outline presented, as well as other procedures recommended in this book, are intended to support an orderly approach to the task at hand. This outline provides a framework for the grand strategy of the overview meeting. The tactics ought to be as individualized as the topic, the student, and the individual faculty members require. The chairperson's role, though, is multifaceted, not confined to directing the course of a meeting. Several other sides of that individual's responsibility are indicated next.

A *record-keeping function* falls to the chairperson. Most keep a personal folder on each doctoral advisee in their own offices, in addition to the student's official departmental file. The personal file has copies of official records plus the transient and incidental notes necessitated by day-to-day advisor-student interactions. In connection with the overview meeting, the advisor needs copies of the official document (the proposal, the signed decision of the committee) plus notes taken at the meeting. If both the advisor and the student take notes, they can compare them after the meeting to produce a more complete and reliable picture of what transpired. That is particulary important if the overview proposal is approved subject to conditions. The chairperson, during steps 9, 10, and 11, reaffirms the conditions the committee has agreed to with the student. Some are substantive, requiring that specific parts of the proposal be altered. Others may be procedural. For instance, final approval of some changes may be left to the chairperson while others may need to be seen by one or more other committee members. Records of these conditions are obviously highly important; it is up to the advisor to assure that they are part of the written history of the meeting and that they are conveyed fully and accurately to the student.

Support of the student also ranks high as a role of the chairperson in the overview meeting. One advisor reports a premeeting conference with each student during which these things are said.

1. "I am going into this session as a strong supporter. I would not have agreed to hold it now if I did not think you are ready and that the proposal is a good one. I, and all of your committee, have confidence in your ability and want you to succeed."

2. "Do not be surprised if changes are suggested in your proposal. Even though you obtained reactions earlier from all these individuals, and adapted to their reactions, almost every proposal review meeting produces some new ideas that call for amendments in the document."

3. "Answer questions as directly and simply as you can. If you don't know, say so. In any event, keep your responses straightforward, short, and to the point."

4. "This is not an examination. Rather, it is a review of your proposal, a proposal that these faculty members helped you prepare. They want it to be a good plan for a good study, and their questions are aimed at making the proposal more solid, both conceptually and procedurally."

5. "As your advisor, feel free to look to me particularly for assistance in the meeting if you have questions or if there seems to be misunderstandings. I will try to clarify questions and to explain their reasons, if you ask me."

Sometimes an advisor agrees to an overview meeting while still unsatisfied about the readiness of either the student or the proposal. Some students insist, and some apparently cannot be convinced of the weakness of their work other than by committee rejection. In such cases a comment like that in item 1 would be unsuitable, though 3, 4, and 5 would still be appropriate sentiments to voice. Each advisor's way of transmitting a supportive feeling to students is unique. Students, too, differ in the amount and kind of support they need. The essential point, though, is that the student be made aware that the advisor is an ally in the overview meeting.

It is sometimes difficult to accomplish one job of the chairperson, namely to *assure balanced participation* by those present. That does not mean equal time for all. There are some occasions when a committee member is so carried away by an idea that no others can get the floor without aggressively interrupting. The chairperson can note when others want to participate, and when an idea has been discussed sufficiently, and can then transfer attention to other speakers or topics. Occasionally it is necessary to invoke the prerogative of the chair arbitrarily to shift the topic to one waiting to be discussed by another person. In this connection, the chairperson, too, must beware of being the offender by monopolizing the floor.

The behavior of the chairperson *establishes the tone of the session*. A quiet, thoughtful manner, respectful and considerate of others, sets a good example. Good humor and receptiveness, too, are fine attributes to bring to the situation. It is definitely out of place, however, to harass the student, to take advantage of position, or to make the student the butt of dubious pleasantries. The way the chairperson sets the tone of the meeting has a great deal to do with how everyone will respond.

Probably no one else at the meeting knows the background and the style of thinking of the student as well as the chairperson. It is especially necessary, then, that the chairperson be alert to how questions are asked, to be sure that the student perceives their true import. From time to time the chairperson may clarify questions by asking that they be rephrased or by doing the rephrasing. The same is true for responses by the student. This can be a very delicate matter, for few people tolerate well the feeling of being corrected. Also, the chairperson should not intrude in ways that actually change either questions or answers.

Overriding all other roles for the chairperson is that of *maintaining the focus* of the meeting. Few people other than university faculty members are so easily stimulated to divergent thinking. A meeting that reviews a proposal for an investigation is an enticing invitation to a brainstorm bout that moves farther and farther away from the main purpose of the gathering. So the chairperson must hold a firm enough rein to minimize irrelevant discussion and at the same time encourage creative consideration of the matter at hand. These items do not exhaust the functions of the chairperson. They are, however, some of the salient ones.

(Special Note: In some universities the chairperson is appointed administratively as a nonvoting committee member simply to convene and conduct the meeting. In such cases most of the preceding information would apply, though the role functions would be divided between the chairperson and the T/D advisor.)

Committee Members' Roles: Individual committee members have fewer of the overview meeting management tasks to occupy them. Collectively, though, they carry more weight in the approval of the study plan than does the chairperson, for approval takes their majority vote (sometimes unanimous vote, depending on local regulations). Each committee member is, of course, chosen for particular competencies. In the end, however, each must voice an opinion on the overall merits of the proposal that is up for review. Thus, each committee member is expected to be familiar with all parts of the potential study.

Committee members can help the process to get under way smoothly by being on time for the meeting, by bringing with them all materials they need, and by falling in with the style of the meeting that the chairperson conducts. It is a reasonable consideration to the chairperson to spring no surprises; if a last-minute question or problem about the proposal surfaces, collegial and procedural courtesy demands that the chairperson be made aware of it prior to the meeting or during the preliminary stages. If the student is involved, as might often be the case, the committee member and the chairperson should bring that individual into the matter in a way they decide between them. The guiding principle is that the student is entitled to a thorough, helpful, professional review of the study proposal, and all efforts should be made to ensure that.

Criticism of either the study plan or of new ideas advanced at the meeting should be dispassionate and constructive. Animosities occur among university faculty just as they do elsewhere, and sometimes those personal differences are fed by conflict over ideas. Committee members, when they take on the role, accept with it the obligation to abjure emotionalism. Further, part of the committee member's role is to aid and assist rather than to ridicule or denigrate.

Direct physical or technical assistance from committee members is sometimes needed by the student in the course of the overview session. It can range from something as simple as help with a projector in a slide display to something as involved as the demonstration of a complex piece of testing or instructional equipment with which one of the committee is expert. Committee members can put students at ease and help them to assure that their proposals are well understood by offering such assistance. It is best, of course, if that kind of physical or technical assistance is planned before the meeting, but impromptu participation is appropriate and appreciated if the need arises.

Perhaps equal in value to every other part committee members can play is that of the encouraging consultant. Students often doubt their own abilities. When a committee member openly expresses confidence in a proposal's worth and feasibility, even while suggesting some changes in it, the student's self-confidence is maintained or elevated. Evidence of another's confidence can strengthen the student's resolve to carry T/D work on to completion, rather than become one of the all too many who do stop at the all but thesis (ABT) or all but dissertation (ABD) level.

Finally, any committee member who accepts the role does so with the understanding that it might be necessary to take over the chairpersonship. Things can happen that take the chairperson out of the picture: health problems, changes in jobs, family considerations, and the like. In such cases, it is usually in the student's best interests that someone familiar with the proposal from the beginning act as chairperson.

Student Participation in the Overview Meeting: This section deals with two forms of student participation. The first is that of the student whose proposed study plan is being reviewed. The second is attendance at the meeting by student observers. Much of what has gone before is relevant for students and for faculty members alike. Only a few items need to be addressed solely to students who are preparing for the approval of the proposals. They are:

Pay attention to little things. Faulty spelling and punctuation, grammatical errors, and incorrect sentence structure can interfere seriously with transmitting the ideas in the overview document. So can improper collation of pages or tables. Blaming such things on the typist or the computer does not provide absolution in the committee's eyes; it compounds the matter.

Prepare for the meeting. Rehearse the introductory statements to be made. Ask friends to listen and critique them. Plan what to wear. Make a checklist of all the material needed at the session. Look at the room where the committee will meet.

Be rested. Organize the day before and the day of the meeting to avoid excessively tiring activities.

Share any concerns with the advisor. Schedule a premeeting visit or phone call to ascertain that all details are in order or can be arranged.

These four items become second nature to experienced investigators prior to important conferences at which they will make proposals. For a student who is just acquiring proposal presentation experience, they must be attended to consciously.

There seems to be a tendency to open overview meetings to students. Where that is done, ground rules protect the participants while giving advanced students the benefit of learning by watching actual sessions in progress. Reasonable regulations may include:

Only the portion in which the student is introduced and the consultation and discussion takes place is open to observers.
Observation must be with prior consent of the student and the committee.
No participation or potentially distracting behavior is allowed.
Ample space is provided so the observers are clearly physically separated from the meeting participants.
The chairperson (and committee members, if they wish) are available after the session to interpret what occurred and to respond to questions and comments by the observers.

In a number of schools, individual faculty members employ simulations to prepare students for overview sessions and for final oral examinations. These, of course, can be designed to bring out specific problems for which students should be prepared.

Whether in in real life, in observation of real life, or in simulation, the quality and completeness of the student's study plan and the student's own academic and professional readiness to conduct the study are the key matters at issue. These will be revealed in how the student states the problem at the outset, how the student responds to committee members during the meeting, and by the nature and degree of the conditions the committee imposes on approval at the close of the session.

AFTER THE OVERVIEW MEETING

Earlier it was pointed out that the overview session concludes in one of three ways: rejection of the proposal, approval with conditions, or unconditional approval. In any of these eventualities, follow-up by the chairperson and the student is necessary.

Rejection: This action is rare. When it does happen, the chairperson ordinarily makes the reasons a matter of record in a letter that summarizes the committee's decision. A copy is filed in the student's record with the statement in the school's file. Another copy goes to the student. Rejection does not *necessarily* mean that T/D work must be abandoned. It may mean that this proposal is not acceptable, but that another proposal might be. The intent of the committee in this regard should be explicated in the letter that notifies the student of the rejection.

Approval with Conditions: By far the most frequent outcome, this decision should be discussed in detail between the advisor and the student. It is most important to establish the conditions precisely and to make clear what will constitute satisfaction of the conditions. Often the student is asked to circulate a brief memorandum to committee members specifying the significant changes to be made. In most cases it is advisable to agree upon a time schedule, too, for meeting the conditions.

Unconditional Approval: Even in this happy case a follow-up meeting of student and chairperson is very desirable. Almost always there are incidental details which can be clarified by discussion between the two.

Presuming that the outcome was positive, the student has reached the close of one very important phase and is about to start a new one, the conduct of the study itself. Many of the same principles that guided the proposal phase apply also in carrying out the investigation. The next chapter is devoted to the operational stage of the T/D. It will illustrate further application of the principles just alluded to, plus others.

Formal Topic Approval

Some faculties ask that the topic be presented and agreed to in a regular faculty meeting prior to the overview proposal preparation and the formal appointment of a committee. Where that is the case an outline form like the one in Figure 6-2 is useful. In some cases the formal Presentation for Topic Approval by Faculty includes a statement about the relevant background of the advisor plus a list of the proposed committee members and the reasons for their selection. If desired, that information can be added to the form shown in Figure 6-2.

From the student's perspective the formal topic presentation has advantages. It heightens pressure at exactly the point that is crucial: settling upon a topic. It gives the student and the advisor

Figure 6-2 Presentation for topic approval by faculty.

Student:_____ Check: Honors___ Masters___ Doctoral___

Advisor:_____ Presentation date:_____

Topic:_____

I. Background of topic: (approximately 150 words to set the stage and, if necessary, define terms and topic focus)

II. Description of study: (approximately 200-word nontechnical statement on what will be done in conducting the investigation)

III. Study rationale: (approximately 100 words indicating the professional/academic/scholarly significance of the topic)

IV. Professional or academic relevance of the study: (approximately 150 words on what impact the results might have on theory or practice, i.e., relevance in terms of application)

V. Relevant background of investigator: (how the student's training and experience provide preparation for this kind of T/D)

an immediate objective, in a formal sense, that precedes the preparation of a proposal. Every time a faculty meeting passes without the student's topic approval having come before it is plainly a missed opportunity.

The topic approval ought not be confused with T/D approval. They are quite separate, with topic approval being a kind of official endorsement for moving ahead with preparing a T/D proposal. However, the fact that the school or department approves should be a powerful stimulant. Also, the practice entailed in getting a brief summary together should prove helpful when writing the full proposal.

A number of instructors who conduct T/D seminars have remarked on the value of the type of topic approval form shown in Figure 6-2. They use such forms to give seminar students guided practice in putting together topic elements in very short preliminary form. We encourage students to include this step in personal Time Line construction.

SUMMARY

This chapter emphasizes T/D work leading to the approval of the study plan. The interactions of chairperson, student, and committee members are highlighted. The purpose of the study plan and the characteristics of an acceptable study plan are pointed out. It is shown that assessing their adequacy, plus that of the student to implement the study, constitutes the common agenda outline for every overview committee meeting. Preferred practices before, during, and after the overview committee session are described.

7

Conduct of the Study

TIME

Leading researchers discipline themselves when they conduct a study by setting specific, short-term objectives to be accomplished at given times. Students can employ that same action principle through the use of a "To Do By ..." List (Fig. 7-1). We recommend that students use the list, or one similar to it, in connection with the Time Line proposed earlier. The "To Do By ..." List becomes a set of action-objectives to guide movement from one point to the next one on the Time Line. Also, it is a convenient place to record items on your computer or by hand that require attention and might otherwise be overlooked or forgotten. A list of this kind should be *routinely checked and updated every morning* or at some other regular time each day. An advantage of doing it first thing in the morning is the assistance it gives in setting the day's schedule.

We and others put great store on the importance of self-management and independence of action on the part of the investigator. Advisors are usually pleased to help students in formulating

Figure 7-1 "To Do By ..." List.

Item	Projected date	Completed date
Make backup of computer files	_____	_____
Next progress report to advisor	_____	_____
Next progress report to committee	_____	_____
Final revised and approved proposal to advisor	_____	_____
Update and record notes on computer	_____	_____
Questionnaire to be printed	_____	_____
Questionnaire to be mailed	_____	_____
Conference with archivist on	_____	_____
Other	_____	_____

their initial "To Do By ..." Lists. It is good to work out the starter list with one's advisor. Also, from time to time it is useful to bring one's list (and Time Line) along to a conference and to review them in the advisor's company. But *self*-sufficiency and *self*-direction should be an overriding goal for the student. The advisor wants to see those qualities grow, too. One of the places that personal autonomy in research conduct becomes most evident is in the careful use of time.

Time and the Individual

For an individual time is a limited resource. There is no way to purchase additional time; the amount available is finite. However, it is possible to use time wisely, to get more out of a given amount of time than do other persons. That means to waste less time.

Our major point is simple: if completing the T/D is a very high priority, then recognize it and admit that many other profitable and enjoyable experiences will have to be postponed or missed. Honestly face the question of commitment. Is the T/D worth all the time and effort it will take? If it is, we have some suggestions for using time wisely and guarding it jealously.

Using and Guarding Time: When the overview is successfully completed, there is a dangerous tendency to relax and lose momentum. The approval of the overview is the signal to accelerate, to press oneself to renewed effort directed at getting on with the study itself. We have found that the best way to get started is simply to get started. It is surprising how clever we are in thinking up excuses and rationalizations, all very plausible and reasonable, for avoiding a start. Often we are not even conscious of the tricks we play on ourselves. There is always something more important, more interesting, more urgent to do than that act of getting started.

In getting under way again, save your time by using others' time where possible. One illustration is in typing. Few students are expert enough to justify doing their own. A professional typist is faster, more accurate, and probably knows more about style and format than students or professors. There are university typists who moonlight and who know precisely the typing requirements and style system of your school and university. A few well-directed questions can usually turn up an excellent person. Typing one's own chapters, except for early drafts, usually turns out to be penny wise and pound foolish.

Recently, students have turned modern typing and computer technology to their advantage by using word-processing equipment. These devices allow one to store typed material in the computer's memory, display it for revision at any time, edit it, proofread it, rearrange it, make insertions and similar changes, construct tables and figures, and prepare contents, footnotes, bibliographies, and other matters all without committing them to paper until one wishes. With the help of a skilled word-processing operator, students tell us that they can save hundreds of hours while gaining the advantage of almost mistake-proof storage and reproduction in printed form on demand.

Other ways to get help are through the use of graduate student assistance, fellow students, and university printing, duplicating, and mailing services. Some of these services can be obtained at little or no cost. University libraries offer free or low-cost services that can save time, such as hard-copy duplication of important microfiche documents. Libraries also can help with searches, and they usually provide free interlibrary loan services for important works. Computer searches of many large databases are often offered at no cost or for a small fee. Use of these can save time. Specialists in the library (bibliographers, archivists, reference specialists, to name a few) are powerful allies and thoughtful and skillful helpers both in technical and in substantive matters. We urge students to explain their research ideas and needs to members of the library staff and to consider them as valuable professional consultants.

Another university service that is often available is advice on the conduct of the study. For instance, one university has an office of measurement and evaluation at which students can obtain consultation at no direct cost. The following brief description was adapted from the University of Pittsburgh (undated mimeo).

The Office provides without charge a consulting service to assist with questions relating to research design, measurement, and statistical analysis. The service staff is office personnel and advanced assistants from the Department of Educational Research.

The consultants do not become involved in the actual conduct of the study. This is a student responsibility in order for the final product to be a reflection of the student's own work. No keypunching or verification of data is done but these skills will be taught, if desired.

Final decisions regarding graduate student research are the responsibility of the student, the advisor, and the committee. In some cases a consultant may wish to speak directly with the advisor to clarify an issue or to voice an opinion regarding the study. Each consultant reserves the right to refuse to assist with an analysis which is considered inappropriate from a research standpoint. In instances where the proposed research requires skills beyond those which the student has developed, relevant coursework and/or reading may be advised before consultant assistance is continued.

Long-term tutoring and complete reliance on consultants for data analysis are not possible through this service. Names of individuals who may be willing to undertake such projects on their own times and at their own specified fees can be requested from the office staff. (p. 1)

Most universities have this kind of office. Set up an appointment and find out how to make best use of it.

PERT and Other Scheduling Helps: The program evaluation and review technique (PERT) (Cook, 1966) is a formal system of planning and control which is probably overcomplicated for most T/Ds, but the ideas embodied in PERT are definitely applicable. If one wants to reach a goal within a specified time and if reaching it requires a number of complex and interrelated steps, it is wise to lay out the steps sequentially and then estimate the time each step will take to achieve the desired goal. It is usually best to work backward, that is, back from the time of anticipated date of completion. That procedure is extremely helpful in highlighting *what* has to be done *when* in order to finish on time. It is well illustrated in the Time Line (Fig. 1-1). There are also project planning programs for computers that can be very helpful.

In most situations, the expected time of completion of the investigation is no mystery. Doctoral programs, for example, have stated expectations for the time it should take from proposal approval to final defense. The time period for a thesis will have an implicit or explicit expectation, too. The important thing is to use the Time Line with the expected time of completion as the target date and work back systematically to the present, including each important task in sequential order. Recheck it periodically and prepare a progress report. This is an antidote for procrastination because it usually is made manifest in the process that there is no time to waste and that one has to get started now to be finished on time.

Simulation and Pretesting

Often the results portion of the study can be written with simulated data before the actual data collection stage, with surprisingly useful consequences in terms of clarity of the writing, accuracy of the simulations, and the helpfulness of the questions faced beforehand. If the results chapter cannot be simulated on the basis of various projections of dummy data, one might raise the question of whether the actual chapter can be written based on the real data one intends to gather.

Another useful technique to ascertain the relevance of the proposed data and the adequacy of data-gathering instruments is to *pretest* any instrument before its use in the real situation. This concept is similar to the idea, developed previously, of a pilot study; indeed, one purpose of a pilot study may be to pretest an instrument. The instrument is pretested for a number of reasons. First, bugs appear in procedures, especially with newly developed instruments. If intended for live subjects, use of a small group like the intended respondents can tell the researcher what may be wrong with the instrument. If the instrument is for inanimate data retrieval, a trial run on real sources can detect defects. For best pretest results develop a system to collect and heed the formative evaluative comments of those who take part.

Second, the data received or simulated in the pretest should prove conceptually sufficient to respond in some clear way to the hypotheses or research questions. If not, it is a danger signal. Perhaps the wrong questions are being asked, the wrong data collected, or the wrong subjects used. Whatever the problem, correct or avoid it before the data collection phase starts.

Selective Data Collection Advisable

Another bit of advice gleaned from our interviews and experience with T/D direction is to be parsimonious about the amount of data one gathers. The search for data should be focused and explicit.

Students who go out to gather a mountain of data often end up under an avalanche. The amount of data should be just enough to answer thoroughly the questions being asked in the proposal and no more. Quality of data cannot be replaced by quantity. In general, marked selectivity in both quantity and quality of data is a sound guideline. Leave some work for other student researchers who will come along later to extend, even if ever so slightly, the frontiers of knowledge, understanding, or professional practice.

Using Available Data

Finally, some advice about available data: the world is full of data, much of which is already there for the asking. Schools, businesses, newspapers, government units, health and welfare agencies, laboratories, test publishers, archives, stock markets, and many other sources have been collecting and banking information for years. The data may be in any form, from very limited, primitive filing systems to highly sophisticated technology exemplifying the most advanced data storage and retrieval capability. The key point here is to *not waste time* by spending it generating data that are already available.

A clinical psychologist we know produced a dissertation based on the analysis of patterns of responses to dozens of items on an individual intelligence test administered to several hundred subjects. It would have taken two years just to administer the tests if the data had been generated that way. Instead, permission was obtained to use existing test records from two large city school systems. That approach allowed an even more controlled management of the population, too, since it could be drawn from the larger universe to suit specific preset criteria. The data were gathered in two weeks of concentrated effort, not two years.

These suggestions are just the beginning; a few hours spent following leads in the university library will turn up a great deal more data that has been gathered, checked, verified, and published, often at great cost, by some official agency. This knowledge can have a major impact on the time and energy devoted to the conduct of the study.

Figure 7-2 Recommended Note-Taking Format.

This design is recommended for its simplicity, adaptability, and convenience in handling. The format lends itself to computers (notebook, laptop, or desktop), to electronic memo devices, to voice-activated tape recorders, or to handwritten 5″ × 8″ cards. The lines numbered (1), (2), and (3) across the top allow for recording (1) principal author's name, (2) subject, and (3) a designation of your own that fits a special organized scheme for the study being done. Space (4) can carry the full reference in the style required by the school or department. Space (5) shows how many cards belong together for an entry; if only one is used the space would read: (5) 1 of 1.

Systematic Data Recording

Accurate, systematic notes are essential to every investigator. Each individual takes and uses notes differently, but there are some experience-based principles that should be considered.

Notes can be arranged in various files (we recommend computer files) and then can be sorted according to categories depending on current need. After use in one chapter or study, some can be recycled for later chapters or related studies. A common filing method is alphabetical, but one may want to file alphabetically by chapter, or within categories of publications such as journals, books, and newspaper articles. Notes can also be rearranged into subject areas. In fact, the possibilities are great as long as there is a way to quickly identify categories. Some common codings that scholars use are: author, subject, or ID number written in the upper left-hand corner.

The usual way of categorizing notes on a literature search is alphabetically by author's last name. That is consistent with many indexing systems investigators use, such as *Readers' Guide to Periodical Literature*. Style manuals also commonly require that footnotes, in-text references, bibliographies, and reference notes be listed alphabetically by author's last name.

Our recommendation is that the reference and bibliographic style be selected before note taking begins. Then the notes will contain the precise bibliographic reference needed ultimately in the T/D. This reference should be near the top of the front side of the note. One reason is that the source of the note is then always at hand. Many of us have taken notes thinking we will surely remember the source, only to forget it when we finally get around to using the material. Also, placing the complete, accurate bibliographic reference in the correct syle on notes means that the bibliography is ready for final typing when the time for that comes. Furthermore, if our recommendations are followed, a note will contain all the information needed for any source footnote. Finally, the notes, properly edited later, constitute an excellent annotated bibliography, a valuable scholarly work that, in itself, may prove publishable.

Individual differences abound in note taking. What may be clear notes to one can be nonsense to another. Try to capture succinctly the points made, use an outline, and write complete thoughts, not a word or two.

Read the first and last part of the work carefully before devoting much time to the rest, unless it is clear beforehand that it is so central to the study that it must be reviewed carefully. Even then, the most succinct notes can often be gathered at the beginning and end of the cited work. If the main ideas are noted in outline form, they can be summarized without fear of repeating material verbatim from another author—assuming, of course, the proper credit is given in the text. Putting page numbers next to ideas on the note card is a helpful practice. In footnotes or in-text references it is often essential to refer the reader to a specific page in the cited work. If a thought simply must be quoted on the note, be sure to include the page number and to use quotation marks. Following those rules helps avoid bad writing habits as well as ethical problems.

We list the call number at the top of the note when we have used a library reference. One is always surprised, usually unpleasantly, at the number of times it is necessary to return to the same work in the course of writing. The call number will save hours of time.

Some investigators expand their category-filing scheme by printing or photocopying the notes and filing copies in different ways, even using them in different but related studies. The copy can be pasted to a card for filing.

These ideas are also applicable to notes on which other types of research data can be recorded. Information about subjects in a study, such as test scores and socioeconomic data, can be recorded and even number-coded to preserve confidentiality. With such data, subgroups of subjects can be identified and quickly pulled from the total file, and needed data can be obtained directly. Such handy, informative recording can be developed for data on many different units of measurement or classes of information.

The advent of computer capability has opened opportunities for keeping notes, files, and records in an orderly way on a computer disk. All that is said above can be applied to computerized notation, and portable computers make it possible to take notes on site at a library or other data source.

For those who are computer literate, there are other, and some would say better, ways of searching, reviewing, and storing data for notes. Databases can be searched by computers. Such searches use search strategies that often depend on the intersection of key words. For example, if one were studying German colonial influence on Papua New Guinea, key words might be *Papua New Guinea, colony, Germany,* or *history.*

Researchers who do their own database searches can quickly find out if the strategy turns up references and if so, how many. If no references are found, then one can immediately try other likely key words—in this case, for example, New Guinea, German colonialism, World War I, Germans, and so forth, until a hit is made.

Computer searches vary. Some will turn up titles, authors, and subjects, and those are very helpful. Others, such as ERIC, provide, in addition, annotated references. Thus one can quickly peruse the computer screen to determine the relevance and usefulness of what has turned up. This ability to quickly screen references is critical to the time of researchers because, for many subjects, the problem is not a lack of references but a surfeit of references. Too many references may mean that the search strategy is too broad or inadequate. Too many references can also mean that the topic is too broad, and unless the list is narrowed in some way, it will engender an enormous time investment.

Once the search is narrowed to the most useful and relevant citations, they and their abstracts become candidates for notes, and possibly for the literature review. The data may be imported to your own computer electronically by importing a data file. Otherwise, a hard copy of the citations is printed and that can be entered in the researcher's computer file either by keyboard or by a scanner, or filed in paper copy.

However entered in the computer file, a system can be devised to make access to a large amount of data possible. One way is to think of the note card system and, in a sense, emulate it. For example, you could use your outline software to create an outline of your project, e.g., your paper, overview proposal, or review of the literature. Making an outline is a good idea in any case. It forces you to think through what you want to say logically, and the software will carry you through step by step, leading you to think about your topics in some orderly fashion, grouping related topics, establishing a subordinate and superordinate relationship where appropriate, and in general helping you to arrange your ideas in some rational relationship, e.g., chronologically, inductively, deductively, or in conformance with a classification scheme accepted by the academic field or discipline. A common outline system looks like this:

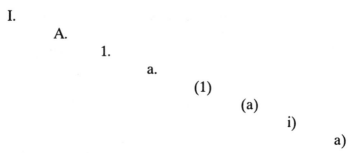

This is not to say that the program will think for you. It will not. But it can be used by you as a prompt to help you think in an orderly fashion.

Once you have an outline, you can create a file and name it for each part of the outline, then fill the file with sentences, notes, paragraphs, and thoughts that you want in that section of the outline. Eventually the file will become the prose file, fleshing out the outline — perhaps a subpart of a chapter with its own heading. We talked elsewhere about breaking up a chapter with major and minor headings to make it easier to read and to help guide the logical thought flow. Consider that each heading in an outline could be the name of a file, and the headings that are grouped together in your outline could be a chapter. The headings (computer file names) that make up your chapter could then be grouped in a logical sequence to make up a directory in your word-processing program, and the directory could be named for the chapter, e.g., *Introduction*, or *Chapter 1*. The example of an outline above is an appropriate size for a chapter. The files that make up the directory would then be about the right size for the purpose of working on them — to add, delete paragraphs, move, replace, cut and paste, and so forth.

As you fill in the outline with information, some of the material will need a citation. Word-processing programs can help you to mark the text where the citation belongs, allow you to enter the citation, and even display the cite on the page or at the end of the file. Some will even help you display the citations in an alphabetized list of references in any common style format you choose. Some allow you to insert footnotes and endnotes as well.

Another useful feature of some word-processing programs is the document summary. This makes it easy to find material when working on a large paper such as a thesis or dissertation. Each file, no matter how large or small, can have a summary prepared by you that pops up when you ask it to, briefly listing the file name you gave it, the date, author, and comments that you insert to briefly identify and summarize the file. This is a very quick way to find pieces of a large document scattered among hundreds of files, some of which you created years ago, and perhaps have forgotten, but still are important to keep. This summary is hidden in the document until you ask for it, and does not print out with the document on file or hinder your working on the document whenever you wish.

Finally, a word-processing program can help you write correctly. Most will check your spelling against a word list of tens of thousands of correctly spelled words. You can add and delete words. There is also a thesaurus, which helps you find an appropriate phrase as you are writing, and it provides synonyms and antonyms for thousands of common words, which not only provide you with choices, but can also be used to define words when you are not sure of their meaning.

Of course, there are many other features of computers and software, and some are much more sophisticated than can be described in this brief summary of the basic features found commonly in such programs. The main point here is to make sure that you know what great help a word-processing program can be to you as you take notes, begin to compile a set of references for your major work, and begin to work on a draft. Learning how to use a word processor now, if you have not done so, can pay enormous dividends, not only in writing the thesis or dissertation, but also throughout your professional and academic life.

Earlier we suggested using a secretary who really knows the system to do the final document. The cost may well be less if you can provide a disk with your overview or T/D on it, already prepared, even in rough form. And, if you are really interested in seeing how close you can come to the perfect document, you can set all the margins and spaces required by your university for the T/D, generate a table of contents from your chapter headings and subheadings, generate footnotes, reference lists, and bibliographies, alphabetized and correctly formatted. Many who begin to work with a word-processing program get so interested, and so good at it, that soon they are turning out documents that appear to be professionally prepared.

USE OF THE COMPUTER

Some uses of computers in T/D studies are for literature searches; for data analysis; for instrumentation in certain educational, psychological, business, and management research; and as the substantive content of research in such professions as library and information science and engineering. A common employment for computers in the research context is to search the literature related to a given topic to help get started on a literature review.

Literature Search

Research libraries may have access to hundreds or even thousands of databases. Online vendors usually provide online access to external databases, and each vendor may have many databases. Examples of vendors are Bibliographic Reference Service (BRS), Dialog, Nexis (Mead Data Central), and Wilsonline. Techniques for accessing the various systems, as well as areas of specialization, vary, and the best bet is to consult the library's reference librarian or information specialist (York et al., 1988).

An extension of the database search is the search of material on disks, either Laser disk or CD-ROM (compact disk-read-only memory). These disks are attractive to libraries because they can store an enormous number of pages of printed material on one disk. In addition, these disks can store the database material, thus providing the search and retrieval capability of an online database without the online connection to a remote location. The disks provide the same retrieval methods and search strategies that are used in the counterpart remote database search. With a printer connected, a disk search can result in a printed bibliography or list of reference notes. ERIC, *Psychological Abstracts*, and *Dissertation Abstracts International*, among others, are available in disk form.

It is important for researchers to become familiar with these forms of searching the literature, for not only are these faster, but they can save hours and days of work and at times can search literature not otherwise indexed, or at least not indexed in a form easy to find. Perhaps most important, as the newer search techniques become more widely available, and more widely used, research libraries, always short of space and money, will tend to drop the printed form when it is duplicated by the library's purchase of a disk or online database search service. Thus the researcher will be forced to learn the new search techniques.

Fortunately, universities often offer short courses in how to work more independently through computer searching. Ask the library about these quick orientation sessions.

Another innovation of importance to the researchers is the online library catalog. Research libraries at universities are now developing such catalogs, and students and faculty will have access to the library's holdings via their computer terminals. Often the libraries themselves have terminals permanently connected to the online library catalog and the catalog may be searched by title, author, or subject, with step-by-step instructions provided on the terminal screen. It should not be assumed that all the holdings of a library, with bibliographic information, are in the online catalog, so it will always be wise to check the print catalogs when more information is needed. However, searching the catalog by computer is fast, convenient, and can give the researcher a good overview of what is available in the library, and where. It is even possible, under certain conditions, to print a copy of a search, and one might envision a future when a researcher can search the major research libraries of the United States from a student or faculty office terminal.

Computer-Aided Data Collection and Analysis

PCS, a portable computer system for observational research, is an example of a software package for collecting and analyzing data on behavior or events (Communitech International, 425 Fisk Ave., DeKalb, IL 60115). Operating onsite with a laptop computer, the program allows the researcher to collect and store data as it appears. The same software can then generate frequency and duration tables and reliability tables and summarize what has been done. Part of the package is also an analysis program able to produce event analyses, time-based analyses, interactions between them, plus others. Moreover, tables created by the PCS program are ready to be imported into programs like SPSS-PC or SPSS-X for additional analyses (see STATISTICAL PACKAGES in Appendix A).

When using the computer as an aid in gathering and processing data, we find that its speed advantage continues to stand out as a major attraction. When an investigation includes survey data, demographic information, large-scale, large-sample polling or questionnaire responses, the computer is the tool of choice for recording, assembling, arraying, and analyzing activities. When well-established statistical procedures are to be employed, ready-made programs can take over. Under those conditions the computer performs at speeds that seem light-years ahead of hand-operated calculators. Even when one's data are mainly observational, subjective, and subtle, there may be parts of the analysis in which the computer can help. Some might be in simple counting and tabling; others might be in testing for observer reliability or calculating central tendency measures. Hardly a month goes by without the discovery of new ways to utilize computer technology in data analysis. Therefore, it pays to review data analysis plans with scholar/technicians who live close to the world of the computer to determine how that burgeoning knowledge might be helpful.

Again we join Sternberg (1981) in the viewpoint that "it is perfectly acceptable to take one's data to a computer consultant, specialist or technician, . . . to run a program for, say, multiple regression analysis of your data. You don't have to have the foggiest notion of how he (or she) wrote up the program so that the IBM could understand it" (p. 129). Gay (1992, p. 476) concurs, saying that *what one needs to know* are the strengths and weaknesses of the analysis procedures chosen and how to make meaningful statements about the results of the analyses. The committee can be expected to pinpoint matters like that and to ask hard questions about them.

Other Computer Uses

Computers too can be major elements in either the treatment in a study or in the delivery or manipulation of a treatment. An example of the first is in computer-assisted instruction. The second might be the processing of a chess match, sports event, or management game via computer. Here the computer is an integral part of some process that is under investigation. Often in studies of this kind the computer's visual display or audible response replaces pencil and paper, a book, a person, or all three.

Another point at which computers surface more and more often is in studies aimed either at discovering how existing computers might be used more efficiently and effectively or even in new ways to upgrade the speed and quality of the work of an academic discipline or a profession. Part of that same category is any investigation that focuses on improving computer usage. From traffic engineering, biology, and energy conservation through temperature control, musicology, and word processing, the academic and professional disciplines are using and enhancing computers and their application in research and development.

Our recommendation is to consider carefully the benefits of investing the time to learn to use a computer, even as a beginner. At many universities, there are free classes for students to help them learn and provide practice, and there are free computer labs set up for students, staff, and faculty to draft and eventually prepare their manuscripts. These labs provide the computers, the software, help from an attendant, and even the printer and paper!

If your institution provides such an opportunity, this is an offer you should not refuse.

USE OF PRIVATE INFORMATION

Confidentiality

To obtain data it is often necessary to promise confidentiality. This is a serious promise; breaking it is an inexcusable breach of ethics. We recommend several procedures to maintain and safeguard confidentiality of data. First, if possible, collect data anonymously. Second, roster data by number rather than name; destroy names and their connections with data as soon as possible. Third, if data are gathered by questionnaire, the questionnaire can be destroyed, returned, or identifying information cut out as soon as there is no further need for it. Fourth, keep sensitive files out of sight and under lock.

Obtaining Needed Permission

Permission is needed in many areas of proposed T/D research. It is not a simple concept; check, if in doubt, with the research advisor concerning the need to ask permission concerning the specific materials to be used or steps contemplated. The need to request permission may stem from custom, common courtesy, or legal rights. Whatever the source, ask permission when in doubt. Some important areas where a need to obtain permission exists include:

1. Permission to use children or persons incarcerated or under guardianship as research subjects, including permission to contact such individuals as jailors, physicians, employers of a business, teachers or principals, armed service personnel, or to systematically gather data in work, recreation, health care, and education settings for research.
2. Permission to use instruments for data-gathering purposes, where such instruments were designed or developed by others, whether such instruments are copyrighted or not, unless in the public domain.

3. Permission to examine, for research purposes, personnel records, student records, and other records containing personal data, where such data are not part of the public domain and open to everyone.

4. Permission to use long passages, charts, tables, and other material from the work of others, whether copyrighted or not, unless such material is in the public domain or unless blanket permission to use it, or reproduce it with credits, is printed on the material in such a way as to indicate that the author and publishers intend the material to be freely used.

Permissions should be obtained in writing, should specify their purposes and limits, should be signed by a person in authority, and should be acknowledged in writing. A useful procedure is to send a letter to the responsible individual with a copy to countersign and return, with the simple statement: "The permissions requested in the above letter have been granted." That, signed and dated, can be valuable insurance as well as a "pass" for use with individuals who have direct custody of the persons, records, or materials to which access is needed.

OBLIGATIONS TO HUMAN SUBJECTS

Researchers have obligations to protect human subjects in their research and to report on their procedures to do so. Because these obligations are legal and bureaucratic, one may at times forget that they are also ethical in nature. Thus, a bit of historical context is in order.

Historical Context

Moral principles of civilized peoples and nations have for centuries contained general prohibitions against harmful experimentation on human beings. Although the moral issue may not be new, it burned itself anew in the consciousness of civilized persons during the Nuremberg Trials after World War II. In the transcripts of the trials we find testimony that human beings in Auschwitz and elsewhere were put through agonizing and maiming experiments (and eventually killed) while under the control of physicians who claimed to be doing medical research. Out of this horror came a number of steps to attempt to prevent a recurrence. A codification of guidelines for research on human subjects was issued in 1947 in the *Nuremberg Code*. The *Declaration of Helsinki* of the World Medical Assembly followed in 1964, containing specific guidelines for physicians doing research on humans.

While America shared in the horror of the concentration camps, most in the United States saw the issues as distant ones, not actually touching our own lives. However, in 1972 when the Freedom of Information Act opened certain government files, the public learned for the first time of the Tuskegee Study in 1932. At that time, the U.S. Public Health Service began an experiment on 399 men in Macon County, Alabama. The subjects were black, poor, and semiliterate. The aim of the experiment was to track the effects of syphilis on untreated black males. To encourage participation, the subjects were led to believe they were being treated, but in fact they were not. Their symptoms were recorded at periodic physical examinations, and autopsies were performed after death. (Jones, 1981).

Gradually U.S. governmental and professional bodies took more seriously the notion that policies were needed to govern the practice of research, with special emphasis on the ethical requirements of doing research involving human subjects. No doubt outrage at the Tuskegee experiment played a role in the increasingly strict regulation of research on human subjects which was to be developed in the seventies.

Another experimental study that brought to the attention, especially of the academic community, the need for guidelines was the famous Milgram study, described in the *Journal of Abnormal and Social Psychology*, in 1963. Although the Milgram study has many defenders as well as detractors, the study is noted here not to take sides in the argument, but because it contributed to the enlargement of the arena of debate. After Milgram, it became clear that not only medical research needed regulation, but social science research as well.

By 1973, the American Psychological Association published its *Ethical Principles in the Conduct of Research with Human Participants*, the Society for Research in Child Development issued a statement of "Ethical Standards in Research with Children," and the President of the American Educational Research Association wrote a strong editorial in the February 1973 issue of *Educational Researcher* calling researchers' attention to the need for ethical guidelines.

During this period, agencies of the U.S. Department of Health, Education, and Welfare (HEW) issued regulations requiring increasingly strict review of research proposals where federal funds were requested. By 1974 the National Research Act extended such reviews to all research on human subjects if done at institutions that had HEW research funds. By 1978 the recommendations of the National Commission for the Protection of Human Subjects of Biomedical and Behavioral Research were published in the *Federal Register*, and after comments were received the Secretary of HEW published a proposed list of recommendations in 1979 and, after extensive dialogue, final regulations in 1981. By 1983, when HEW had become the U.S. Department of Health and Human Services (HHS), revised regulations were published by the Department, entitled "Protection of Human Subjects."

While federal regulations apply to HHS grants, in effect they have encouraged universities to set up committees or boards to review all research involving human participants, including theses, dissertations, class projects or assignments, nonfederally funded research, and institutional research. There are good reasons for this extended coverage.

First, if the regulations are appropriate in federally funded research, then logically they should apply equally when the funds come from some other source. Second, if inappropriate procedures entail liability for the student, the advisor, and the university, that liability would appear to remain whatever the source of funds. Third, with respect to T/D research or any other research done by students, training and insistence on proper and ethical procedures would seem to be an essential part of any university program.

Procedures for Review of Proposed Research with Human Subjects

The first decision a researcher must make is whether the proposed research must be reviewed under university human subject guidelines. Research not subject to review by this procedure would be that research which is not concerned with human subjects — for example, an examination of texts for readability levels, research confined to historical documents (such as a history of the Harmonist Society of the nineteenth century), or research that is restricted to library resources or the use of publicly available documents on or about humans. Note, however, that research using data *on* human subjects *does* constitute research *involving* human subjects and, although possibly involving minimal risk, is subject to the review process.

Under the HHS regulations, each institution is required to set up an institutional review board (IRB) to review research for human subject protection, and to assure that a system of continual review and safeguards will be maintained, and responsibilities will be discharged for protecting the rights and welfare of human subjects of research conducted at or sponsored by the institution, regardless of the source of funding. Several IRBs may operate at an institution; for example, one for the social and behavioral sciences and another for medicine, but each must follow careful written procedures, spelled out in the HHS regulations. These regulations also permit expedited reviews by IRBs, reviews designed for certain kinds of research involving no more than minimal risk, and reviews for minor changes in already approved research. Expedited reviews are designed to be faster, less detailed, and to require less complicated and lengthy documentation than full reviews. Researchers are encouraged to study the regulations promulgated by HHS, as well as their own university's regulations for full explanation of the requirements of the various reviews. Such regulations should be readily available in several places, including the library, at any research university or institution.

IRBs also oversee the protection of human subjects in another category of research: exempt. Exempt research is the category most likely to apply to T/D research. The concept of exempt research does not imply that such research is exempt from review or regulation, but rather that such research is so benign, so nonintrusive, and so commonly accepted that there is little risk of harm to subjects if proper procedures are followed. Examples of such research, from the regulations, would include research conducted in established or commonly accepted educational settings, involving normal educational practices; research involving survey or interview procedures; research involving the observation of public behavior; and research involving the collection or study of existing data. Exempt research at institutions is usually reviewed by subunits under the general supervision of the IRB. Even exempt research must contain provisions for the protection of human subjects.

It is not likely that students preparing theses or dissertations could be principal investigators for research requiring full IRB review. Such research is usually so intrusive or has such a potential for risk that careful protection for human subjects is mandatory.

However, T/D research involving human subjects which would otherwise appear to be exempt research can take an additional risk under certain conditions, and will need a more detailed review than is normally accorded exempt research. Examples include research involving children, prisoners, or incompetent adults; research involving deception; and research that records responses or observations which, if they become known beyond the researcher, could reasonably place the subject at risk of criminal or civil liability or damage the subjects' financial standing or employability. Again, it is our advice to refer to competent authority and to the federal and institutional regulations for guidance.

Informed consent is one of the most important aspects of necessary permission in the conduct of studies that involve human subjects. Past abuses, chiefly in medical or psychological investigations on human behavior or disease, have resulted in a fresh look at the issue. Research institutes and higher-education institutions now commonly require that all research on human subjects be approved in advance by an institutional review board or ethics committee.

The concept of informed consent applies to any investigation involving human participation. Informed consent means the exercise of free power of choice on the part of the human participant, without coercion, deceit, promise of future benefits, or other forms of influencing the participants to act against their better judgment.

Humans subjected to research procedures have a right to know what the procedures are, what the purpose of the research is, the risks and benefits (if any), costs and payments (if any), and the right to refuse or end participation. The subject has the right to know if the results of the study will be published, and to what extent information will be treated confidentially.

The subject also has a right to know what will be done with data after the research is completed. If the subject is receiving some benefit, it should be clearly stated that the benefit will not be withdrawn or changed because of refusal to participate or withdrawal from participation in the study.

Formal, signed consent forms, where appropriate, should be submitted with the T/D proposal. Human subjects have a right to a copy of their signed consent form.

In some cases, separate signed forms are not needed, as in certain mail surveys or personal interviews where the subjects are competent adults who are evidently fully free to refuse participation. In such cases the respondent, as long as he or she is fully informed, may be presumed to be indicating consent by returning the survey, or by responding to questions from an interviewer. This concept of presumed consent depends, however, on the provision of enough information to the subject that tests for *informed* consent can be satisfied. For example, one would want to tell the respondent who the researcher is, the purpose of the research, the provisions to protect anonymity if anonymity is promised or implied, the degree of confidentiality with which the data will be treated, how the data will be used, the plans for publications resulting from the study, what will happen to the data after the study has been completed, and describe the voluntary nature of the responses.

Federal agencies, notably the Department of Education and the Department of Health and Human Services, as well as professional organizations such as the American Psychological Association, have promulgated formal statements and guidelines for both practitioners and researchers. These are periodically updated, so it is advisable that students, professors, librarians, and administrators be alert to the most recent views of such significant groups on this important matter. Refer to the federal regulation, particularly Section 46(16), for detailed general requirements for informed consent (U.S. Department of Health and Human Services, 1981).

The line between human participation that does or does not involve potential human risk is not always clear. For example, consider a policy that indicates that an activity involves risk if participation has a potential, greater than negligible, for harm to the subject physically, psychologically, or socially. Clearly, these determinations require professional judgments rather than yardstick measurements. It is for this reason, as well as the fixing of institutional responsibility, that an institutional committee is both advisable and helpful. In a large university, each major academic unit should have a human subjects committee, in addition to the universitywide one. The aims should be to protect the rights and health and welfare of human participants and to provide appropriate models for graduate student research.

To help assure an orderly and systematic procedure to protect human participants, we offer five recommendations.

First, the concept should be communicated to faculty and to students. This may be done by memos, workshops, colloquia, faculty meetings, and certainly should be a part of classwork in overview seminars, research seminars, and courses in research methodology.

Second, research proposals, such as T/D proposals, should contain signed assurances that the student and the principal investigator, that is, the research advisor, are aware of the school and university policy with regard to the protection of human subjects.

Third, in the institution, we recommend the establishment of a faculty-chosen board or committee with student observers to make judgments with regard to the degree of human participation and degree of risk involved in proposed studies, as well as the proper procedures to assure the necessary human protection without destroying opportunities to conduct appropriate research.

Fourth, we recommend that where there is a possibility, or even a question, of participants being at some risk because of the proposed research, including those who would conduct it, the proposal should be submitted to the committee in the third recommendation. Such submission is designed not only for an approval and informational purposes, but also to elicit advice on the conduct of the proposed study from the members of the committee, who are the experts in the institution.

Fifth, we recommend that, as a part of the orderly and systematic review procedure, students, faculty, advisors, and the committee or board keep accurate records and communicate in writing. Ethical considerations and legal liability indicate the wisdom of conducting studies within the letter and the spirit of the policy, as well as having the evidence to show that it was so conducted.

No recommendation can, of course, be appropriate to every school. These five are minimal. Any serious attempt to set up a school policy and procedure should involve faculty of the institution who do research and should include a thorough review of the literature, a good deal of which can be found in the reference list.

MAINTAINING COMMUNICATION

The best way to guard against unpleasant surprise in any aspect of the T/D study is to keep in constant contact with the advisor. This does not mean to be a pest, but it does mean to make an effort to keep the advisor informed of the progress and problems. The regular progress report is basic to serve that purpose. However, there are needs for added personal contact, too. Often this can be done informally by telephone. The student should keep a log of calls, including date, time, and subjects discussed. It may also involve writing a letter to the advisor from time to time summarizing the calls and the decisions and reports made in the calls, and requesting further clarification, if needed. When visits are necessary to the advisor's office, schedule them in advance with the advisor or the secretary. Advisors, like students, are busy people with many roles. Determine whether your advisor is usually available for a drop-in visit or whether appointments are preferred.

Normally the committee does not expect to see the student researcher as often as the advisor. Much of the nature and quantity of the student-committee interaction is a result of the particular style of the advisor. The advisor often serves as a communications medium with respect to the committee expectations. Within that framework, it is wise to let the committee know of progress through the progress report and to offer to meet and share additional information with any committee member who has time to receive the student.

MATERIAL AID FOR STUDENT RESEARCH

Significant changes in support for student research have been in progress in the second half of the twentieth century. They were accompanied by equally significant alterations in how research is conducted. Both the changes in funding and procedures have important implications for student research (AAU, 1990; Bowen and Rudenstine, 1992; CGS, 1990b).

1. Projects have become larger and more complex. For instance, some have subjects samples as large as 5% of all the nation's youth of given ages. As projects become more complicated,

they involve more variables and more different styles of data analysis.

2. A research team is more often used as opposed to a single researcher. A staff of 5 to 10 persons is not uncommon on one investigation. The principal investigator of a major project devotes increased time to management and administration, with less time for direct research.

3. Two or more institutions may form a consortium to conduct one study.

4. Investigations frequently extend from three to five years and sometimes longer.

5. An increasing proportion of research is developmental, case study, evaluative, historical, and survey, in contrast to experimental.

6. The cost of individual studies has mounted, often being in excess of a million dollars.

7. Universities, corporations, pension systems, unions, defense departments, school systems, health agencies, and state social service agencies have established offices to facilitate the search for funds to support studies. These agencies maintain central accounting staffs to monitor the use and flow of research funds.

8. In universities, the proportion of faculty members with "research" prefixed to their professional titles has increased, creating a faculty subculture distinguished by being outside the tenure stream and carrying few teaching or student advisement responsibilities.

9. More graduate students are supported in their advanced studies by working on research studies conducted by faculty members.

10. Funding agencies set and publicize substantive and methodological priorities for the research they will consider supporting. They also usually require that proposals, progress reports, and final reports be prepared in a prescribed format.

The total amount of money available for research related to the academic disciplines and the professions each year tends to increase gradually (corrected for inflation).* That means every year from public and private sources a great deal of new money, probably in the billions of dollars, is added to that already expended. Also, the 10 points just stated constitute important parameters with respect to the flow and the utilization of that money. T/D advisors and students face the challenge of finding ways to tap into that potential wellspring of support. Any probes made in the major stream of funding need to have two qualities to start with, namely, a focus on a relevant problem and a clearly written, succinct proposal embodying a methodology that promises to get nearer to the heart of the problem.

To obtain material support it is essential, first, to know where to look and how to look. Your librarian can help you find funding sources, like directories of foundations. For example, the Henry J. Kaiser Family Foundation [Quadrus, 2400 Sand Hill Road, Menlo Park, CA 94025, (415) 854-9400] is interested primarily in projects that address health problems, broadly construed. More about this and other foundations with other interests can be located in the directories.

Your computer can help speed your search for a source of support that matches your interest and capability. For one example, the U.S. Air Force Office of Scientific Research supports basic research on several topics in the life sciences. That office can be reached by telephone (202) 767-5021/5022, or by E-mail: COLLINS@AFOSR.AF.MIL anytime. For another example, American Psychological Association members have free access to a bulletin of research funding announcements from a wide variety of federal agencies and private foundations. Accessed by BITNET or INTERNET, the data in the bulletin are updated biweekly. For further information, contact the APA Science Directorate by E-

---

*This is an estimate of the situation by the authors, based on informal conversations and observations. A careful analysis of the situation to answer the question definitively would make an excellent dissertation.

mail at APASCDCF@GWUVM.BITNET or by phone at (202) 336-6000.

Ask your advisor and other committee members if they have specific suggestions about where and how to look for aid with your particular topic. Keep in mind, too, that if your T/D proves to have outcomes that suggest the need for additional research, you will have a firm basis for seeking support to extend your research efforts into a long-range program.

T/D Work as Part of Funded Projects

Sometimes students have opportunities to do their studies as parts of projects being conducted by faculty members, projects supported by local government, state, federal, or private agency grants or contracts. These can be excellent opportunities. They often grapple with real problems. The investigations have social, theoretical, and professional significance, and it is possible to establish truly collegial relationships with the project staff and the faculty members leading the work. At the same time, there can be sticky problems in such situations for both T/D advisors and students to consider (AAU, 1990; LaPidus, 1990). Some of the potential complications are these.

Whose Problem Is It? One desirable characteristic of T/D work should be that the student has the major role in generating the problem to be studied. That may be difficult to achieve if the matters to be investigated are largely predetermined by the language of the funded proposal that was written by someone else.

Time Pressure Can Arise: Most funded research is committed to a time frame. If it coincides with the student's projected schedule, all may be well. An interruption in the student's work can ordinarily be accommodated. But if there is a tight linkage to a strict project time sequence, there is much less flexibility to adjust to other factors. Any protracted time out for the student, even if necessary, might mean the student would have to abandon the partly-done study to allow its completion by another project staff member.

How Independent Is the Investigation? Funded projects of any major proportions tend to operate by distributing work such as data collection, data analysis, and short- and long-range planning among a number of staff members. In such instances, care must be taken to assure that the student has and does exercise the level of independence in such activities that allows the committee to properly assign accountability to the student for the thoroughness and quality of these aspects of the conduct of the study.

What Format Is Followed in Reporting? There can be differences between the school's T/D writing format and the reporting style required by the project. Sometimes the school is flexible about such matters. If not, the student may be contracting to prepare two different reports.

These four specific items illustrate the particular types and the wide range of problems that can crop up. There are potential problem areas of a more general nature, too. There is an atmosphere of concern about possible carelessness and mismanagement in connection with university use of public research, development, and training funds. Some of these malpractices, if they occur, could lap over upon the student and result in litigation and costs or, at least, unpleasant matters on the record. To forestall that, the student would be well advised to obtain commitments in writing, to obtain and keep all financial records, and to be thoroughly familiar with the rules governing disbursements and accounting on the project. Faculty members with T/D advisees doing their work on funded projects should accept a major share of responsibility for safeguarding the student from being victimized by the errors of others in the university in this regard.

Student research done on funded projects can have advantages. Perhaps the most significant point on the positive side is its realism. If all of the objectives of T/D instruction can be attained on a funded project headed by others, and if the independence and integrity of the student and the T/D project itself can be maintained in the context of the larger project, advisors can be expected to encourage their students to make increasing use of that route to the goal.

Specific T/D Funding Support

State, federal, and international agencies, a number of foundations, and many universities give direct financial and other material support to T/D projects. The specific procedures vary among organizations and agencies, but they tend to have these general operating principles in common.

1. The student completes an application form or drafts a letter to the potential funding source, providing specified information.
2. A summary of the proposed investigation is required.
3. The amount of money and/or other material help being requested is indicated, usually with details as to how the assistance is to be used.
4. If a source external to the university is approached, an indication that the university will accept custody and accounting responsibility for the fund is required.
5. There is a limit on the charge the university can make for managing the funds and providing facilities for the proposed study.
6. The funding source specifies how its name may be used in connection with publications and reports arising out of the project.
7. A full-time faculty member accepts responsibility for coordinating, directing, or monitoring the work, with the T/D student being named principal investigator.
8. There are deadline dates for submission of applications for assistance.

Advisors sometimes keep files of potential funding agencies to share with students. Some universities maintain offices which are on the alert for such resources. In a number of cases these same university offices offer consultation on the mechanics of proposal preparation, processing the proposal for official university approvals, and expediting communication with the agency to which the application will be directed. In some research seminars students are required to select a potential funding source and to prepare a mock (or real) proposal in the format of the funding source as a class assignment, and to subject it to evaluation by a group of fellow-students and the instructor. We commend practices like that as excellent exercises leading to independence on the part of the student.

The use of specific T/D funding support has few problems associated with it in contrast to its evident advantages. There is the added work of finding a source and making the application. Timing, in relation to both the application and the wait for a response, can be crucial. But the experience, plus the material support that results if the application is successful, usually more than compensates. It is anticipated that more and more students will try to avail themselves of opportunities for help in this way.

STUDENT DROPOUTS IN THE RESEARCH STAGE

Robertson and Sistler (1971) concluded alarmingly that "the most cited reason by administrators for students dropping out of doctoral programs was 'inadequate personal financing' and the evidence pointed to an increase in this direction rather than an alleviation of the position" (p. 60). As they turned to a discussion of the need for more information, the same writers said, "There needs to be further study to determine the extent of finance as it bears upon the pursuit of the doctoral degree in Education. Part of such studies would include investigations of sources for the implementation of such programs" (p. 72).

We believe that the situation is common. "Money problems" is an oft-cited reason given by students for stopping graduate study, either permanently or temporarily. It no doubt has validity in most cases, too. We suspect it may be a contributing problem more often than it is the primary or precipitating problem, however. The widespread occurrence of money problems and the socially and emotionally neutral tone of the matter may make it a fine cover story for the more personal and potentially stressful real reasons that may actually prompt dropping out (Bowen and Rudenstine, 1992; CGS, 1990b; Monaghan, 1989a).

The loss of a student who has reached almost the end of a training sequence is a serious matter. For the student, it means that major financial and personal time investments do not bring the hoped-for returns. Sacrifices by the student's family often go into that investment, too. Personal and academic or professional life, also, are sometimes materially altered in undesirable ways. For example, one former student is avoided by close friends of an earlier time because they do not wish to listen again and again to the inevitable diatribes against university faculty members the student feels were unfair when they invoked a statute of limitations. Another former student has adopted a personally awarded doctorate, encouraging subordinates and new acquaintances to use it as part of everyday address. That same former student periodically threatens to sue the university and individual faculty members for denying the degree. Both students actually dropped out of school while in the dissertation stage and did so despite encouragement to complete the work they had begun. The true dynamics behind their dropout and their later behavior is not understood. We do not suggest that these illustrations are typical. The problem is that we do not know what is typical, and we should.

There is an institutional loss, too, when student dropouts occur. It has financial aspects. No student pays fully for instruction. Thus, there has been an institutional investment in the student from tax funds, endowment income, and other nontuition sources, and that investment has not achieved the expected return. Add to that the fact that irreplaceable faculty time has gone into the student's program in many ways, from advisement to small-seminar and individual instruction. Faculty time is the institution's most precious resource. Even when a student drops out, it can be hoped that not all that has been done is wasted. But that is a faint hope. When the doctoral process, for example, is left without its capstone, the dissertation, the result is at best a very limited success.

We asked the faculty members we interviewed what their estimates were as to the proportion of doctoral students they knew who completed all course work but never started dissertations.

Forty-three answered. The responses ranged from negligible to 40%. The mean was 19%, or about one out of five. We then asked faculty members for the same information about students who started dissertations (had approved proposals) and did not finish. The range of estimates was again wide, from negligible to 50%. The mean of the estimates was 15%, or about one out of seven.

We have no way to compare those figures with doctoral programs in other professions at other universities. Our feeling is that, for the limited samples we had, the estimates indicate that there is very great variability from faculty member to faculty member in student dropouts.

When we asked faculty members why some students completed all course work and then did not begin dissertations, their answers were of five kinds. In the lead as a cause, they said, were student personality traits such as lack of self-discipline, procrastination, failure to set priorities, indecision, and fear of failure. These are to a large extent matters that can be remedied. Such characteristics are amenable to change. The guidelines set down by advisors and other faculty members can often produce positive alterations in such behavior.

The second most frequent cause clustered around a group of factors that would clearly be influential, though external to the situation. That included economic factors, such as the need of the student to work to keep body and soul together, family problems, and illness. Once a student leaves the university, for one of those or any other reason, the impression of the faculty members we interviewed was that the chances of return to study were slim.

Program inadequacies made up a third significant group of factors, in the faculty members' opinions. They were most critical of program discontinuity, i.e., the lack of developmental stages and smooth transitions between one and another program phase. If the student has been accustomed to course work with the instructor making decisions, that is poor preparation for a sudden shift to almost total independence. What would help would be more experience for students in generating their own ideas.

Inadequacies in the cognitive domain took fourth place as a dropout reason. It was argued that some students who lack enough intellectual ability or who find the rigors of scholarship too demanding cannot readily be located until they are faced with independent study outside the support system of a class or a seminar. Faculty members also felt that there is another group who simply have not learned enough about how to originate, propose, and conduct research. Theirs is not a lack of potential, but a lack of achievement, which could be corrected.

Though the least in frequency, almost 10% of the total of comments dealt with failures of advisors and other faculty members. When a student did not locate a faculty member to identify with, the stage was set for a dropout. The student would find too little help with problems of the kind which should have a legitimate claim on faculty attention, such as discussion of the student's research ideas. Another point made by some was the advisor's failure to alert the student to start early and to plan according to a Time Line based on the experiences of other students. It was suggested, also, that some faculty members may be thrust into T/D advisement without themselves having sufficient background and skill in either helping students to define research problems or to plan and execute investigations.

At present it is not clear how many students drop out just prior to or during the course of dissertation work. If the reasons offered by the faculty members we asked are accepted, many of the causes of dropouts can be eliminated or sharply minimized by the faculty members themselves, either through changes in their own advisement procedures or by repair of program inadequacies (AAU, 1990; Bowen and Rudenstine, 1992; CGS, 1990b, 1991b).

SUMMARY

This chapter is about the conduct of the study. The sensible use of time is emphasized. The resources and commitment needed to conduct the study are explored. Technological advances (i.e., word processing and computer usage) are pointed out. Suggestions are made for systematic data recording. A major section explains the obligations the researcher has toward human subjects. Also, specific suggestions are made for relating to the advisor and for finding financial support. Finally, causes and remedies for T/D dropouts are suggested.

8

Writing the Manuscript

Sooner or later the time comes when the advisor and the student agree that a draft of the entire document should be prepared from title page to appendices and bibliography. From our experience, the earlier that first complete draft is written the better.

THE THESIS/DISSERTATION FORMAT

One of the first things a student wants to know is what a thesis or dissertation looks like. Faculty members, too, need to know if there is distinctive format associated with a particular kind of study or with a specific department or school. In a more general sense, both student and faculty member are recognizing the importance of and the need for some skeletal structure around which to assemble their ideas, the data, and their conclusions. The desirability of a well-planned outline is emphasized by Martin (1980):

> Probably no other aspect of writing so quickly distinguishes between the professional and the amateur writer than the emphasis on structure. The student writer, for example, fre-

225

quently starts writing at the beginning of Chapter 1 of a dissertation with the hope of working his/her way to the end of the chapter with little more in mind regarding structure than the three or four most important points. Such a neglect of structure is the primary cause of the situation most feared by all writers — sitting for an hour in front of a blank piece of paper trying to compose the first sentence. (p. 38)

The most difficult decisions at the full first draft stage of writing have to do with the internal organization of chapters, the structure that supports the flow of thoughts. Special attention is paid to that in this chapter.

A Table of Contents as a Guide

Over many years patterns have emerged for the T/D proposal and for the final document. The final document expands and extends the proposal text. Much the same patterns characterize both thesis and dissertation.

Usually the T/D proposal (see Chapter 4) constitutes a substantial part of the T/D. If the researcher has carefully drawn up the four chapters of the proposal, they become, with some changes including tense changes from future to present, the first four chapters of the dissertation. This would be so if the conduct and reporting of the research were as closely tied to the proposal as it should be. This fact serves to underscore the importance of a clear and carefully thought-out proposal, for such a proposal is not only more sound analytically, but more efficient as well.

The table of contents in Figure 8-1 incorporates a step-by-step excursion through the skeleton structure of a T/D. Note that it is an extension of Figure 4-1 and that it is a generalized outline. Outlines more adapted to specific types of studies are illustrated in Appendix B. Not every student's study will need every heading. For example, some reports may need no tables or appendices. Some students, on the other hand, may need to add headings not mentioned here or subdivide some of these. As said earlier, there is no standard outline that all research reports are required to follow.

AN APPROACH TO THE FIRST DRAFT

Organizing for Writing

This is something only the student can do. Advisors and committee members, though, may offer helpful suggestions. The preferred organizing process starts with establishing a writing schedule (i.e., a certain time each day, with projected objectives to be accomplished by certain times) and sticking to that schedule. Also, organizing for writing means arranging notes, references, and data in systematic and readily accessible form. At this point an ounce of order is worth a pound of clutter. Finally, organizing for writing calls for arranging for a place to write, preferably one that will not have to be moved and can be left as is when work is interrupted and returned to later. Often that can be accomplished at home by staking out just enough out-of-the way area for a computer and other technical equipment workstation, a table, a straight chair, a good light, and storage shelves and boxes for materials and supplies. However it is done, for most people organizing for writing is fundamental if the manuscript preparation is to progress effectively and efficiently.

Using a Dummy

Editors and experienced writers recommend early in the game the construction of a life-sized blank model of the finished document. Starting with the front cover and tentative title, pages with titles at the top are inserted in the order in which material will appear in the completed manuscript. They then can be rearranged, added to, or otherwise changed as progress dictates. Some make the dummy in a large looseleaf notebook. Others use a series of folders, one for each chapter or other section, with pages inserted. Still others construct the dummy as a computer file. Whatever the mechanics, filling in the dummy becomes the operational evidence that the draft is on its way to completion.

The Approved Overview Document

A comprehensive and detailed overview paper pays off first in the project approval stage. Second, it proves of great benefit as a

Figure 8-1 Table of Contents for Theses and Dissertations.

I. Introduction
II. The problem
   A. Rationale, significance, or need for the study
   B. Theoretical framework for the proposed study
   C. Statement of the problem to be investigated
   D. Elements, hypotheses, theories, or research questions to be investigated
   E. Delimitations and limitations of the study
   F. Definition of terms
   G. Summary
III. Review of the literature
   A. Historical overview of the theory and research literature
   B. The theory and research literature specific to the topic
   C. Research in cognate areas relevant to the T/D topic
   D. Critique of the validity of appropriate theory and research literature
   E. Summary of what is known and unknown about the T/D topic
   F. The contribution this study will make to the literature
IV. Research procedures
   A. Research methodology
   B. Specific procedures
   C. Research population or sample
   D. Instrumentation
   E. Pilot study
   F. Data collection
   G. Treatment of the data
   H. Summary
V. Findings
   A. The plan of the study
   B. Procedures
   C. Elements, hypotheses, research questions
   D. Evidence found that supports or fails to support each of the elements, hypotheses, or research questions
   E. Unanticipated results (findings)
   F. Summary of what was found
VI. Conclusion and implications
   A. Conclusions

1. Conclusions to be drawn based on the findings
2. Alternative explanations for the findings
3. Impact of the study in terms of what was learned
4. Strengths, weaknesses, and limitations of the study
B. Implications
   1. Implications for professional practice or decision making
   2. Implications for a scholarly understanding of the field
   3. Implications for theory building
   4. Implications for future research studies
C. Recommendations
   1. Recommendations for further research, or for changing research methodology
   2. Recommendations for changes in academic concepts, knowledge, or professional practice
   3. Recommended changes or modifications in accepted theoretical constructs
   4. Recommendations concerning changes in organization, procedures, practices, behavior
D. Summary
Appendices
   Appendix A . . . .
Bibliography

---

guide to conducting the study, particularly in gathering and analyzing the study's information base. Now, in the first full draft writing stage, the third major value of a sound overview appears. For many studies, the overview document with minor additions and modifications becomes the first several T/D chapters. With careful updating, including tense changes referred to earlier, the overview document gives the student a running start toward the goal of a full-scale first draft.

Style and Other Local Requirements

Costly mistakes can be avoided by an early re-review of the university and school regulations about style, required kind of paper, and other details. Some requirements that applied to the proposal may differ for the T/D document. Also, consistency in style makes for a smoother and more rapid flow of writing and reading. In the unusual case where there may be no mandated style and no preference expressed by the research advisor, two options should be considered. First, if it is anticipated that the T/D might be published in whole or in part as a book or in a journal, choose the style of that particular publisher or journal. If that is not feasible, select one of the numerous published style manuals and follow it. Abiding by one style, and paying close attention to it, precludes making expensive adjustments later.

Copyrighted Material

The most common location for quotations in the T/D is the chapter in which literature is reviewed, though the words of other writers may be cited elsewhere also. An overarching principle to guide researchers in quoting (or otherwise displaying) anything of someone else's is this: the owner of the copyright has the exclusive right to use, market, or otherwise employ his or her material in any form. It is essential, therefore, to stay with accepted practices for quoting, and to obtain permission wherever there might be a use of copyrighted material that goes beyond the standard rules and limits. One's advisor, the graduate office, and the university library are good sources for determining the rules and limits on quotations that apply to T/D writing. A contemporary reference (Gorman, 1987) is an excellent source for both the history and the rationale for protection by copyright.

Studying Other T/Ds

Useful hints about what to include in the dummy and how to present the final manuscript for maximum effect can be found by examining previously approved T/Ds on closely related topics. Some may have been read earlier as part of the literature review. Their procedures and findings may be summarized and critiqued in that chapter. Now is the time, though, to look at those T/Ds for another purpose. How are they organized? How do they present their material? How can their good qualities (and their mistakes) be helpful in preparing this one? These and similar questions ought to be foremost now as previously completed research reports are reexamined.

Studies Previously Directed by the Committee Members

Every faculty member has favorite student research reports that stand out as especially well written. It is perfectly proper for students to ask their advisors and committee members about these and to use them as illustrations. In fact, some faculty members commend such memorable illustrations to their students as models. Truly superior academic, professional, and scientific writing is not easy to find. Students certainly should take every opportunity to review works that their advisors and committee members judge to be exemplary specimens.

Uniqueness

Advisors emphasize the value of building on the experiences of others and of using guides and models (LaPidus, 1990). That can be very valuable. Yet, it must not be allowed to override the essential specialness, the one-of-a-kind quality, every student investigation should display. Thus, we urge students to strive for balance. On one side are stylistic and organizational patterns adapted from the best that past experience can offer. On the other side are freshly minted forms of expression, some perhaps newly invented to illuminate the particular contributions of this specific study. Harmoniously weighted, these can blend to foster the simple elegance of writing and illustrating that characterizes printed communication of the highest quality.

USING ADVICE AND TECHNICAL ASSISTANCE

An old saying has it that advice is the easiest thing in the world to give and the hardest thing in the world to take. So far as we know, there are no old sayings yet about technical assistance but, if we were to coin one, it would probably be to the effect that it too often tends to be heavy on the technical side and light on assistance. We hope to show, however, that both advice and technical assistance can be very useful in this first full draft writing stage, and that there are ways to stockpile each so they can be drawn upon when needed.

There is a real distinction between advice and technical assistance, as the terms are used here. Both, of course, involve communicating useful messages from one person to another. But they differ on these four dimensions.

Advice may be broad and general or pointed and personal; technical assistance is always focused on a scientific, academic, or professional situation.

Advice is frequently unsolicited, offered gratuitously; technical assistance is almost always in response to a request on the part of the person receiving it.

Advice tends to be directive, with the strong implication that it should be heeded; technical assistance is supplied with the understanding that the receiver will consider it but will feel there is no implicit or explicit requirement to act on it.

Advice is frequently, if not generally, oriented to what to do in a given situation; technical assistance emphasizes how to analyze situations and how and why to evaluate possible solutions.

Thus, while there is considerable overlap in meaning between the two expressions, the way they are used here plays up the differences rather than the similarities. The next several paragraphs offer suggestions about roles certain associates of the student might play in supplying both advice and technical assistance.

Other Students as Resources

Other students most frequently advise, though occasionally they also are sources of excellent technical assistance. The experiences of other students with typists, with individual faculty members, with the staffs of various university offices, with library or computer services, with style guides — these are valuable resources that can be mined for profit. And fortunate, indeed, is the writer who finds a student friend or acquaintance with skill and interest in academic, scientific, and professional writing in the same or an allied field. The nature and the degree of help that can be expected is, of course, a personal matter to be settled between the two individuals. We consider student-to-student advice and technical assistance to be both appropriate and desirable, and we encourage it. Both parties can learn and practice important skills in the process. Such interaction between and among colleagues is recognized as valuable in the real life of the learned professions. Two cautions, however, must be observed. First, the manuscript must be the student's own work; advice and technical assistance from others must stop substantially short of their literally writing the T/D. Second, advice and technical assistance that have a significant bearing on the concepts, format, or writing of the document should be explicitly acknowledged, either in the preface or by suitably placed footnotes.

The Chairperson as a Primary Consultant

The committee chairperson is usually a primary source both of technical help and of information about where to get such assistance, in this as in other parts of the research process. Students have the right to expect that. The chairperson, too, has the burden of deciding when to take on technical assistance consultation directly and when to refer the student elsewhere. To make that decision responsibly, chairpersons need to know and acknowledge their own limitations. They also must be aware of the competencies of other committee members and the strengths of other faculty members who may not be on the committee. A chairperson who cannot openly admit to limited knowledge about something puts the advisee in jeopardy by filibustering, bluffing, or ignoring a real need on the student's part. Equally dangerous are chairpersons so enraptured by their own pursuits that they know very little about their associates' academic and professional interests and capabilities. Such "one-person committees," where they occur, are evidence of inadequate quality-control monitoring of the T/D process by the faculty in general. In any event, students do well to initiate and maintain regular contacts with all committee members. That will be reinforced by thoughtful chairpersons by using opportunities to refer to others when students come to them and request technical assistance. As in all other aspects of the research enterprise, the committee chairperson has the major faculty role, and the way that role is played sets the tone for all the other participants.

Recourse to Other Committee Members

The committee members, as mentioned earlier, are chosen with several criteria in mind (i.e., knowledge about the topic, representativeness of departmental and other university involvement, graduate faculty status, experience). It is assumed, too, that they are all willing and able to provide technical assistance of various kinds. If a committee member is expert in statistical analysis, opinion polling, qualitative research, graphic displays, achievement testing, or group dynamics observation, it is reasonable to expect that person also to be knowledgeable about preferred practices in writing about or otherwise presenting information on the same topic. Thus, the committee member who renders consultation on procedure might well give technical assistance in how the material might best be presented in the T/D manuscript.

Technical Help from the Typist

The typist's experience with manuscripts can be of great importance. There are many who are speedy and accurate. But not many combine those qualities both with knowledge about the special requirements that attach to T/D typing and with good judgment in applying their skills and knowledge. That desirable mixture of qualifications can usually be found in two situations. One is the commercial typing, computer, and copying services that have multiplied in recent years near campuses. A number of them advertise T/D typing and printing at established rates. The other is the departmental secretary who does student papers and other contracted typing outside office hours at a per-page rate. In either instance, two precautions ought to be considered. First, learn from students or from faculty members how satisfactory the work from those specific sources has been in the past. Second, meet and talk with the person who would actually do the typing or word processing and assess his or her understanding of what is needed for a fully acceptable product. The more care taken at this point, the more likely it is that confidence can be placed in the typist's advice as to the combination of style, format, and mechanics that will meet all regulations and present the document in the most favorable light.

THE REVIEW OF THE FIRST DRAFT

As the first draft nears completion, it is increasingly trying for the student to hold to the idea that it is merely a first draft. So much effort has gone into it, so much time and money may be invested in it, that it becomes difficult to think of making even minor alterations in it, much less major changes. Ideally, the first draft should be so complete, so accurate, so well thought through, and so soundly written that it calls for very few modifications. That is a goal well worth the student's and committee's striving. Yet in reality it is rarely attained. So it is well if the student maintains a "first draft" attitude, a disciplined certainty that variances, some imperative and some only desirable, will be proposed. Adjusting to those proposals, and using them to make a good manuscript even better, is a significant part of the learning process inherent in this stage of the work.

Critiquing and Revision

Complicated and difficult parts of the draft may be profitably rewritten a number of times. Few persons find deathless prose flowing from their pens or word processors on the first try. Good writing is closely related to clear thinking, and neither comes easily or quickly to most writers. This is especially true of scholarly, technical, and scientific writing. Readable, clear, direct prose is usually the result of polishing, correcting, rephrasing, and rewriting any number of times. It is at this point that composing, editing, and rewriting on the word processor shows its merits most clearly. Changes on the screen are easy, and the new section or sentence can be seen and revised immediately.

Some students wait for their advisor to read and critique each draft of a section or a chapter before rewriting. This is a waste of time. Any intelligent, critically thinking person can read a T/D chapter and ask pointed questions about its meaning. If it is not clear to another person of good intelligence, it is probably not fully clear to the writer, nor will it be clear to the committee. At this stage, in fact, it is probably better *not* to have the proposal critiqued solely by another professional who is knowledgeable in the field of the proposal—there may be too much tolerance for the jargon and obfuscation that are the bane of the professional and academic lives. It would be well to trust one or more critical readings of the draft to an acerbic veteran of 10 to 20 years teaching composition and expository writing to high school or first-year college students, a person who knows little or nothing about the subject of the proposal.

The advisor's review of the draft is important, of course, but others can suggest improvements to the draft between appointments with the advisor. This will save the advisor's time and also impress upon the advisor that the visit is regarded as serious by the student, as evidenced by the grammar, spelling, wording, clarity, and neatness of the draft each time.

This is a good time to look again at Figure 5-1, a form that is sometimes used by committees to help to evaluate a T/D. To supplement that form, we also suggest using the checklist for theses and dissertations (Fig. 8-2). It need not follow the table of contents exactly. The central point is to assure that the document answers the checklist questions well.

Obtaining Reactions from Committee Members

The obvious way to learn what the committee members think of the material in its first full draft form is to ask them. The quality and thoroughness of response, however, are influenced greatly by the manner in which the student makes the request. Committee members report that they feel they can be most helpful when the student behaves in an orderly, organized way, as in the following illustration.

The student makes an appointment and delivers the document in person. That gives time for the two to update each other on their activities with respect to the project and to talk about any matters that need to be discussed.

Allowing enough time for the committee member to read the draft in its entirety (usually a week or two weeks), an appointment is made to meet again for the student to receive the reactions directly. In preparation for the follow-up appointment, the student does these things, if they are appropriate:

Asks for agreement that the meeting might be taped so it can be reviewed by the student after the meeting.

Raises specific questions about the draft and calls attention to the parts of it in which the committee member might have particular interest.

Indicates that reactions from all committee members are going to be listened to and reviewed with the advisor before final actions are taken on them.

Encourages the committee member to make notes, changes, and comments on the draft itself while reading it.

Asks the committee member what other preparations, if any, should be made for the follow-up appointment.

In ending this meeting with each committee member, the student leaves information about how to be reached (by telephone or other message) prior to the follow-up appointment, should a committee member need to have clarification of something while reading or should circumstances require a change in time or place for the meeting.

Not all committee members look for precisely the same approach. There are differences in style, and students need to accommodate to them. The paramount point, though, is that the conference is for the benefit of the student. It is the committee member's obligation to be constructive, to guide, and to teach. The probability that the committee member will fulfill that obliga-

Figure 8-2 Checklist for Theses and Dissertations.

Introduction and Problem Statement
Is the problem stated both in a general and in a specific way?
Is the purpose of the study stated?
Are the questions or hypotheses stated?
Does the reader get a general view of both the rationale for the
     investigation and its relationship to a supporting theoretical base?
Is there a transition to the next section?

Review of the Literature
Does it show thorough knowledge of the research, theory, concepts,
     ideology, and opinion related to this topic?
Is the reader made aware that the review has been selective and are the
     criteria for selection and relevance explained?
Is there any critical assessment of the reviewed literature?
Does the review reveal the relation between what has previously been
     done by others and what is proposed in this study?
Are suitable headings used to help the reader sort out the sections of the
     review?
Is each section summarized?
Are transitions provided from one section to another?
Is there a final summary that clinches the need to do the study, including
     gaps in the literature this study fills?

Method or Procedure
Does it explain what was done to gather the information essential to the
     investigation?
Would it be possible for another person to gather data and analyze it
     exactly as in this study simply by reading and following the
     statements in this section?
Is the specific research method used related clearly to a more general
     design known in the research methodology literature?
If human or animal subjects are used, are they adequately protected?
Are the variables in the study identified and described?
If controls are used, are they explained in sufficient detail?
If materials or apparatus are involved, are they described, illustrated, and
     their history and usefulness indicated?
Is the setting of the study specified?

If any directions or explanations are given to subjects by the investigator
in the course of the study, are they included?
Is debriefing necessary? If so, is it explained?

Results
Does the reader learn how information in raw form was summarized?
Descriptive statistics? Content analysis? Other?
Do tables contain all essential information so they can be read without
references to the text?
Does each table stand on its own, clear and self-explanatory?
Are results grouped in relation to questions or hypotheses?
Are incidental findings not immediately related to the questions or
hypotheses reported? Are there unforeseen results?
Is redundancy eliminated or minimized?
Is this section free of interpretations of results?

Discussion and Conclusions
Are the meaning and importance of the results indicated?
Are conclusions drawn about each question or hypothesis?
Are the limitations on conclusions specified?
Are alternative explanations for the findings identified and discussed?
Does the reader learn how successful the investigation was and what
further study might be needed on the topic?

tion well increases if the student takes a hand in setting the stage
for productive interaction by planful behavior similar to that illustrated in the list.

If the initial arrangements proceed satisfactorily, the follow-up
session for feedback should start in an easy, yet focused and
objective, way. The great bulk of the student's time should be
spent in listening and observing. Notable points for the student
are:

Be sure to understand the committee member's statements. If
uncertain, ask to discuss them.

Avoid conflict. This is not the time to argue about whether a
change should be made or how something should be pre-

sented. Keep in mind that all committee member reactions
are to be discussed later with the chairperson before deciding
if or how they will be used.

Stay open, not resistant. The gist and the value of what is being
said can escape if one is preoccupied with being defensive.

At the close of the meeting, make an oral summary of the salient
points covered to be certain that nothing the committee
member considers important has been overlooked.

Sometimes more than one meeting, even a series of meetings,
is necessary to obtain all the technical assistance to come from a
committee member. Time invested at this point pays dividends
and interest by reducing the number of challenges and surprises
later when the T/D defense must be made.

Coordinating Committee Reactions with the Chairperson

Under an ideal condition the student and chairperson would have
little to do when reactions to the first draft come back from committee member review. That ideal condition, though, is unusual.
Since committee members were seeing the work in its entirety for
the first time, they were almost certain to find gaps that they
assumed were filled with data analyses or discussions that they felt
were flawed or inconsistent. Moreover, the student sometimes
finds that two or more committee members offer bewilderingly
divergent ideas about changes that should be made in the same
part of the draft.

The effective chairperson at this stage helps the student in at
least three ways. These include the reconciliation of conflicting
recommendations of committee members, the restructuring of the
manuscript to include missing components or to make clarifica-
tions and corrections, and the preparation of a smooth second
draft that embodies the alterations.

In the first of these activities, the chairperson must remember
that the student may be very inexperienced in merging different
points of view, especially when they are voiced by persons the stu-

dent regards as superiors. Frequently the student can be prepared for the work to be done if the advisor points out that it is the values and relationships of the ideas or concepts that are to be thought about, more than the personalities of the differing faculty members. It may then be advisable to liken the task to that faced in writing a paper in which the varying viewpoints of several authorities need to be compared, contrasted, and, if possible, related to a larger and unifying conception. Alternatively, sometimes the student must be led to examine the conflicting expressions of different committee members and to reject one or more of them in favor of another. In that case, it is the chairperson's place to help assure that the student is prepared to support the decision. In all of this, the student's growth in competence to handle such situations is the central concern. The advisor intrudes or supports only to the extent necessary to achieve closure in a reasonable time. The student should feel the primary responsibility for whatever course is chosen or decision made.

If restructuring of the manuscript calls merely for the excision or rewriting of a paragraph or a sentence here and there, it is a minor matter, more an annoyance than a problem. When the recommended shifts are big ones, though, it may signal the need for a thorough redrafting of the document. Prior to embarking on such a comprehensive reformulation, it is usually advisable to arrange a conference to include the student, the chairperson, and the committee member(s) from whom the proposed alterations came. Such a meeting can clarify for the student and the chairperson the expectations that prompted the recommended changes. Sometimes, too, such a meeting reveals that the revisions proposed are not as drastic as the student originally thought. In rare cases, the variances requested by a committee member are substantial and far-reaching and the committee member is adamant. The committee chairperson, in that case, may need to call a full committee meeting to attempt to resolve the matter. The overriding consideration must be that the student receives fair treatment. In extreme cases, the student may need to lodge a grievance through the channels provided by the particular college or university.

A truism we referred to earlier has it that an ounce of prevention is worth a pound of cure. That certainly is accurate for the writing of the initial complete draft. The more care exercised in putting the first full draft together, the easier it should be to incorporate the changes, deletions, and additions into an even-flowing document. Chairpersons tend to impress that notion on students from the outset.

In addition to the three major kinds of assistance students can expect from chairpersons during this coordinative stage, there are countless other little ways in which a spirit of confidence and support can be conveyed. Some advisors maintain an "open-ear" policy, encouraging the student to telephone to discuss any problem that may be temporarily troublesome. Others describe and explain their own effective work habits, giving students opportunities to test them for themselves. Still others deliberately reinforce productive behavior on the part of students and then discuss with them how and why they did so. Whether they employ these or other procedures, advisors who are remembered as good models are the ones who offer advice and technical assistance in connection with the review of the first draft that helps the student over rough spots, who show respect for other committee members, and whose help enhances the quality of the report.

Rewriting the First Draft

Most experienced writers on professional and academic subjects agree that they can improve first drafts by laying them aside for a week or 10 days and then rereading them, editing along the way during the second reading. Our recommendation, therefore, is to rewrite the first draft in a two-step process (if rewriting proves necessary).

First, go through and make all of the corrections and changes that were agreed to in the coordinating session with the chairperson. Then put the material aside for a week or two. (Most students have plenty of other things they can do in the interim, such as obligations they have postponed while concentrating on the T/D.) During this time it is a good practice to arrange a rereading by others, some of whom, as we suggested earlier, are expert in clear prose composition and who are not specialists in the student's field.

As a second step, after an interlude, begin with the title page and read through the entire document, editing again for clarity and accuracy. Again we emphasize the enormous help that a good word-processing program can be in such editing. Recheck all references. Delete excess words. Check every compound and every complex sentence to ascertain if it would not be more readable if broken into simple sentences. Critically examine each paragraph that takes more than half a page to see if it might better be broken into two, or shortened by leaner writing. Look again at transition points from topic to topic and from chapter to chapter. If they are not present, construct short summaries and introductions as route markers to lead the new reader over the trail of reasoning that the writer can easily follow now without landmarks because it is so familiar.

Chapter 10 contains suggestions about writing style adapted from statements by editors of major professional journals. The hints are intended primarily for would-be writers for journals, of course, but they are equally applicable to T/D writing when the focus is on fat-free prose.

Finally, in the rewriting, attention should be paid to the material in the next section of this chapter. While some T/Ds must go through several drafts before presentation for final defense, the student who is alert to committee member advice and technical assistance and who approaches rewriting in an orderly way will face fewer disappointments.

WHEN THE WRITING IS FINISHED

There are really two different final drafts of the T/D. The first is the one that the student defends before the final oral examination committee. The second is the document that is accepted and entered into the school's records as part of the fulfillment of the degree requirements. The difference between the two is a function of the amount and kinds of changes that prove necessary in consequence of the battering the study takes in the final oral session. Some emerge virtually unscathed. Others, though ultimately approvable, may need major repairs. More will be said about this when the final oral examination itself is discussed. In the meantime, what appears next can be taken as relevant to both final documents.

The Student's Standards

The standards a student shows in writing do not emerge suddenly; earlier work with term papers and the like reveal the patterns of writing behavior the student brings to the task. In some cases an excellent foundation has been laid in prior work. But in a woefully large proportion of students the basics of composition are shaky or missing, to say nothing of skills essential for scholarly writing.

Obviously, it takes even more than ordinary intellectual prowess and determination for a student weak in written expression to attain acceptance for advanced study. More often than not students with that handicap find that the overview is an almost insurmountable hurdle. It can be questioned, of course, whether sheer ability to communicate well in writing should be a determining criterion. (See Disabled or Handicapped Students, pp. 63–64.) We would want the option to make exceptions if other circumstances appeared to warrant it. But where the ability to master the mechanics and styles of high-quality written communication is demonstrably within the student's range of potential, we would argue for holding it as a requisite for T/D preparation.

Students' standards for language usage and mechanics are, as noted before, predictable from earlier samples of written work. A great deal of disappointment can be avoided, therefore, if faculty members will maintain high criteria for quality of writing in all courses and seminars, and simply not accept sloppy and inaccurate sentence structure, spelling, punctuation, capitalization, paragraphing, and other recognized elements of correct writing. Both carelessness and ignorance are remediable, and the process should not be deferred until research work starts.

Equally important are the students' standards for the content and the thought processes and the arguments that should tie the T/D into a coherent, complete report of the study, from inception to conclusions and implications. These standards, too, are not likely to flower in the context of research proposal and report writing unless they were rooted, nourished, and budding during prior professional and academic study.

The standards that students internalize can be influenced by example. A direct and straightforward way to provide positive influence is to bring students into frequent contact with high-quality original research reports in all of their courses. Discussions with students suggest that a great many of them never see or touch an actual T/D before beginning work on one. Even then, they may review them principally for hints on how to set up a table of contents, chapters, and chapter subheadings.

We urge that students be introduced early to investigative studies and to the rationale for their place in preparation for roles in the learned professions. The use of T/Ds as models for scholarly writing is part of that theme. It is not a panacea, of course. Actual remedial instruction in composition may be essential for certain students before they can be fully admitted to advanced study. However, the early and consistent employment of selected, illustrative T/Ds offers both a most promising and a very readily accessible means to exemplify for students high standards of quality for mechanics, process, and substance in professional and academic authorship.

The Chairperson's Standards

We queried experienced chairpersons about how they acquired the standards they use in judging the merits of student research. Also, we listened to their views on what criteria ought to be applied in determining whether a document is ready to be presented for the final oral examination session.

Senior professors frequently regarded their own preparation for student research direction and committee work as less than satisfactory. It was too frequently based on incidental, spotty, and haphazard personal experience. What they learned, they said, was picked up for the most part from observing what other chairpersons did and by occasionally asking questions. Thus, inconsistency could be expected in standards from one to another chairperson. With recognition of the insecure bases for their views, however, chairpersons did say that they look for these characteristics, so far as student research writing is concerned.

The problem is clearly stated and well conceptualized.
Ideas are communicated in clear, readable language.
The student demonstrates significant analytical skills.
The writing is succinct, not verbose.
The presentation is well organized.
The thought processes are well defined and internally consistent.

Not every chairperson will consider those six statements to be either an essential or a sufficient list by which to access the adequacy of T/D writing. Also, they may not be objective or operational enough, in the view of some, to form the basis for a rating scale. Yet the odds seem to be good that most of those items will be high in the priorities of chairpersons when they judge the quality of writing and that documents that fall short on them will be returned to the student for more work.

The advisor cannot be expected to teach the fundamentals of composition. There may be occasional basic errors the advisor will detect and correct in the student's writing. But the ability to write plain prose which is grammatically correct seems to be a reasonable prerequisite, not something to be first learned from the advisor.

Another important role for the advisor, though, consists of increasing the student's awareness of the desirability to attain high standards of quality in writing with maximum economy and precision. By economy is meant using only as many words as are necessary. We are all familiar with sentences that ramble, repeat, and trap our thoughts in a tangle of verbiage. Improved mastery of the simple declarative sentence in writing should be one of the outcomes of T/D study for students. It is well within the scope of the advisor's authority and responsibility to keep that goal before the student.

Precision in writing calls for at least equal attention. Students who are otherwise fluent and even creative writers often need more of the discipline that scholarly writing requires. For instance, a student reports that the literature review included "reading everything that Robert Browning wrote." The student may need to be asked if the review did not actually include only "reading all of Robert Browning's known published works, as listed in [a given reference]." Another student may write that "Americans were the first to make a landing on the moon." That student may need to be shown that a more precise (an altogether accurate) statement is that "Americans were the first to set foot on the moon." This form of polishing is a very important kind of instruction the student should expect from the advisor and committee members. It extends from making the title say exactly what is intended, through table headings, statement of the problem, writing footnotes, and drawing conclusions, to the phrasing of the implications of the investigation.

The College or University's Standards

We were unable to find any statements, as such, that colleges or universities published as standards for satisfactory writing in a T/D. The same is true for professional schools. Many institutions and schools do require compliance with certain style guides. The inference can be drawn that adherence to the style guide, coupled with correct spelling, usage, grammar, and punctuation, would meet the standards for the mechanics of composition.

In a more general sense, several professional schools do exercise a form of quality control. At the University of Michigan's School of Education, for instance, a sample of T/Ds is drawn from each year's crop for special review. The selected T/Ds are sent to a jury of acknowledged leaders at other locations for assessment. The letter that accompanies the documents asks for a critical analysis of each and a rating as to its worthiness. The responses are then distributed to all faculty members, with the expectation that the faculty's future standards and actions will be influenced constructively by the reports of these annual checks. In another professional school it was reported that one associate dean perused every T/D approved by final oral committees. They numbered over 200 per year. Aside from the almost incredible amount of reading that entailed, there were no indications that systematic feedback occurred. It may have been felt that simply the knowledge that someone in authority would look at all the products would stimulate efforts toward higher quality.

Actually, apart from either recommended or required style guides, most higher education institutions' standards seem to be no more and no less than an amalgam of the various views of the faculty members who serve on T/D committees. That amalgam itself is rarely analyzed to determine where it constitutes a consensus on anything. In short, the institutional criterion for satisfactory writing is, in most cases, whatever a final oral committee approves. Neither concomitant with nor beyond the committee's positive decision is there any other check on quality.

School and Departmental Standards

Even a casual examination of T/Ds from different units in a school will reveal some variations in what is acceptable. One expects, of course, differences in topics, and that has been discussed earlier. There are also understandable differences in sources, emphasis, terminology, and, sometimes, investigative methodology from one division or department to another. Studies about very early childhood may depend heavily on more or less quantified information supplied by third parties who observe the infants and toddlers. Investigations involving teenage youth may, in contrast, draw mainly on data generated by or from the adolescents themselves, such as autobiographies or test responses. Research on supervision may use material drawn from interaction analysis. Work in administration and management may employ actuarial information, costs, and other facts. Trend analyses in history or in political science may use library resources, primarily, though all of the above depend heavily on library facilities, too.

But even though sharp substantive and procedural differences legitimately appear, the quality of student research writing ought not vary significantly from one school or department to another or from one document to another in the same school or department. When it does, the most probable culprit is the faculty, for failure to establish and abide by standards. The immediate losers, in that case, are the students, because inferior work will not be discriminated from high-quality work. The distinguished products of excellent students will be diminished through association with the shoddy work of others. The students who offer inadequately written T/Ds will not be informed that they are weak, and the ones who could do better will not be helped to improve. The long-range losers are the school or department and the higher education institution, for they, over the years, come to be judged mainly by the products of their graduates.

Thus, the generators and guardians of T/D writing standards are and should be all of the faculty members of the higher education institution. The graduate faculty, that elect group vested with the power to guide and approve, should spearhead the total thrust for superior writing.

Application of Standards with Objectivity

Ultimately, the decision about whether the T/D is in final written form, ready for submission for the final oral examination, is the decision of the student. It is a decision that, ideally, should have the full concurrence of the chairperson. But that is not always the case. If the student insists that the manuscript needs no further work, even though the chairperson does not agree, the student's choice should prevail. And both the advisor and the student may feel that their view is objective.

High on every priority list of scholarly qualities is an attitude of objectivity. It includes objectivity both about one's own work and about the work of others. It is not divorced from a humane attitude, for that, too, deserves a high priority on the same list. But objectivity is a distinct quality. It allows one to make clear decisions about what degree of credibility to assign to any academic or professional matter. It is behind every reasoned evaluation. Objectivity allows the weighing of variables that can make the difference between sound judgment and sheer guesswork. Objectivity is a chief determinant of the confidence one has that one's present procedures and future projections have substantial foundations. Objectivity is a necessary precondition to believability.

Surely objectivity is emphasized in many ways in the course of collegiate preparation. Probably many students possess highly developed levels of objectivity as part of their entry behavior when they start T/D work. One of the tasks of the research advisor is to determine the degree to which that quality is already present in the student, and to reinforce and strengthen it as needed until it is firmly established. One of the questions that should be answered in the affirmative by the committee before final approval is given is: "Has the student consistently demonstrated an adequate level of objectivity in professional and academic matters?"

The chairperson is obligated to ascertain that the student is aware of all the objective standards that may legitimately be used to measure the product. Also, the chairperson is responsible for informing the student objectively how and in what ways the proposed T/D does not measure up, if it does not. And, of course, the chairperson's advice and technical assistance should be available to the student. But if the student either ignores the cautions of the chairperson or mistakenly believes that the chairperson's questions have really been satisfied, the die is cast.

The usual outcome of the application of standards is a happy one in which the student moves ahead to the next step with confidence that the chairperson is fully supportive. In such cases the confidence usually proves to be fully justified.

SUMMARY

This chapter is chiefly about writing, with suggestions about how to accomplish it with dispatch and with superior results. Writing includes attention both to mechanics and to clear exposition of thought. The judicious use of both advice and technical assistance is advocated. The significance of institutional roles, regulations, and standards is emphasized, as are the roles of various persons in providing guidance and interpretations. The meaning of objectivity and its applications are discussed. The preeminent position of the student in decision making is made clear, as is the high stake both student and institution have in the production of excellent student research.

9

Defense of the Thesis or Dissertation

The research project is not finished until the student has submitted to an examination on it, made whatever adjustments are shown to be needed as a consequence of that examination, and received a signed statement of faculty committee approval. This chapter deals with those matters, how they are to be carried out, and the factors that influence and guide faculty decision making.

STRUCTURE OF THE ORAL EXAMINATION

The oral examination in most institutions is the final procedural step in student evaluation in the degree process. It concentrates on the study, the findings, and their interpretation. However, questions regarding the academic and professional preparation of the candidate may also legitimately arise.

In the historic tradition of great European universities, the rite of passage from the rank of student to the community of scholars was marked by hours and even days of examination by established scholars. Invitations would be issued to learned persons throughout the country to attend, and every visiting scholar felt obliged to

253

ask erudite questions. The candidate was fair game as long as the questions were in the candidate's field of expertise, for the candidate was, after all, seeking admission to the community of scholars who had the high distinction of being titled "master" or "doctor" (Haskins, 1957).

Modern examinations do not normally follow those traditions, but knowing something about them may help all concerned to put the process in a conceptual perspective and to see why the final defense committee may not limit its questioning to the investigation itself. In most contemporary cases, the examining committee focuses on the written evidence of scholarship before it. The time set aside for the final defense is usually too brief to allow the committee to do much more than that. Today, most final orals are conducted in two- to three-hour sessions. Those present are usually limited to the candidate and the committee, with perhaps one or two guest scholars or students.

Scenario of the Examination

The candidate and the committee meet at a designated time in an office or seminar room. Each committee member has presumably prepared for the examination by reading the document carefully and by making note of any items needing clarification or questions to be asked.

The chairperson may begin the session by asking the candidate to make a brief statement about the results and findings of the research, after which each member of the committee is encouraged to ask questions or make comments. The candidate responds, where appropriate, to the questions or comments. At the end of the appointed time the candidate is often asked to leave the room while the committee discusses what decision it should make on the basis of a review of the document and the final oral examination, as well as any other information revelant to the academic competence of the candidate. Usually then the candidate is brought back into the room, the chairperson announces the committee's decision, and a short discussion ensues concerning the conditions attached to the decisons, if any. At this point the defense and the oral exam is considered over. The purpose of the final defense has been accomplished, namely, to establish whether the candidate has qualitatively and quantitatively met the standards of the institution and the faculty in the completion of the research and in the program of studies.

Criteria for Excellence

The oral examination gives the candidate a chance to defend the way the study was done, the validity of the findings, and the importance of the conclusions and their implications. The committee is interested in how well the candidate demonstrates the ability to cite, explain, analyze, and conclude, in a scholarly way, in the chosen areas of expertise and research. It will become clear, in a properly conducted examination, that the work is the candidate's own, that the candidate learned a great deal from the work, and that the candidate is able to conduct other similar research independently.

An excellent oral defense is one for which it is clear to the committee that the candidate has prepared well. The document presented is in excellent shape. The answers to the committee questions are concise, clear, to the point, and informative. The oral presentation is tightly reasoned. The impression made on the committee is one of quiet confidence and competence. There is little doubt at the end that the candidate has the ability and integrity to carry on competent research without detailed direction from a senior colleague.

The Evaluation Procedure

Final defense committees commonly use four options in deciding what action to take after the oral has been held. Two of the options are unusual: the committee may find the T/D so well done that it may approve the T/D as executed and written, or it may be so poorly written that it will be denied approval. Both decisions are extreme in the sense that they seldom happen and in the sense that they have a powerful effect on the student. The other two options are the witholding of approval until major revisions are made, or approval with minor modification. These will be discussed later in this chapter.

Whatever the option chosen by the committee, there must be specific reasons for it, and those resaons must be stated orally in the final defense session. They are usually summarized for the committee and the candidate at the end of the session by the chairperson after the committee decision is reported.

PREPARATION FOR THE EXAMINING COMMITTEE SESSION

Examining committee sessions require preparation and prior planning, perhaps several months in advance. Refer to the Time Line for compliance with local rules on this. The preparation is the responsibility of a number of persons, but the two principal roles belong to the candidate and the chairperson of the committee.

Chairperson's Responsibilities

Before a committee examination can be firmly scheduled, the research advisor must be satisfied with the draft of the T/D that is to be the basis for the final oral. This draft then is sent to the rest of the committee for review. It should, in the student's mind, be considered a final draft. It should include changes and reconcile conflicts raised by committee members in earlier draft reviews.

If the advisor at this stage seems too strict or too demanding in the eyes of the student, it is well to remember that the advisor's reputation is also at stake. By authorizing the draft's distribution, the advisor is saying that it is ready to receive the careful review of the committee. A conscientious scholarly advisor would be embarrassed to give permission to circulate a document full of errors. Sending the draft to committee means that the advisor has reviewed it carefully and critically and believes that it is ready for committee review. After the committee has received the final draft, the advisor sets aside a reasonable amount of time for the committee to review the document. We suggest at least two weeks, if there is no specific time set in local regulations.

If the advisor has been successful in helping the student put together a well-formulated and well-written report, the committee will usually not request further revisions prior to the examination. However, one or more members may request improvements in a more formal way during the meeting of the examining committee.

Time, Location, and Notice of Examination

We recommend that the advisor circulate copies of the final draft along with a memorandum that gives notice of the time, location, and membership of the meeting of the final defense examining committee. This may be made the candidate's responsibility, but the chairperson should then oversee it. The university process for notifying students and the faculty committee of the time and place of the meeting usually includes some procedure to also notify other members of the graduate faculty and to allow them to read the T/D before the meeting. They can then attend with some knowledge of the subject and can assess the document against the standards of the institution.

Preview of Procedures for Student

It is good form for the advisor to preview procedures with the student. The student is often unaware of role expectations in the committee meeting, is unsure of preparation that should be made, and is not knowledgeable about the support or nonsupport of the advisor during the examining committee meeting. These, and any other matters raised by the candidate, ought to be very thoroughly discussed in the advisor's office. The advisor may offer some advice about the steps the candidate might take to prepare for the final defense. The advisor should make sure that the candidate has gone through all the mechanical steps that accompany the final stages of the T/D process and eventual graduation. The two persons might again go over the limitations of the study — limitations that are unavoidable and not remediable at this point. Problems may be anticipated in this preview session, but the role of the advisor should be to make the candidate feel at ease and self-controlled. After all, the candidate has done the best work possible, and the advisor has approved what was done; although the product may not be perfect, it is their expectation that a favorable outcome will result.

This is a good opportunity for the advisor to review the formalities of the session, how questions will be asked, and how long the session is likely to be, and, as well, a description of how the advisor will chair the session, including a perception of the advisor's role as chairperson of the examining committee. Finally, there ought to be some frank talk about the role of the candidate in the session, and how that role might be seen as functional to the achievement of the goal. We provide our own recommendations regarding the role of the student subsequently. It is also valuable at this point to read again what we said earlier about the overview meeting, for much of it applies.

Candidate Responsibilities

The first responsibility is to be well prepared. The second is to be completely frank and open with the advisor about the problems and weaknesses of the study and any other possible difficult issues, from the point of view of the student, which may come up in the final defense. This committee session will have much more the atmosphere of a scholarly examination that any prior meeting of the group. Students must be ready for that and all that it implies about student-faculty interactions during the examination.

Availability of Needed Equipment

At some examining committee sessions the candidate needs special equipment for the final defense. This may be audiovisual equipment needed for a presentation or some displays or examples. It may be a tape recorder to capture the deliberations of the session, used so that accurate recollection of suggestions can be recorded. Whatever the special equipment required, it is the candidate's responsibility to check with the chairperson to ascertain if it is permitted in the examining committee session. If so, it is the candidate's responsibility to obtain the equipment and place it in the examining room before the session, and to make sure it works.

If the equipment is not portable or if it is so specialized that a special room is needed for the examination sesson, it is the responsibility of the candidate to schedule the room with the concurrence of the chairperson of the T/D examining committee.

Freedom to Observe Oral Defense Examinations

The final defense ordinarily is publicly announced and is open to interested members of the university community who wish to observe it. Graduate students and faculty should be especially welcome. If not, it may be an indication that the process is not open to public scrutiny because of institutional insecurity about the quality, rigor, or fairness of the process. The final defense is too important to faculty and graduate students to keep them from seeing examples of it operate. Further, an open and public final defense is in the finest scholastic tradition, and on the face of it there does not seem any good general reason to keep appropriate observers out.

Use of Simulation for Preparation

Once there is a recognized structure and procedure to the final defense committee meeting, a fairly realistic simulation can be designed. Students can work together to constitute an examining committee, simulate the whole meeting from beginning to end, and even pass, fail, or amend the candidate's presentation. If the simulation is taken seriously, as it ought to be, fellow students often ask harder questions and grill a candidate with less mercy than faculty in the same situation. A candidate who has been through a number of tough simulations will probably have anticipated the questions that will be asked in the real defense and will have formulated thoughtful answers to the questions anticipated.

The simulation process can be carried to a fine art. Fellow students from the candidate's department can assume the roles of specific faculty members on the committee, reflecting their backgrounds and research interests and probably predicting many of their questions. Having gone through the final draft of the T/D, the student-colleagues who are playing out the roles of faculty members on the committee should be able to perceive the weaknesses in the study and anticipate the insightful queries one would expect of well-prepared faculty examiners. As well, it should be an education for those who help in the simulation, students who may soon have to face their own final defense. These students will then have an opportunity to model their behavior on a colleague who may be a little more advanced. In case this process seems a little too playful, let us point out that several observers have described a process very similar to this as having been used successfully to prepare high public officials to face more effectively a potential barrage of wide-ranging and difficult press conference questions and to prepare law students for trials.

Actually, we recommend beginning simulation sessons quite early in the final writing stages. If some tough unanswered questions or some gaping holes in early drafts become evident, they can, perhaps, be repaired before the document goes to the committee. In effect, the best preparation for the final defense is a document written and argued so tightly that there is very little room for embarrassing questions. Committees usually like such T/Ds because they are well done and because the committee can spend most time during the defense exploring the implications of the study and looking to the future research needs it reveals rather than tinkering with errors in grammar, style, research design, or methodology.

CONDUCT OF THE ORAL EXAMINATION

If there is sound preparation, it is unlikely that the final oral will hold any great threat. A half-century ago Edwards (1944) alluded to this when she said that in many cases the final defense is seen as a pro forma meeting. That condition prevails when the student investigator has produced an excellent study, fulfilled the promises made in the proposal, worked closely with advisors, and communicated fully with committee members. In such cases the advisor and committee members have a common view that the graduate research was well done. The final defense then becomes what many faculty hope for in every case — a lively and informed discussion of an important problem and field of interest in which the candidate and faculty participate essentially as colleagues. The discussion focuses on the growing edge of research, explores the implications of the results of the study, examines the interdisciplinary effects of the study findings, and brainstorms new research ideas to push back the frontiers of knowledge, understanding, and professional practice. Such final orals are exciting and enjoyable for everyone; in the best of circumstances they become the focus of interest and intellectual excitement of a much broader circle of scholars than just the committee. In our view, this is a state of constructive intellectual ferment to be sought at colleges and universities that aspire to be "great" or "excellent."

Role of the Chairperson

If the chairperson is also the research advisor, there is some role conflict inherent in the examining committee session. The advisor has worked closely with the candidate, approved the proposal, the research design, the methodology, the conduct of the whole study, read the drafts of the document, and finally approved the work in a form to come before the committee. Hard as one may try, it is impossible to be completely disinterested in the outcome of the process. For many advisors, the candidate's product becomes almost a part of the advisor.

The committee chairperson role has expectations that are somewhat different from those of the research advisor. The chairperson is expected to conduct the session in an impartial way. The role is not one of defense of the candidate or defense of the chairperson's own deep involvement in the work of the candidate. The role is rather that of an impartial judge, who assures a fair and open hearing for the candidate, and also for each member of the examining committee, even the most junior member. The chairperson has the obligation to set the conditions and guide the process so that all the participants can come to a fair, equitable, and reasoned decision as to what is the best course of action under the circumstances.

Balanced Participation

It is essential that the oral examination be conducted in such a way as to be equitable and even-handed with respect to all parties. The one person most responsible for maintaining that equilibrium is the chairperson, though each faculty member shares it. Balanced participation means operationally that every person on the committee has a fair and equal chance to ask questions and make comments and that the candidate has a fair and equal chance to respond to questions or comments and to put forward others where appropriate. It also means that all members of the committee have the same opportunity to participate. If the persons who have a role in the oral examination feel that the session has been partial, biased, unbalanced, or unfair, the results of that feeling may well spill over to create other committee problems, and perhaps other problems for the candidate. Moreover, such feelings may well engender formal grievances.

Tone of the Session

If there are observers, the chairperson is responsible for arranging seating for them that separates them physically from the candidate and the committee members. Also, the observers should be addressed by the chairperson before the examination begins to explain that comments, questions, or other forms of participation or expression by them are to be reserved while the examination is in session.

As the convener and as the presiding university official, the chairperson is in the position to set the tone of the meeting. It is a serious undertaking, most of all for the candidate who has invested so much in the study, and the session is expected to have a serious and a moderately formal quality. The most important tone, however, is conveyed by the verbal and nonverbal behavior of faculty. The behavior should indicate that the individual faculty member cares so much, values so much, the candidate's work that no effort was spared to read it carefully, and that while the faculty member is supportive of the candidate, nothing short of excellent work will be allowed to pass the committee. It is best if this tone can be established and maintained from the beginning by the chairperson.

Clarification of Questions

The chairperson is also looked to for clarification of technical or substantive questions on the T/D and on the examining committee process. For example, if the student's work has been part of a larger program of investigation directed by a faculty member, the degree to which the student has been able to maintain independence would be a reasonable area of inquiry. Another example: suppose the student has made significant use of a consultant from another university. What kind of monitoring has that consultant's participation had from committee members? For a third example, what if the candidate is deaf and will be using an interpreter to facilitate communication during the committee examination session? How can one be certain of accurate interpretation? It is important to anticipate such questions and to have explanations readily accessible before the session if one is in the role of chairperson. In cases where the questions are clearly for the candidate, the clarification role may be simply to supply a communication link between a faculty question and a student's attempt to understand the question. In any case, the role of the chairperson does not include answering faculty questions clearly directed at the candidate concerning either the investigation or what the candidate has learned through the program.

Signaling Completion of Examination

There is no magic number of minutes the session is required to last. Based on our data, the total time, from calling the meeting to order to notification of the candidate of the outcome, typically ranges between one and one-half and two and one-half hours. After every faculty member has had a chance to ask questions of the candidate, and the candidate to respond and ask questions, the chairperson should be able to sense that the time for ending the examination is drawing near. The chairperson should then try, without being arbitrary, to bring the session to a close. There are always individuals who may find it difficult to stop talking; dealing with those individuals within the context of an oral examination is the responsibility of the chairperson.

Committee Member Roles

The role of the committee member is to be a judge of quality and specifically to ascertain if the quality of the T/D is sufficient to admit the candidate to the ranks of those holding an honor's master's or doctorate. In our view, this is the essential element of the role, and it is carried out in a number of ways. The oral examination, in effect, gives the committee a chance to ascertain the quality of the document and the quality of the student's work, but beyond that the committee is treading on thin ice. It would seem, for example, that the candidate's life-style, political orientation, or championship of popular or unpopular causes is beyond the purview of the final defense committee, at least with respect to present-day academia's mores. The issue may seem different, however, if the candidate is known to be engaged in dishonest, unprofessional, or illegal activities, but even here committees are reluctant to make judgments, *in this situation* on anything very much beyond the written and the oral presentation. They tend to see such judgments as outside their role unless the activities have to do with the research itself.

Committees do assess the depth and range of the candidate's knowledge about the document at hand and the methodology used to do the study. If the candidate cannot answer detailed questions about his or her own work, including the review of the literature and the methodology, the role of committee members is to delve deeper and question reasons for this apparent ignorance.

One important thing the committee members look for is the congruence between the promises made in the proposal and what appears in the final draft of the study. One role of the committee is to exercise approval over any changes the student wishes to make in the study plan after the overview committee has met and approved the proposal. If the approved proposal has the attributes of a contract, then *both* parties must adhere to it. Therefore, the committee will be looking for the final draft to show how the originally approved study proposal has been carried out in the conduct of the study.

Students sometimes assume that the acceptance of the final draft by the committee for the purpose of the oral examination signals its acceptance as a document of sufficient quality to meet all the requirements of the university and the committee. That is a false assumption. What the committee action means, in fact, is that the members individually have reviewed the draft carefully and are satisfied that it is good enough to provide a basis for an oral examination. Problems that remain with the final draft will be brought out at the examination. They may or may not be communicated to the student or the advisor beforehand. That depends on the time constraints on the individuals, whether or not there is good communication among them, and whether the problems were actually identified earlier. Some issues do not surface until there is the interplay of minds during the examination itself. In any case, the problems that remain in the draft that goes to the committee will be worked out in committee and may become a part of the substantive revisions that must be made before the document is finally approved.

Role of the Candidate

Preparation is the key to success. The final oral examination is the culmination of a long preparation process. The candidate has been guided in pre-T/D study by an academic advisor, a person who is usually a member of the committee. The candidate has thoroughly reviewed the literature, designed the methodology, and conducted the study under the guidance of the advisor and committee. Finally, the T/D was written with the advice and consultation of the whole committee. Every committee member had a chance to see it and comment on it before the final defense meeting. With all that background, there should be no great surprises and the final defense should go smoothly.

Yet, it is not uncommon to find important problems at the end. Why? We have put down a list of three main reasons reported by colleagues and from our own experience.

1. The advisor has been misled about how much of the work — the design, the literature review, the data gathering, and analysis (including the knowledge base from which these are drawn) — was really done or understood by the candidate. Because of that, serious weaknesses come out at the final oral, and then are pursued by the committee, often to the point where it becomes acutely embarrassing and uncomfortable for everyone.

2. The advisor errs in allowing the candidate to come to the final defense before the research is thoroughly and carefully done, and before it represents a work of excellence. Sometimes the candidate is convinced that he or she is ready for the final defense and convinces the advisor of this when, in fact, there is a good deal more work to do. Often there is pressure of time, such as a statute of limitations, a baby due, an upcoming job in another city, or a tenure decision to be made on the candidate who is a faculty member at another institution. Sometimes there is simply a factor of fatigue, when the advisor and the student have revised the work over and over again, and, in effect, throw themselves on the mercy of the committee.

3. Occasionally, the candidate is unrealistic in assessing personal skills, ability, commitment, or the amount of time and detailed work required to complete the T/D, and the advisor is unsuccessful in communicating with the candidate about the problems. The advisor then decides to bring the full force of committee rejection to bear to convince the candidate.

The role of the candidate in the final defense meeting is important. In our view, the role is one of *openness, honesty,* and *mature* expertise. Openness about the data and problems of the study is the only ethical way to approach this final test. Honesty is the one most important attribute of a researcher. Maturity motivates candidates to do their own work, accept the responsibility for all that was done in the study, live up to the promises made at the time of the proposal, and treat colleagues in an ethical and unbiased, objective manner.

Responsiveness of a positive, constructive kind is another essential attribute. The final defense is not the place to become "defensive." It is a time for calm, reasoned responses to questions or suggestions. Where a response is appropriate, a direct, to-the-point answer is usually best. There is nothing fatal about a straight "I don't know" when that is the simple truth, either, though that response should not often be necessary. In most cases, the candidate's thorough knowledge of a fairly specialized subject area means that the candidate has the most expert knowledge in the committee room. There is no reason, though, for the candidate to flaunt that knowledge. Such behavior is unnecessary and dysfunctional. The time for the candidate to expound with great erudition and wisdom is (if at all) after the awarding of the degree, not during the defense of the research for the degree.

In addition to responding to questions and comments of the committee, the candidate's role includes that of note taker regarding changes suggested by the committee during the oral examination. Sometimes this responsibility can be delegated to a fellow graduate student who is sitting in on the oral examination. The chairperson and committee members take notes, too. In any case the responsibility lies with the candidate to see that in one way or another the job is done. Remember, too, that not all changes proposed during the examination survive the critical appraisal of the full committee during the committee's end-of-session deliberations. It is what is conveyed to the candidate by the chairperson after the examination that really counts so far as required changes are concerned. It is the candidate's role to raise any question if suggestions for change agreed upon in committee are not clear. It is also within the student role to defend against suggested changes in the T/D that seem unfair, inconsistent with the promises of the research proposal or overview, unethical, or untenable in light of the research. Of course, one would want to be very careful in resisting suggested changes, and perhaps substantial reliance on the views of the chairperson would be appropriate at this point. In our experience, however, there have been very few cases in which a final defense committee suggested a change that was not also seen as desirable by the candidate.

All the above chores are simplified if a voice-activated tape recorder is switched on during the examination. It may be under the control of the chairperson, with the tape remaining in that person's custody. It could then be listened to by the candidate afterward for the purpose of assuring that the committee's requirements regarding changes and additions are clearly understood and verified.

DECISION MAKING REGARDING THE ORAL DEFENSE

Applying Criteria for Approval

Whatever criteria for approval the committee uses should be made explicit. The T/D Evaluation Form (Fig. 5-1), was designed to help achieve that purpose. It is useful both at this point as a last-minute check before the final defense and earlier in the T/D process as the draft version is being written. *It seems essential* to us that *all* criteria that have significant weight be stated on the T/D Evaluation Form. The committee owes that to the candidate, to the institution, and to themselves. Ambiguities and hidden agendas create misunderstandings and disputes; clarity and openness help to prevent them. Thus, the T/D Evaluation Form has multiple uses. In effect, we are recommending its use at this point as a summative evaluation form as we recommended it for formative evaluation purposes throughout the preparation phases.

Conditional Approval

There are two forms of conditional approval. If the document is essentially acceptable but minor revisions are needed, the committee will often simply indicate where changes should be made and rely on the candidate and the research advisor to make the alterations before the final document is sent to the appropriate office under the signatures of the committee and research advisor.

Under these circumstances, the candidate makes the minor revisions, submits them for a final review by the research advisor, and then circulates the corrected copy to the committee. Committee members rely on the candidate and the research advisor to make the changes.

The second level of provisional approval is much more tentative. It may be used with a final draft which has major problems, but ones which the candidate understand and can probably clear up in a reasonable time. In this case, the candidate is instructed to carry out the major changes and to bring the complete T/D or the altered portions back to a committee meeting or for approval by individual members. This form of provisional approval is short of failure, but if the revisions are not a sufficient improvement over what the committee reviewed at the oral examination, the candidate simply does not pass. The process of getting back to the committee varies, but in any case the responsibility is on the candidate to make the substantial revisions on a timely basis and get them to the advisor and, after advisor approval, back to the committee. In such cases, individual committee members do not sign the approval form until completely satisfied that the revised document reflects credit on the candidate, the advisor, the committee, and the university.

Formal Voting

Practice varies from institution to institution, but usually a final oral committee is comprised of an odd number of members, which implies that a vote, if taken, should not be a tie. Usually, only members of the graduate faculty may vote, although others, even from outside the institution, may serve on the committee. Whether or not the chairperson votes depends on the institution, as does the issue of whether a passing vote must be unanimous, simply a majority, or a specified number of members.

Our own experience and research indicate that there is seldom an issue about the vote. The committee tends to work as a group and, with the help of the chairperson, arrives at a consensus acceptable to all. If one member, or a minority of members, is adamant about a point or decision, usually the committee hears all the arguments at great length, weighs the issues carefully, and comes to a conclusion that seems as fair as possible under the circumstances. A committee can be persuaded to take an action by one member, if that member's arguments are good enough and if those arguments support fairness and the concept of high quality in graduate research standards. Usually, the committee chairperson knows what the formal votes will be before passing the official approval form around because agreement on the wisest course of action has been reached by voice vote in committee. When the committee members sign the formal approval form, they are, however, casting formal votes that become a matter of record and for which they are accountable.

Notification and Interpretation to the Candidate

At the end of the oral defense the candidate should clearly understand the decision of the committee. Sometimes that decision has to be interpreted to the student. The situation may be stressful, or the student may simply not understand the implications of the decision. A common point of misunderstanding, we have found, is where the committee is calling for major revisions and the student hears the call in terms of minor modifications which can be accomplished in a short time. Committees usually remain calm and quiet, at least in front of the candidate, and speak in low tones and shorthand sentences, and the atmosphere of the final defense session may mislead the candidate to believe everything is going well when in fact it is not.

The research advisor ought to interpret at the end of the meeting what the committee meant by what is said and did, and the specific implications for the candidate's future work. A good procedure is to have the candidate describe what was said, what was decided, and what changes are being required in the draft. A session with the candidate right after the oral examination is in order to debrief the candidate, to pull the threads together, and to prepare to work on whatever it is the committee recommends. Further sessions should also be scheduled to check progress. This keeps the candidate focused on the future rather than on rehashing the committee meeting and perhaps indulging in resentment or self-pity. Some of the latter is natural and human, particularly if the final oral examination did not go well, but it is dysfunctional to the task. It is best for the candidate to start immediately on what remains to be done.

FOLLOW-UP AFTER APPROVAL OR DISAPPROVAL

Usually this period is one of extreme feeling on the part of the candidate. If the study is approved, the candidate may be so happy that it is easy to forget to make the revisions and do the other procedural things that are necessary before graduation is a reality. If the results of the oral examination seemed disastrous, the candidate may understandably exhibit avoidance behavior with respect to the whole process and everyone attached to it. Neither extreme is functional or task-oriented with respect to reaching that difficult, time-consuming goal everyone agreed to at the beginning. The thing to do is to immediately start picking up the pieces.

Candidate and Research Advisor's Roles

Whatever happened at the defense, the advisor's role is to help the candidate calm down, reassess, reevaluate, and redirect toward whatever it takes to reach the goal. Failing the oral defense is not necessarily irretrievably final. Candidates have successfully renegotiated with their committee and redone the same or different research with a high degree of excellence. It will take more time. Sometimes it means the learning of new skills, the taking of additional courses, and the appointment of a new committee, but it can be and often has been done. On the other hand, it may be that the candidate either does not have what it takes, or does not want to put that much effort into the process. In that case, the advisor has a counseling role to help the candidate arrive at a realistic self-perception. It may also be possible for the candidate to do better in another department or another university or school.

Even when the T/D has been approved, the advisor's role is still difficult and time-consuming. Although there is a feeling of joy and a tendency toward relaxation after approval, the situation is rarely one in which the advisor or student has nothing left to do on the study. There are usually some revisions to make, and sometimes these are substantial. All of the rules of the university concerning the filing of abstracts, corrected copies, binding, and rules concerning the mechanics of actually becoming a graduate of the university have to be followed after the successful examination session. Both the candidate and the advisor have to guard against the temptation to let things slide by because the major work has been done. For both, whether the time is one of sadness after disapproval or happiness after approval, this period is one that should be devoted to reexamination of original goals, the determination of the relevancy of these goals in light of the final defense committee's decision, and, if appropriate, the renewed determination to reach the goals.

Disseminating the Results of the Study

In major universities dissertations are copyrighted, microfilmed, and indexed in *Dissertation Abstracts*. There is a fee attached to these services. The copyright is designed to protect the author's work from use by others without permission. Microfilming and indexing the document through the University Microfilms process makes it available to other scholars and to libraries for review and even purchase. In using University Microfilms, the author agrees to permit these uses and under certain circumstances receives a royalty. The author is often offered the opportunity to have the dissertation listed in the survey of earned doctorates awarded in the United States, and these forms are available at universities that grant earned doctorates.

University Microfilms will make available to authors printed copies of the abstract of the dissertation written by the author. These abstracts can be used effectively to disseminate the results of the study. In some cases, a dissertation will be accepted for inclusion in one of the storage and retrieval systems mentioned earlier. That can bring wide dissemination. Abstracts may also be sent to professional societies having a professional interest in the subject of the dissertation for printing in their publications.

Professional societies provide another dissemination opportunity. In almost every case there are annual meetings where authors read papers. There are journals and reviews of research that publish not only some of the papers given at the annual meetings, but also manuscripts submitted for review by the journal. While a journal would rarely publish a whole thesis or dissertation as such, it may be happy to publish an article or chapter from one. For publication, revision is usually necessary to make the work fit into the style and format of the journal.

We recommend using the professional societies for dissemination purposes because the process not only makes the study available to others, but it also contributes to the recognition, security, and standing of the author. In fact, we recommend that the advisor and candidate explore the possibility of sharing findings, where appropriate, even before the completion of the T/D. For a student to give a paper at an academic or professional meeting is a great learning experience. Often the help of the research advisor is critical to providing the opportunity.

Finally, there are some investigations which by their nature lend themselves to publication commercially. Historical studies, for example, sometimes find their way into a book or a number of articles. If the work has enough general interest or is topical at the time of publication, it may be successful commercially. That means it will sell as a general work, as a textbook, or as a professional work of merit. In this case, the author may be on the way to more publications and some success as a writer. All of these possibilities are addressed in more detail in the next chapter.

SUMMARY

This chapter explains the process of T/D defense, including the oral examination, suggestions for preparing the examining committee session, and the conduct of the oral examination. The kinds of decisions and how they may be arrived at are discussed. Finally, the need for follow-up after the final defense and the need to disseminate results are described.

10

The Completed Thesis or Dissertation and Future Growth

Faculty members believe students should do theses and dissertations for future-oriented reasons. Some are:

To add to the body of knowledge necessary to solve the many problems with which academics and professionals now grapple, like undereducation, job dissatisfaction, unemployment, crime, accidents, and others.

To establish the ability to write about professional and academic discipline data in ways understandable to people who need such information.

To prepare the student for participation in research as part of a career.

Plainly, the faculty members who told us those things in interviews or through their writing envisioned links between what might be learned during the completion of research and certain tasks students would need to perform during their future careers. Also, there was a clear indication that the results of research ought to lead to possible resolutions of current or future problems. The question, then, is not whether there should be a tie between student investigations and future work, but rather the question is how best to encourage that viewpoint and to actively implement it. Myers (1993) says it well:

> What is needed is serious contemplation of the achievement, thoughtful consideration of what changes the achievement will bring to the self-concept of the student, and reinforcement of the sense of ownership of both the product and the process just completed. Without dedicated attention—largely on the part of the sponsor—to the final step in this developmental task, the meaning of the enterprise can be lost. (p. 336)

AFTER THE RESEARCH IS APPROVED

The last four decades brought marked changes from the days when completed T/Ds were simply covered and sewn together by a local bookbinder. Distribution then included a copy for each committee member's office shelf and two for the institution's library. A national list of T/Ds was published occasionally, and interlibrary loan was the only means of wider dissemination.

Now, almost all dissertations and many theses find their way onto microfilms and can be obtained readily at a modest cost. Also, many are referenced in databases which can be searched by computer. Storage and search and retrieval resources and procedures are as common now as library card files have traditionally been. With access so convenient, why go to the trouble of revising the document for another form of publication? There are several widely acknowledged reasons.

Learning to write for publication is valuable in itself, for it develops a set of skills that can enhance all written communication. Members of the academic disciplines and the professions must be able to write material that is well organized, clear, and interestingly stated. Memoranda, directions, reports, letters, evaluations, policies, proposals, regulations, lesson plans—the list of styles and forms of written expression in which scholars must perform well is almost endless.

Security and recognition are often tied to publication productivity. In higher education one of the criteria for continuation of employment and ultimately for permanent tenure relates to the quality and quantity of authored articles and books. (It is important to remind oneself here that sheer publication does not give assurance of job security. The published material must be of high quality, there must be enough of it, and other characteristics such as teaching ability are weighed, too. But publications are essential if the criterion of quality and extent of published work is to be assessed at all.) It is also true that initial and continued employment and promotion in research and development centers, state and federal agencies, and other public and private positions can be influenced positively by growth in one's own list of scholarly writings in print.

Career exploration and direction, opportunities for testing new paths, can be significant outcomes from reworking the T/D for possible publication of a book, article, or monograph. Some learn for the first time that they enjoy editorial activity and that they have hitherto unrealized capabilities for it. Others, during the rewriting, find their interest kindled or quickened in planning a programmatic set of investigations based on the research already done. That may be only one step from seeking and obtaining financial backing for a several-year research and development effort. Still others are turned in new directions by job or consultation offers that come to them because of the interest generated in prospective employers by initial and follow-up publications stemming from their research.

Contributions to knowledge may, of course, be found directly in the research reports themselves by anyone who searches them out. But it is the nature of the T/D that it is phrased very carefully. Committee members tend to counsel restraint both in what is said and in how it is phrased. Some committee members may urge the candidate to cut loose in the final draft, particularly in the section on implications. By that time, though, the candidate is writing with such ingrained caution that boldness is out of the question. Thus, a journal article may afford the first real opportunity to be more daring, to point out more explicitly how the results and conclusions might be used to add to wisdom and to improve practices. Appearance in the forum of public print also invites comment and discussion, so important to the weighing and balancing that ought to take place before new concepts or changes are fully accepted.

Dissemination of new information still lags. Great gaps yawn between where knowledge is located (e.g., in T/D pages) and where that knowledge ought to be if it is to be used. Publication is one way to narrow those gaps. In addition to the conventional print forms, the delivery of papers or participation in panel discussions is another means of dissemination. Writers who cite relevant T/Ds in their own publications are aiding in dissemination, too. (It was mentioned previously that publication could reinforce academic and professional security and recognition. The same is true of citation. A large number of citations of a scholar's work in the publications of others suggests that it has extraordinary significance.) The T/D supplies an excellent database from which to disseminate new ideas, information, or concepts, whether through print, oral presentation, or via citations. Committee members and other faculty members who encourage students in those directions are making a contribution to both the students and to their professions.

WRITING FOR PUBLICATION

William Strunk, Jr. (Strunk and White, 1979) said it best in *The Elements of Style*:

> Vigorous writing is concise. A sentence should contain no unnecessary words, a paragraph no unnecessary sentences, for the same reason that a drawing should have no unnecessary lines and a machine no unnecessary parts. This requires not that the writer make all his sentences short, or that he avoid all detail and treat his subjects only in outline, but that every word tell. (pp. ix-x)

Few thrills match the first acceptance of an article for publication. It is a great feeling for the author, and it can rightly be a prideful event for the faculty members who tutored and encouraged the author. Surprisingly, relatively few publications about professional or academic publication appear in any field's literature. Etzold's (1976) article is one of the rare ones to address the matter seriously. It provides a tightly knit and thought-provoking process guide to the writing, submission, and acceptance of scholarly manuscripts. It offers practical assistance that can benefit both beginners and experienced writers.

Guidelines on Writing

A brief set of guidelines on writing for publication follows. It draws in part on Etzold's (1976) suggestions, in part on our own experience, and in part on what colleagues told us. The outline has two major components, one dealing with writing the article and the other with getting the article published.

Writing the Article: This step calls for particular attention to three procedures.

First is deciding on the form in which the content will be presented. Journals tend not to employ the conventional T/D format for articles. They prefer shorter pieces; they often merge the problem statement and the literature review; and in many other ways journal articles have organizational qualities of their own. What they have in common, though, and what successful manuscripts require, is a systematic sequence of content that enhances communication of concepts. The structure (outline) decided upon ought to reflect one's scheme for proceeding in an orderly way with the different components and facets of the topic. Preplanned organization should be flexible. Some excellent ideas occur while writing, and it should be possible to fold them into the article's outline as they occur. But an overall plan to start with is essential.

This is the time to review your computer files, checking each one for items and ideas you think could be worked into the article you have in mind. Also, this is the time to start a new outline to

fill in and store in your computer, this time an outline for an article.

Second, the article should begin with and maintain a firm fix
on its main theme. Every paragraph or larger section ought to
move that same theme ahead, building on the foundation of the
earlier paragraphs or sections. Anything that deviates from the
main line of development should be reexamined, either to bring it
into the main current of the article, to justify it as a necessary side
step, or to eliminate it. One can help oneself to monitor the forward movement of the text by posing this question: Does the first
sentence of every paragraph stick to the core theme of the article
and does it follow sensibly the first sentence in the immediately
preceding paragraph?

Third, make absolutely sure that all grammatical, spelling, and
other mechanical and structural composition details reflect preferred practice in contemporary usage. Quality of expression and
correct usage can be upgraded for almost everyone by taking
advantage of the standard features of most word processor programs. These not only can call the attention of the writer to such
basics as correct spelling, but also can offer synonyms and even
check a manuscript for overuse of trite phrases. All of that help,
and more, can be had almost automatically, if the proper commands are entered into the keyboard. Correct language cannot
make an otherwise weak article into a good one. But few factors
can distract an editor from the positive qualities of a manuscript as
quickly and as emphatically as sloppy and inaccurate writing.

Successful authors reach out for the counsel of friends, associates, previous teachers, and others who promise honest and ener-
getic criticism, plus suggestions to remedy the defects they detect.
It is extremely unusual that the first draft of a manuscript turns out
to be the one that ought to be submitted to a journal editor.

Achieving Publication: The article, once written, calls for tuning in
on a number of conditions that influence editorial acceptance.
Three of the main variables are discussed briefly.

First, pick a periodical to match your topic. Ask your committee members to make suggestions. Journals that cater to social

work studies seldom find room for reports of studies in engineering or business. If a paper has a focus on a matter of interest to professionals only in one state or only in one region (i.e., the Nebraska Association of School Psychologists), then a journal that deals mainly with that state or region's concerns would be the target of choice. If the article is a theory, opinion, or development piece, it would be better aimed at a publication that is known to carry many such articles, rather than at one whose annual index of titles shows only statistical studies. One good source of information on the characteristics of publications is the *Directory of Scholarly and Research Publishing Opportunities*, carried in most public libraries.

Second, find out what author guidelines, if any, the chosen journal provides. If the information does not appear in each issue of the journal itself, write or call the editor and make an inquiry. We have adapted and constructed in the section following this one a sample set of notes that might be supplied to prospective authors by a simulated journal.

Third, be ready to try another journal if the first choice rejects the manuscript outright. Peters and Ceci (1980) offer evidence from a cleverly designed and executed investigation that rejections are often the result of differences in judgment on the part of editors rather than lack of merit in a proposed article. We believe that it is a rare topic that cannot be matched sooner or later with the publication interests of more than one journal. Usually, too, whether the rejection is outright or conditional, the author is given the main reasons for the decision. By taking those reasons as constructive criticisms, it is often feasible to prepare an improved draft that may be accepted on a second go around.

There is a great deal of competition for journal space. Editors of high-quality periodicals annually receive many times the number of articles that they can publish. Standards for acceptance grow in rigor each year, as more and more journals state their criteria more explictly and as an increased number of journals use a referee system that screens potential articles through groups of volunteer associate editors who are specialists in the journals' domain of special interest. Achieving publication, therefore, depends in large measure on doing a superior job of putting together a well-composed, tightly organized manuscript and directing it to a periodical the style and publishing interest of which match with the article's content.

Illustrative Journal Guidelines

We have simulated guidelines that could have relevance for all who are trying to write for professional journals. They cover guidelines for manuscript preparation. They will not fit every journal, but study of them will help illustrate the similarities and differences between T/D style and article style. These guidelines will help to produce an article that reads well and is a consistent, unified publication:

1. Select the *time perspective*. Write in the present tense or in the past or future, but be *consistent*.
2. Write in the active voice: "Jones believes that clear enunciation helps to communicate well" *rather than* "It is believed by Jones that. . . ."
3. *Keep sentences simple, short, and logical.* (Rambling, convoluted, page-long sentences turn people off.) Write with known peers in mind — not abstract "scholars."
4. Employ subheads to break copy into readable segments and to guide readers in making transitions. One subhead per three typed pages is a minimum rule.
5. Avoid quotes unless they are essential or unique in style. Identify the fact and the source. Provide copyright permission for quotes of 50 or more words and for charts or figures or models.
6. Make use of the graphics capability of your computer both to present concepts and to clarify procedures or methods used. Consult key sources for displaying data and for showing very complex theoretical constructs (Tufte, 1983, 1990).
7. Extract the *most quotable brief statements* (for use as highlights at tops or sides of pages), at least one for every three pages.

8. Keep footnotes to a minimum. Put them at the end of the manuscript in the order in which they appear. They are appropriate to acknowledge: the basis of the study (e.g., doctoral dissertation, paper presented at a meeting, and so on); a grant or other financial support; scholarly review or assistance in conducting the study or preparing the manuscript.

9. The *reference* list cites only works that are referred to in the article. Every work cited in the text must be listed in the references. A *bibliography* cites other works for background. Do not duplicate items on the reference list in the bibliography.

10. State the names and correct titles of institutions of all *authors*. List them in author order on the last page of the manuscript.

11. On a separate cover page include professional biographical information: name, title, unit within larger institution or organization or legal name of the institution or organization, and mailing address.

12. Prepare the *manuscript double-spaced on one side*, with margins of at least 1.25 inches. Do not reduce. Send the original and one clear copy.

13. If human or animal subjects have been used in the study, include a statement (or a photocopy) indicating that the investigation was approved by the appropriate human or animal subjects review committee at your institution.

14. Identify specifically any computer programs and any individual consultants employed in statistical analyses reported in the manuscript.

15. Copies of signed, dated, and witnessed release forms should be included for any photographs of humans to be used, and care should be taken to conceal identities.

16. In your cover letter to the editor offer to provide electronic copy of your manuscript, if desired, for example, in Word-Perfect or ASCII on a 3.5-inch or a 5.25-inch double-sided/double-density diskette. This often speeds reviews by readers and facilitates technical editing to the journal's requirements.

17. If you have the copyright to your material and wish to retain it, make your desire clear immediately to the editor. Many journals insist on receiving assignment of the copyright as a precondition for publication. It is appropriate and ethical to negotiate for the arrangement you wish *prior* to review of your manuscript.

18. A dissertation or thesis is considered a publication. Thus, any article based on a dissertation or thesis should cite the dissertation or thesis in the article's text and bibliography.

These directions illustrate the principle that journals have their own preferences for mode of expression. Guidelines, on the one hand, help publications to maintain and express their own journalistic styles and, on the other hand, offer assistance to the author while the manuscript is still in the early stages of composition. The guidelines for periodicals may vary markedly, one from another, as reflections of their differing editorial policies and purposes. Thus, it is advisable to obtain and to work directly from the guidelines of the particular publication to which the article will be directed.

IMPROVEMENT OF ONE'S PROFESSIONAL OR ACADEMIC DISCIPLINE

Part of the rationale for requiring research projects is that students who complete them are, in consequence, better prepared to bring about improvements in their fields. The same rationale holds that the studies themselves, if disseminated and applied, can influence change for the better.

Research and Professional Improvement

Guba (1967), in analyzing the relation of educational research in general to educational improvement, said:

Ideally, research develops the basic findings, the "new truths," the empirical data, upon which improvement decisions should be based. In education we have been singularly short-sighted in the past in constructing mechanisms by which research products are moved into practice. (p. 12)

While Guba's sentiment applied to educational research, it seems to us to have relevance for investigative studies in general. The "new truths," also, may arise as a result of taking new looks at old data, seeing things from changed perspectives. Students, while still engaged in the research process, should be guided by their advisors to think of the possibilities of weaving the results of their work into the fabric of their field's future. That task ought to be kept before students as a responsibility. Now students and advisors too often tend to close the door on research activity as if it is a completed episode that stops with the faculty committee signoff after the final oral examination. Instead, students should be guided to see their approved theses and dissertations as points of transition, not simply ends in themselves.

There is solid evidence that journal publication does follow shortly after the dissertation is completed for many graduates. For example, Schuckman (1987) studied publications by recent Ph.D. recipients in psychology and biology, finding that it was not uncommon for three to five publications per student to appear within four years after graduation, although a substantial number did not publish at all in that same time period.

Schuckman also produced evidence that the number of post-doctoral publications per student was not related to gender. Not only was there no significant relationship between frequency of publication and male or female gender, but also it did not seem to matter whether the student's advisor was male or female. In other words, Schuckman's (1987) study provided no evidence for the belief that the sex of the graduate student's advisor had a significant impact on the student's publication rate following graduation.

The encouragement of publication by graduates is a major responsibility of advisors and committee members, according to the professors we interviewed. Many advisors wished graduates would ask them to help in moving the dissertation, or a study based on it, into the mainstream of journal articles.

Translation into Theory and Practice

There is an obligation to put the significant findings of both T/D and other research and development into the hands of potential users. That obligation includes the analysis, interpretation, "repackaging," and dissemination of research results and other pertinent information for a variety of specific, nonresearch audiences. The main purpose is to provide operating agencies and individuals with a sound and growing research and development information base for evaluating and modifying current programs or planning and implementing new ones, including the facilitation of more rapid adoption of tested professional innovations and new information.

Students amass data of various kinds in the process of their research. Some is about people, some is about things like books or other objects, or about procedural policies, or schedules. Still more is about interactions of people and things, such as how teachers and students and parents design and use individualized education programs, the attitudes of citizens toward public welfare and taxes, or the dynamics of collective bargaining. Taken together, enormous quantities of data are collected and processed in some way annually. For the most part, the information is seldom used again after serving its function once in a T/D.

Yet, if it is accessible, it has many additional potential uses. Accessibility is becoming less and less a problem, with increases in the understanding and the technology necessary for easy and inexpensive data storage and retrieval. Knowledge availability systems have burgeoned with computers, modems, online search capabilities, fax machines, and a large variety of software becoming common as part of the library service, in schools, homes, offices, businesses, and other public and private organizations.

Thus, one of the significant contributions of student research may well be found in the data collection itself, quite apart from the specific use to which the information may have been put in the particular T/D for which it was gathered and processed. The contribution: ready, low-cost access to significant amounts of the raw material for inquiry, concept building, hypothesis testing, and decision making.

While it is still uncommon, a related and preferred development in student research is to build into the process itself an appreciation for the importance of what Guba (1967) called a "linking mechanism" between the T/D and practice. That calls for enlarging greatly on the implications section of the document and devoting an entirely new section to a presentation on the potential applied significance of the investigation's outcomes. After the development of that implications material, the student is almost certain to feel a greater stake in building on the scholarly insights and knowhow engendered during the design, conduct, and reporting of the research itself.

FOLLOW-UP STUDIES BASED ON T/D RESEARCH

Completion of the T/D can bring relief from taut nerves and a strong temptation to turn away from the tension source to put it out of mind. Sensitive committee members, aware of that syndrome, prepare advisees to recognize and to think about other, more positive ways to slide from student-researcher to researcher-student, a more mature form of the scholarly species. That transition can be fostered by guiding the advisee to prepare for questions in the final oral examination that bear on what kinds of follow-up investigations the findings of the investigation ought to stimulate. It is only one step from that to helping the advisee to sketch out procedures that could be used to pursue the suggested studies.

Potential studies that capture and hold students' interest after the T/D is finished vary in kind. Three forms of follow-up do kindle more than ordinary interest: those which replicate, those which expand, and those which refine instruments.

Replication is a great research need. The literature is replete with one-shot studies, many with major possible significance but with sample, locale, or other limitations that minimize generalizability. Even with results of investigations that are broadly applicable, replication is usually needed in additional settings in order to create a critical mass capable of firing an adoption of changed mood in the enormous bodies of scholarly community and business systems. There are, of course, some studies that, by their nature, cannot be replicated. For them, closely related, companion investigations are needed to confirm and extend the credibility of the originals.

Expansion presses the original research work outward to new horizons. It answers questions like: How much farther will this principle reach? Where else can what has been found have influence? What other professional practices are amenable to study and analysis in this way? How does what has been uncovered in this study link to other scientific laws or academic concepts? Expansion carries the implication of a programmatic approach to additional inquiry stemming from the T/D findings and motivated by them.

Instrument refinement is a possibility for further study when the student research requires the use of ratings, scales, questionnaires, tests, observation schemes, interview protocols, apparatus, formulas, or other tangible date collection aids. Sometimes, too, the study itself may not involve instrumentation, but it may unearth reasons why existing tests, scales, or similar items should be improved, with suggestions about how the needed polishing should proceed.

Replication, expansion, and instrumental improvements are only three directions that follow-up studies can take. Whether one or more of these paths or others seem feasible, it cannot be overemphasized that committee members have the obligation to try consciously to engage the creative imagination of their students in thinking about follow-up. That needs to be done early in T/D work, too, and reinforced frequently if it is to carry the student through the typical tendency to let down after final approval.

REINFORCEMENT FOR FOLLOW-UP

Two of the most effective motivators for degree-seeking students are financial support and faculty approval. Strategic patterning of these can create powerful forces that foster continued research activity subsequent to T/D completion. Following is a list of a number of possible ways to join reward systems to follow-up activities on the part of students.

When financial support is given during research, whether as tuition remission, job opportunities, or as outright grants, include in the application and the award statement language that indicates expectation that follow-up will be done.

Establish as standard practice a post-T/D approval committee meeting that is devoted to consideration of possible follow-up work. The agenda could include:

   Student ideas about possible follow-up activities
   Governmental or private foundation resources
   Suggestions about journals to which to submit
   Organizations or agencies interested in the kind of investigation done by the student
   Identification of other faculty members doing related research
   Practical suggestions for making a start on follow-up

Hold competitions for best T/Ds. Provide for a sufficient number of categories, with several awards in each category, to assure that all truly meritorious studies receive recognition. Include students as judges.

Arrange for student presentations about their completed research to local audiences of other students and of faculty members. Presentations can range from class or seminar discussions to formal papers at colloquia or in faculty meetings. In all cases make it a requirement that at least one-third of the presentation deal with potential or planned follow-up activities.

Publish a school periodical that contains summaries of completed student investigations. A necessary part of each summary may be the student's projections about possible related continuing research activity.

Hold an annual school or departmental event (luncheon, dinner, one-day conference) that highlights graduates who have published articles, presented papers, or carried on studies that built on student research they completed in the recent past.

One of the most frequently voiced concerns of advisors is that too many students have become discouraged from continuing research by the time they complete the T/D. Some end up embittered by the experience, rendered hostile to anything that relates to research. More than 30 years ago James (1960) made the essential point this way.

> It is important to keep the candidate . . . in mind. Some candidates are treated so harshly that, for them, research study in later years is something carefully to be avoided. . . . It is of major importance that the candidate's efforts to identify a problem, to plan and carry out the research, to present the results, and to defend . . . results among . . . older professional colleagues should constitute a "success experience," and not a passage through pergatory. (p. 148)

We carry James' notion a step further by emphasizing the potential positive impact of thoughtfully designed end-of-mission activities. It is to be hoped, of course, that pleasant experiences will predominate all along the student research trail. If there are substantial difficulties, it is to be expected that committee members will help students work their ways through the difficulties objectively, without abrading feelings in the process. Finally, we encourage the deliberate employment of reparative and rewarding professional acknowledgment and encouragement to enhance the likelihood that the solid satisfactions of inquiry and investigation will remain dominant in those who complete T/Ds.

FUTURE TRENDS

During 1973 and 1974, the Educational Testing Service (Educational Testing Service, 1974, pp. 62-63) reported on the trends in graduate education in its report *Flexibility for the Future*. Significant for T/D study were these summary recommended actions:

... That the practice of evaluating all graduate schools and their faculties in terms of research be re-examined;
That all doctoral students spend time doing off-campus work related to their major fields;
That efforts to recruit women and minority group members for faculty positions be intensified;
That faculty be allowed more time for seeking solutions to society's major problems; and
That institutional policies governing such matters as student residency and fellowships be made more flexible. (Educational Testing Service, 1974, p. 63)

Each of those recommendations remains as fresh today as when they were first made. Without exhausting the possibilities, these are some examples. About the first recommendation, one could ask what role *student* research has and should have in that reexamination? As for the second, to what extent might that recommendation be instrumental in promoting student studies in off-campus settings, with attendant influence on the nature of T/D topics? The third recommendation not only opens the way to studies of women and minority persons' recruitment itself, but also promises to bring more subjects of concern to women and minority groups into the pool of potential student research topics.

The fourth recommendation focuses on faculty time for addressing the world's chief problems. For the professions, that immediately suggests investigations that attack such national problems as aging, union-management relations, education for literacy and values, and studies about population control, to name only a few. The academic disciplines have at least as urgent an agenda.

With regard to the last of the five recommendations, two difficult problems for T/D students are embedded in it: residency and financial support. Residency usually refers to the time spent in study while on the campus. It is increasingly difficult for students to continue in residence (so defined) while conducting research, and particularly dissertation work, because of the extended period of time often entailed. The chief problem is financial support for the student and the student's research during that period. Moreover, when financial support is available from the higher-education institution, it is usually in exchange for performing some task other than the T/D work. Thus, the student is the captive of the job for which the payment is given; that captivity effectively limits the range of action of the student to investigate certain potential topics. More flexibility in residency requirements and financial support are objectives worth pursuing.

SUMMARY

This chapter begins to chart some of the largely unexplored terrain beyond the formal completion of graduate research work. The contributions of such investigations to the growth of the individual student are discussed on the one hand, and on the other hand, the functions of the T/Ds in the development of the professions and academic disciplines are considered. Suggestions are made for how faculty members and students may further their own development by means of intelligently planned activities coincident with and following the conclusion of the officially prescribed research process.

Appendix A: Research-Related Computer Terminology

The 30 expressions below are used at various places in the chapters of this book and many readers may already be familiar with them. For those readers to whom the terminology is new or not well known, this glossary should prove helpful.

Many other words and phrases from information science and technology are used in this book, too. However, they are sufficiently defined in context as to present few, if any, questions as to their meaning.

ACCESS CODE refers to a set of letters and/or digits which, when entered into a computer by an operator, gives that operator freedom to use the computer. Access codes are used primarily to keep unauthorized persons from operating the computer. Access codes also can trigger an accounting system in the computer to keep a record of usage by person or by department and keep track of the date and amount of time, the hour of the day, and the nature of the usage. (*See also* MAINFRAME and PASSWORD.)

BBS, or Bulletin Board Service, operates from a computer program that allows one to confer with multiple users through notes, messages, or files left on the mutual-use bulletin board. Using a modem, one can dial into the bulletin board and trade information and thoughts with other users. Most colleges and universities have at least one bulletin board and some have several. BBS is a good place to get acquainted with others who have similar research interests. The bulletin board idea has been developed by some companies into a multifeatured instrument service with individualized monthly or hourly fees. Examples of organizations that offer the basic bulletin board message transfers and information services plus many more features like stock quotations, travel agency and information, shopping, and news reports are Prodigy, CompuServe, and America Online.

CD-ROM is the acronym for compact disc read-only memory. CD-ROMs resemble CDs found in record shops. Computers can read them but cannot write on them as they can on other data discs. Small as it is, one CD-ROM can hold at least 600 million characters of type. A researcher can own one CD-ROM with the key writings of Charles Darwin, 650 color and black-and-white images, natural sound recordings, a 1000-entry bibliography, and more. The accompanying software allows, among other things, searching and browsing by word, author, subject, or title (Lightbinders, 2325 3rd St., Suite 320, San Francisco, CA, 94107). Another example is the Britannic Electronic Index, one disc providing 16,000,000 references to the 1993 *Encyclopaedia Britannica* (Encyclopaedia Britannica Educational Corporation, Toll Free 1-800-554-9862). Increasingly, too, the entire texts of scientific and professional journals may be obtained on disks. These are but a few examples of the values of the CD-ROM. And it can be much easier to find topics of interest by searching a disk than by examining a book. The researcher can then readily print out relevant passages. Databases are generally sold in the CD-ROM form, and they are relatively inexpensive, considering what they contain. Moreover, many may be accessed through university libraries at no cost to bona fide students.

DATABASE means a body of interrelated information that is organized or managed by a computer. It puts the information into a rational structure, much like a person doing the organizing would, so that it can be easily located and retrieved. For the researcher, it is possible to put material on computerized index cards that may then be numbered, put under topics, alphabetized, prioritized, or brought together in any other way that might be desired. Material can be added, changed, or deleted. For the investigator, most important is the fact that the one can sort the information according to any set of rules one gives the computer.

E-MAIL is a system that lets computer installations in different locations share messages. It functions between adjoining rooms or around the world, so long as the proper connectivity network is in place. Many colleges and universities now make computers available to faculty members in their offices and to students in "labs" or "centers" at various convenient campus locations. With the proper authorization, one may compose, exchange, forward, query, or route copies of a message, even with lengthy documents attached, to one or more other computers without using a scrap of paper. The researcher can use e-mail to maintain communication with consultants, advisor, committee members, and other researchers. Six or seven Windows e-mail packages, each having many kinds of options, are available.

FAX-MODEM (*See* MODEMS.)

FILE refers to a collection of information stored in a computer memory under a single name. The computer treats a file much the same way you would deal with a file folder in your file drawer. Just as a researcher might move the folder to another location, make copies of all or part of the contents, change the name on the folder, add to or remove some of the contents, or discard the folder entirely, the researcher can command the computer to do the same things to a file. Since a file can, on command, hold, change, organize and reorganize almost anything (data, instructions, correspondence, graphics, plans, and more), it is one of the most useful aspects of computer memory utilization.

FLOPPY DISC DRIVE and FLOPPY DISC combine to make up a common form of information storage. The drive is a mechanism accessed by an opening usually on the front of the computer. A floppy disc is slipped into the opening and the mechanism can then write on it or read from it, using tiny induced magnetic fields.

Fairly inexpensive, floppy discs are very useful to researchers for moving information from one to another computer and for exchanging or storing data in a conveniently accessible location.

FONT is the technical term for a style of type used in printing. It is advantageous, often, to present typed material more attractively and in more readable fashion by altering the font from text to headings, for highlighting in the text, for very significant quotations, for footnotes, and for lists, tables, and other items to which the researcher wishes to call particular attention. T/D students have more freedom to do that in preliminary documents like the proposal; the final T/D draft may have more conservative style constraints. Word processor units often come with a variety of fonts; others can be purchased. Font cartridges can be purchased for printers, too.

GRAPHICS refers to the ability to construct, display, and print charts, graphs, pictures, data-flow diagrams, conceptual schemes, and other figural representations in black and white, shades of gray, and color, with integrated text, titles, headings, labels, and the like. The presentation of research ideas, procedures, findings, and conclusions is frequently much clearer when such means are used to help convey what the investigator has in mind, especially when employed to supplement text and when placed so that text and illustration can by viewed simultaneously. Software is widely available for this purpose. There are numerous programs designed for specific application to certain professions or academic disciplines.

HARD DISC DRIVE and HARD DISC constitute the main mass information storage component of a computer. The hard disc (or fixed disc) cannot be put in and out of the computer like a floppy disc, but the reading and writing processes function in the same way. For the researcher, hard discs are proving essential because of their ability to store and to retrieve vast quantities of information very quickly. If cost and speed are balanced, the hard drive is the most efficient means of information storage by computer for almost any form of research activity.

KEYBOARD (*See* MAINFRAME and TERMINAL.)

MAINFRAME refers to a large, multipurpose computer, usually in a fixed location, that services all, or a major portion, of an institution of college or university size. Most mainframes store and manage enrollment data, scheduling, and the like. In many instances there are terminals strategically located on the campus for officials and for students to use in their investigations and writing. The terminal in most such cases consists essentially of a display screen (monitor) and a keyboard, much like that of a typewriter, used to issue the commands to the computer that cause it to perform specified tasks.

In schools where the mainframe facility is made available to students, there are short courses of instruction required prior to receiving permission to use it. The student is then typically given an access code and is required to record the time and the procedures used, called logging in. At one time the mainframe was the chief resource for students, and it is still a good one, but the rapid recent growth of microcomputer use has tended to move them into the forefront for the kinds of procedures T/D students require.

MODEMS allow telephone line communication, short or long distance, between computers and the linking of one system to another. With a modem, one can access the resources of other PCs, minicomputers, or mainframe systems of universities, of research centers, of businesses and foundations, and of other public or private organizations. An investigator can use a modem at home to dial into and use an office computer (or the reverse). The portability of a modem (about the size of an average textbook) is one of its great advantages. Recently there have been advances in the design of a fax-modem, one that more and more approaches the capabilities of a faxing machine and of a modem. The fax-modem promises to greatly increase the capability of researchers to bring together all relevant material on a topic electronically and to arrange for research collaborators or research subjects to both view and read the same material at the same time and give reactions speedily. Also, some newer computers, including laptop and notebook types, are designed with both fax and modem capabilities built in or readily added.

MONITOR designates the display screen on which the computer operator sees the words, the graphics, the tables, and whatever else has resulted from the commands the operator has given.

NOTEBOOK designates a portable personal computer (PC) style that has enormous advantages for researchers whose investigations require them to travel or to work for significant periods of time away from their offices or laboratories. Modern notebook PCs are powerful, fast, and truly portable, measuring about 9″ × 12″ × 3″ and weighing 7 or 8 pounds, with battery. Advances in miniturization promise increasingly capable notebooks now and in the immediate future.

OPERATING SYSTEM designates the main program that tells the computer the way to perform basic functions like writing on discs, reading discs, responding to input from the keyboard, managing files, and similar fundamental activities. To be of any use, a computer requires an operating system. The system called MS-DOS, or Microsoft Disc Operating System, became the industry standard when adopted by IBM in 1981. About the same time Windows was introduced as a graphic extension of MS-DOS to make a number of operations simpler to use. Since compatibility is essential between the computer's operating system and any added software package, the researcher must recognize that fact in planning computer usage at any stage of an investigation.

PASSWORD is similar to access code, except that a password is more often used to allow entry to a specific program. If the researcher wishes to keep private the content of a particular program or file, the computer can be directed to allow it to be run only if a particular term or expression known only to the operator is used to call it up from memory.

PRINTERS, of which there are three types, are accessories to computers that make it possible for the researcher to turn stored information into typed documents. The three widely used printer types, dot matrix, ink jet, and laser, all can be of use to the researcher. For preparing final documents, however, laser printers offer the most advantages and are technologically the most advanced. Their reproduction approaches typeset print in quality; they are fast; they handle graphics well; and they are reliable for producing large numbers of documents.

SHAREWARE refers to software usually created by a person to help deal with a particular and specific problem for which commercial software packages are not available. There are shareware products for almost every computer-amenable task imaginable. They usually are amateurish, lacking the svelte quality of professional work. The researcher who wishes to search for a program in the shareware category can do so by using computer bulletin boards, programs at conventions of persons interested in the researcher's field of study and investigation, and by communication directly with persons who have published recently in the same research area. The shareware in existence is usually inexpensive, but it does pay to test-run it to ascertain if it has any serious flaws.

SMARTPHONE is a telephone that incorporates a variety of functions ordinarily found in a computer. The more versatile the smartphone, the greater its potential usefulness in data gathering and organizing and in other ways saving the time of the researcher. These technologically advanced marriages of computer and telephone are marketed by several companies, so it is best to examine several to see which best fits the individual researcher's needs.

SOFTWARE, or program, is a group or a collection of instructions that spells out or directs the computer as to what to do. Software is typically organized into files in the computer's memory, the files being simply lists of instructions. When the computer is told to run a piece of software, first it opens and loads the file into memory, and second, it starts executing the commands one after another. The execution results in a computer program — a database or a word processor, for example. Software is made up of information, as opposed to hardware, the material components and wiring of the computer.

SOFTWARE PIRACY is white-collar crime against software vendors. Companies that manufacture software (Lotus, dBase, Word-Perfect) defend themselves vigorously against anyone who obtains and uses their products without paying for them. Any university or other agency using unlicensed software faces heavy fines and possibly other penalties. The same is true for individuals. Research integrity includes knowing and being guided by institutional standards and personal honesty.

SOUND, including actual or imitated human voice and noises of the natural environment, may be added to most computers by employing an expansion board. In some cases there can be stereophonic effects, and real electronic piano keyboards may be incorporated. Also, mixtures of sound and graphics bring multimedia potential to computer output. The possibilities in this extended computer capability in doing and reporting research in the arts, the sciences, and the professions are extraordinary.

SPREADSHEET refers to a program designed to allow the user to readily manipulate numbers or symbols. A spreadsheet appears as a grid on the display screen. Numbers or other characters may be typed into the grid blocks. The program may then be directed to compute almost anything from simple sums or averages to regression analyses. Available programs (e.g., Lotus 123, Microsoft Excel, Microsoft Works) can also be directed to produce graphs and charts, in some cases in color.

STATISTICAL PACKAGES are programs that perform designated analyses on data provided by the researcher. An example is SPSS, or its updated version SPSS-X, which stands for Statistical Package for the Social Sciences (Norusis, 1982, 1983). This package is probably available to students and staff in more college and university LANs than any other. A module called SPSS for Windows Base allows data and file management and has color, analytic graphics, and a report-writing facility. The statistical component of the package includes summary statistics (univariate, crosstabs, exploratory data analysis), mean comparisons (means, t-tests, one-way ANOVA, and ANOVA with covariates), correlation (bivariate and partial), 16 nonparametric tests, and analysis of multiple response data. A more advanced module called SPSS Professional Statistics includes nonparametric correlations, proximity measures, hierarchical and k-mean cluster analysis, factor and discriminant analysis, multidimensional scaling, and item analysis.

To decide which of the many available packages is most suitable for a particular investigation, the student will probably need help from the T/D committee or a consultant suggested by the advisor. The reason: some packages provide more information than others; some are more fine-tuned than others; some express and display results in different ways than others; some are more complex to use than others; and some are more expensive than others. A good rule: determine from the committee what will be the minimum essential statistics that need to be reported in the final T/D document. Then choose the statistical package that will give those essentials with least effort and expense.

Colleges and universities that offer T/D work now usually have a centralized computer and consultation service center. In large institutions individual schools or departments often have their own facilities. Such centers are good places to seek advice on statistical packages, as well as on other aspects of research procedures.

TERMINAL designates a location from which commands can be given to a computer. It consists primarily of a keyboard much like that of a typewriter, plus a lighted screen on which input and output from the terminal to the computer and back may be displayed. (*See also* MAINFRAME.)

VGA is the acronym for video graphics array, the most common computer display format for presenting information in other than verbal or numerical form. Grayscale presents graphics in black, white, and shades of gray. Color VGA permits displays in up to 16 colors. Super VGA, allowing up to 256 color variations, is available, too, but not all graphics programs are designed so as to take advantage of it.

VIRUS is a term borrowed from physiology to refer to any destructive program of unknown origin that might enter a computer without the owner's knowledge, reproduce itself, and attach itself to and damage other programs when they are run. Sometimes a virus causes the computer's memory to malfunction. The best safeguard against a virus is prevention by avoiding shareware, write-protecting your disks, using software bought from the manufacturer, and avoiding file trading. Your computer can be invaded by a virus only if it is carried by a program you run.

WORD PROCESSOR is the electronic typewriter in its ultimate form, a device on which one can do everything from create to publish, and which all but thinks for its user. Word processors come in two basic forms, both widely utilized. One is basically an elaborated typewriter able to perform all the "processes" listed below. A second form of word processor is a program to be run in a computer, allowing it to perform the same "processes," which include:

Create text	Edit text	Reformat text
Check spelling	Check grammar	Punctuation
Outline	File	Paginate
Change type	Make tables	Paragraph
Add text	Delete text	Insert text
Move text	Footnote	Citation
Bibliography	Store text	Print text
Insert paper	Draft text	Thesaurus
Typo check	Display text	Word count
Phrase alert	Error check	Mailing list
Right justify	Make copies	Word search
Phrase search	Title	Subtitle
Time line	Date calendar	Merge text

Word processors of both types can be instructed by the one using them to do all of the above, and other tasks, as well. For the researcher for whom discourse, verbal description, argument, and the like make up the content of the T/D being prepared, probably the augmented typewriter form of word processor is quite satisfactory. But for most researchers, the word processor program plus the computer will prove much more useful because of both its greater flexibility and the many ways other features of the computer can be integrated with or added to the word processor features.

Appendix B: Suggested Proposal and Project Guidelines

The following three outlines supplement material that appears in the text and may stimulate students to consider additional ways to structure their thinking about theses and dissertations. It is possible to combine parts of these outlines, to add or delete parts, and, of course, to create new outlines. As we have said, there is no fixed recipe for outlining research projects. There is no substitute for thought. These are examples, only, of ways to structure thought and problems.

The outlines illustrate ways to set up frameworks for thinking through various types of problems or issues of significance to the professional and academic disciplines. It can be seen that they all have a common theme: the identification and specification of some matter for study and the orderly process of working toward a solution. Students are encouraged to adapt these, and others that appear in the text, to suit the particular studies they wish to address.

Example A: Empirical Investigation Outline
 I. Statement of the problem
    A. The general concern that makes this a matter of significant and current interest.

B. The specific practical problem that needs to be researched in order to enhance practice or understanding, design policy, or determine action.

II. The theoretical framework
   A. Name(s) and brief description(s) of relevant theory(ies) to be utilized in approaching the problem.
   B. Review of major concepts and their interrelationships derived from existing theoretical work.

III. Review of literature
   A. Discuss how the theoretical framework or its components have been used in existing empirical studies.
   B. Relate the literature review to the utilization of concepts in the current study. Show how existing literature points to the need for the specific investigation proposed.

IV. Methodology
   A. The research problem — the statement of a relationship to be tested (general hypothesis). In some cases of exploratory research, it may not be appropriate to formulate hypotheses. Instead, state precise research questions with a specification of variables to be included.
      1. Specification of variables: give objective definitions of each variable that will be controlled, measured, or manipulated.
      2. Specification of interrelationships between variables: the dependent variable(s) (goal or result), the independent variables (factors that relate to the goal or result), and the intervening variables.
   B. The specific working hypotheses.
      1. Break down the general hypothesis and state specifically the exact type of relationship expected between the independent and dependent variable(s).
      2. State the exact type of relationship expected between each of the identified subpopulations and each of the subresults expected. (How will the introduction of intervening variables affect the general results?)

C. Operational definitions: Define each term in the statement of the relationship to be tested so that it is carefully
delimited. This includes each of the variables of concern
and the population under study.
D. Limitations and delimitations: Specify each under the
appropriate subheading.
E. Procedures.
  1. Procedures for collecting data.
    a. General plan: State in words and provide a diagram,
      if feasible.
    b. Population and sample: Indicate how selected and
      criteria used.
    c. Date and instrumentation: Include all relevant data
      and instruments.
    d. Mode of analysis: Describe both the techniques and
      their application.
    e. Time schedule: Utilize a Time Line or PERT for-
      mat.
  2. Pretest and results.
Overview Takes Place Here
 V. Collection, analysis, and interpretation of data
  A. Collection of data.
  B. Processing and tabulation.
  C. Carrying out appropriate tests for analysis.
  D. Interpretation of data.
VI. Summary and conclusions
  A. Generalizations from research results to theoretical
    framework.
  B. Serendipitous findings.
  C. Practical implications of research results (professional
    development, for practice, for policy, for action, and so
    forth).
  D. Limitations of the study.
  E. Implications for further research and practice.
Example B: Policy Analysis Investigation Outline
  I. Statement or definition of the problem

A. The general concern(s) that make(s) this a significant problem of current interest.
B. The specific point(s) of focus of this proposed study within the general concern(s).
II. Conceptualizing the problem for analysis
   A. Outlining the dimensions or the parameters of the factors of concern.
   B. Demonstrating the interrelationships of these factors for a general framework of approach.
III. Relevant literature: Discussing sources, including theories and principles, from which the problem conceptualization was derived, including any studies that have been made use of or can be related to the problem conceptualization or some aspect of it.
IV. Specifying the problem of analysis
   A. The specific questions or propositions to guide the analytic effort.
   B. The concepts or variables that will be used systematically in the analytic effort.
   C. Operational definitions of concepts.
   D. Strategy or design for making inferences about data.
V. Procedures
   A. For collecting evidence or data.
      1. General design.
      2. Sources of evidence or data.
      3. Instruments or techniques for collecting/extracting evidence or data.
      4. Mode of analysis planned.
Overview Takes Place Here
VI. Collection and analysis of evidence or data
   A. Carrying out the library and/or field research.
   B. Carrying out the specified mode of analysis.
   C. Analysis and interpretation of findings.
VII. Summary and conclusions
   A. Relating the findings to the original conceptualization of the problem.

B. Serendipitous findings.

C. Specifying the implications of the study for the policy concern.

D. Suggesting further efforts in policy analysis with some specific reference to limitations of the present study.

Example C: Theoretical Synthesis Investigation Outline

I. Statement of the problem

A. The general concern(s) that make(s) it relevant and desirable to attempt a synthesis of a particular body of knowledge or theory or of two or more related theoretical or conceptual perspectives.

B. Describe the specific points of focus of this effort within the general concern(s).

II. Developing a framework for theoretical synthesis

A. A concise but comprehensive overview of the major concepts in the knowledge, conceptual, or theoretical body(ies) of concern.

B. Specification of the perceived problems or gaps in knowledge, conceptual, or theoretical coherence.

III. Relevant literature: A preliminary review of existing conceptual and theoretical work in the area of concern(s), including key empirical studies employing relevant concepts and theoretical constructs

IV. Methodology

A. Specifying the problem for synthesis.

1. Identifying the specific dimensions to be addressed in the synthesis (e.g., conceptual confusion, conceptual conflicts, conflict in research findings relevant to theory).

2. Operational definitions.

a. Of major concepts.

b. Of variables standing for concepts as used in research.

3. Strategy or design for synthetic efforts (identifying the relevant population of sources and how they will be sampled, if appropriate).

B. Procedures for collecting and analyzing relevant information for synthesis.
 1. Sources of analysis for conceptually and theoretically relevant material.
 2. Sources of relevant research to shed light on conceptual or theoretical adequacy or to assist in resolving conceptual or theoretical conflict.
 3. Techniques for extracting systematic information from secondary sources.
 4. Planned mode(s) of analysis.

Overview Takes Place Here
 V. Collection and analysis of information
 A. Carrying out the library and related informational source research.
 B. Carrying out the specified mode(s) of analysis.
 C. Analysis and interpretation of results of inquiry: toward a conceptual and theoretical synthesis.
 VI. Summary and conclusions
 A. Presenting a new model for conceptual or theoretical approach(es) on the basis of the inquiry.
 B. Specifying the implications for the further study of professional problems or issues under the guidance of the new model.
 C. Suggesting the implications for further concept or theory building with specific reference to limitations of the present study.

Appendix C: Course Outline

This course outline is designed for faculty who teach or plan to teach courses on thesis or dissertation research and preparation. The outline below is the result of years of development by several faculty with many classes and students.

The two aspects of the course that over the years have seemed most successful have been the required weekly written preparation leading to the draft overview, and the classroom simulation. Thus every student, in a step-by-step sequence, has to provide a draft overview document in order to successfully meet the course requirements. Also, every student must become familiar with the overview meeting by simulating each role actually present in the real overview meeting.

Students are expected to be important contributors to the seminar learning process and thus are required to review critically their own work, the work of their peers, and disserations completed by others. The experience of the authors has been that the overwhelming majority of those who successfully complete the course successfully defend the overview proposal in committee.

RESEARCH SEMINAR

Term:_____
Time:_____
Place:_____

Instructor:_____
Telephone:_____

SEMINAR OBJECTIVE AND CONTENT

The objective of the instructor is to help students use research as a tool in seeking solutions to significant problems by developing dissertation proposals.

The seminar is concerned with the problems of designing and conducting dissertation research. More specifically, the course is designed to assist the student with the following:

1. A critical review of selection studies.
2. Identification of the trends in the body of research in order to become familiar with current concerns as well as to point out research needs.
3. Formulation and evaluation of researchable problems.
4. Development of a research design that employs appropriate methodology for dealing with the formulated problem.
5. Experiential learning through a simulated presentation of the overview to a committee comprised of class members and the instructor.

WHO SHOULD TAKE THE COURSE

The seminar is appropriate for students who are nearing the end of required graduate study, and who are ready to begin serious work on the dissertation proposal. Thus, the instructor assumes that each student:

1. has successfully completed the required graduate courses in research methodology and disciplined inquiry;
2. has identified a dissertation topic, or topic area, that is acceptable to the research advisor;
3. has established a schedule that will make it possible to be in frequent contact with the research advisor about the topic as it develops;

4. has established a schedule that will permit concentrated work over the time of the term, having as a firm goal the completion of the overview (dissertation proposal) in draft form by the end of the seminar.

EVALUATION

This seminar is designed for graduate students who are prepared to engage in serious and scholarly preparation of a dissertation proposal. Students in this course are expected to assume a collegial role, and their substantive and methodological contributions to class discussions and colleagues' work are expected to be substantial, scholarly, and informative.

Given the above, and the fact that grades are required, evaluation will be based partly on the quality and relevance of class contributions, including evidence that members of the class have read, understood, and are able to critique the readings.

Therefore, it should be clear that for your education, as well as others, a commitment is necessary. Your presence and contribution is important and is required for a successful class. Please do not waste the time and money of other students by coming to class unprepared, or by failing to be present to contribute your insight into the work of your colleagues. Unexcused absences are evidence of lack of commitment to study, and will be considered in the evaluation. Absences and incomplete work will, of course, be part of evaluation and may result in an incomplete or failing grade. If you cannot make the commitment, or are unwilling to undergo the discipline of class requirements, the first meeting of the class is the point at which it is appropriate to drop the class.

Each student will be asked to demonstrate computer proficiency or attend a computer workshop, designed to demonstrate the uses of the computer in the development, design, writing, and execution of the dissertation proposal. Those who are already computer-literate will be expected to perfect their skills by, for example, learning to use software designed to help write proposals and scholarly papers.

An acceptable dissertation proposal must be submitted before the course is successfully completed. That means that a proposal draft, acceptable to the research advisor, must be submitted to the instructor before a letter grade is awarded.

TEXT

Mauch, J. E., and Birch, J. W. (1993). *Guide to the successful thesis and dissertation* (3rd ed.). New York: Marcel Dekker.

In addition, each student is asked to have available a recent edition of *one* of the style manuals acceptable to the school. Students will be required to conform to *one* style manual in completing class assignments. The following style manuals are commonly used and are available at the book store:

American Psychological Association (1986). *Publication manual of the American Psychological Association* (3rd ed.). Washington, DC: Author.

Turabian, K. L. (1987). *A manual for writers of term papers, theses and dissertations* (5th ed.). Chicago: University of Chicago Press.

COURSE ASSIGNMENTS

Assignment 1

Describe your topic to be developed as an overview proposal. Length—one page or less, single spaced. Include: Name and Date, Title, Problem Statement, and Proposed Methodology. Prepare sufficient copies to be distributed to the class for the discussion. Each seminar participant will provide written comments to the writer of the description. Each person will be given a short period to discuss the project during the seminar and to receive additional feedback from the other participants.

Assignment 2

Based on comments from class, prepare the introduction and problem chapter of your proposal. This is a draft. Concentrate on writing clearly what you want to tell the reader in three or four pages. Substance and clarity are more important than format. Avoid big words, use your own language. Make enough copies for class, so all can read and critique.

Assignment 3

Each student will be required to attend a workshop, designed to provide experience in using the computer to search the university online library catalog, containing over 1/2 million citations. Additionally, during this same class, students will have the opportunity to do computer searching of a bibliographic database programmed for retrieval, such as ERIC, Dissertation Abstracts, Dialog.

Assignment 4

Based on comments from class, continue, as above, with the review of the literature. This could be 20 pages easily, but more important than length is the submission of something for colleagues to review.

Assignment 5

Review and evaluate three dissertations relevant to your chosen topic. Prepare a written critique of each, one or two pages in length. Be prepared to present this in class.

Assignment 6

Based on comments from class, continue as above with the research design.

Assignment 7

Based on comments from class, continue as above with the preparation of the reference list.

Assignment 8

Develop a dissertation proposal (overview) to be presented to a simulated overview committee composed of class members. Length — minimum of 15 pages, maximum of 25. Copies should be available one week prior to the presentation to the committee.

Each student will be assigned to serve as a research advisor and as a committee member for other students. Research topics should also be discussed with student advisors as soon as possible.

Assignment 9

Review of the Literature, Research Design, Bibliography. When the parts have been put together, revised, and shared with the research advisor, they become the draft overview.

The dates of assignments may vary with the scheduling of instructional resources.

RESEARCH SEMINAR SCHEDULE

Meeting no.		Content/assignments
1	9/8	Introduction, objective, assignments. Text: Chapters 1, 2, and 3.
2	9/15	Description of proposed dissertation overview. Assignment 1 due. Chapter 4.
3	9/22	Introduction and Problem Statement. Assignment 2 due. Chapter 5.
4	9/29	Research sources. Assignment 3. Chapter 6.
5	10/6	Review of the Literature. Assignment 4. Chapter 7.
6	10/13	Dissertation Critique. Assignment 5.
7	10/20	Research Design. Assignment 6.
8	10/27	Reference List. Assignment 7.
9	11/3	Completion of draft research proposal. Assignment 8 due. Chapters 8 and 9.
10	11/10	Simulated overviews through last class. Assignment 9.
11	11/17	1._____ 2._____
12	11/24	1._____ 2._____
13	12/1	1._____ 2._____
14	12/8	Class evaluation and review. Chapter 10.

References

Adler, A. G. (1991). How should we cite references — Or should we? *American Psychologist, 47*, 424–425.

Allen, D. C. (1968). *The Ph.D. in English and American literature.* New York: Holt Rinehart and Winston.

Allen, G. R. (1973). *The graduate student's guide to theses and dissertations: A practical manual for writing and research.* San Francisco: Jossey-Bass.

American Association of University Professors. (1981). Regulations governing research on human subjects. *Academe, 67*, 358–370.

American Educational Research Association. (1973). Editorial. *Educational Researcher, 2*(2).

American Institutes for Research. (1967). *Creative talent awards program.* Pittsburgh, PA: Author.

American Psychological Association. (1963). Ethical standards for psychologists. *American Psychologist, 18*, 56–60.

American Psychological Association. (1975). Guidelines for nonsexist use of language. *American Psychologist, 30*, 682–684.

American Psychological Association. (1982). *Ethical principles in the conduct of research with human participants.* Washington, DC: Author.

American Psychological Association. (1983). *Publication manual* (3rd ed.). Washington, DC: Author.

Anderson, S. B., Ball, S., and Murphy, R. T. (1975). *Encyclopedia of educational evaluation*. San Francisco: Jossey-Bass.

Andrews, F. M., Klem, L., Davidson, T. N., O'Malley, P. M., and Rogers, W. L. (1981). *A guide for selecting statistical techniques for analyzing social science data* (2nd ed.). Ann Arbor, MI: Institute for Social Research, The University of Michigan.

Asher, W. (1990). Educational psychology, research methodology, and meta-analysis. *Educational Psychologist, 25*(2), 23–28.

Association of American Universities and Association of Graduate Schools in the Association of American Universities. (1990). *Institutional policies to improve doctoral education*. Washington, DC: Author.

Atkinson, R. C. (1990). Supply and demand for scientists and engineers: A national crisis in the making. *Science, 248*, 425–432.

Baker, E. I. (1978). Evaluation dimensions for program development and improvement. *New Directions for Program Evaluation, 1*, 59–72.

Barass, R. (1978). *Scientists must write: A guide to better writing for scientists, engineers, and students*. New York: Wiley.

Barzun, J. (1985). *Simple and direct: A rhetoric for writers*. New York: Harper and Row.

Barzun, J., and Graff, H. F. (1985). *The modern researcher* (4th ed.). San Diego, CA: Harcourt Brace Jovanovich.

Baumrind, D. (1964). Some thoughts on ethics in research: After reading Milgram's "Behavioral Study of Obedience." *American Psychologist, 19*, 421–423.

Baumrind, D. (1971). Principles of ethical conduct in the treatment of subjects: Reaction to the draft report of the committee on ethical standards in psychological research. *American Psychologist, 26*, 887–896.

Becker, H. S. (1986). *Writing for social scientists*. Chicago: University of Chicago Press.

Bernstein, T. M. (1978). *The careful writer*. New York: Atheneum.

Blanton, J. S. (1983). Midwifing the dissertation. *Teaching of Psychology, 10,* 74–76.

Borg, W. R., and Gall, M. D. (1983). *Educational research: An introduction* (3rd Ed.). White Plains, NY: Longman.

Borgman, C., et al (1984). *Effective online searching: A basic text.* New York: Marcel Dekker.

Bowen, W. G. (1981). *Graduate education in the arts and sciences: Prospects for the future.* Report of the President. Princeton, NJ: Princeton University.

Bowen, W. G., and Rudenstine, N. L. (1992). *In pursuit of the Ph.D.* Princeton, NJ: Princeton University Press.

Brooks, P. C. (1969). *Research in archives: The use of unpublished primary sources.* Chicago: University of Chicago Press.

Brown, J. H. U. (1980). The philosophy of an institutional review board for the protection of human subjects. *Journal of Medical Education, 55,* 67–69.

Buros, O. K. (Ed.). (1972). *The sixth mental measurements yearbook.* Highland Park, NJ: Gryphone Press.

Burstein, L. (1980). Issues in the aggregation of data. In D. C. Berliner (Ed.). *Review of research in education.* Washington, DC: American Educational Research Association.

Calfee, R. (1981). Cognitive psychology and educational practice. In D. C. Berliner (Ed.). *Review of research in education.* Washington, DC: American Educational Research Association.

Callahan, L. G., and Glennon, V. J. (1975). *Elementary school mathematics: A guide to current research* (4th ed.). Washington, DC: Association for Supervision and Curriculum Development.

Campbell, D. T., and Stanley, J. C. (1963). *Experimental and quasi-experimental designs for research.* Chicago: Rand McNally.

Campbell, W. G., Ballou, S. V., and Slade, C. (1986). *Form and style: Theses, reports, terms papers* (7th ed.). Boston: Houghton Mifflin.

Carnegie Commission on Higher Education. (1970). *Less time, more options: Education beyond high school.* New York: McGraw-Hill.

Castetter, W. B., and Heisler, R. S. (1980). *Developing and defending a dissertation proposal.* Philadelphia: University of Pennsylvania.

Clark, B. R. (1983). *The higher education system.* Berkeley, CA: University of California Press.

Clemente, F. (1973). Early determinants of research productivity. *American Journal of Sociology, 79,* 409–419.

Cone, John D., and Foster, Sharon L. *(1993). Dissertations and Theses From Start to Finish.* Washington, DC: American Psychological Association.

Connell, R. W. (1985). How to supervise a Ph.D. *Vestes, 28,* 38–42.

Cook, D. L. (1966). *PERT: Program evaluation and review technique applications in education.* Washington, DC: U.S. Government Printing Office.

Cook. T. J., and Campbell, D. T. (1979). *Quasi-experimentation: Design and analysis issues for field studies.* Chicago: Rand McNally.

Cooley, W. W., and Bickel, W. (1986). *Decision-oriented educational research.* Hingham, MA: Kluwer Academic Publishers.

Cooley, W. W., and Lohnes, P. R. (1976). *Evaluation research in education: Theory, principles and practice.* New York: Halstead Press.

Cortada, J. W., and Winkler, V. C. (1979). *The way to win in graduate school.* Englewood Cliffs, NJ: Prentice-Hall.

Council of Graduate Schools. (1988). *Enhancing minority presence in graduate education.* Washington, DC: Author.

Council of Graduate Schools. (1990a). *Academic review of graduate programs.* Washington, DC: Author.

Council of Graduate Schools. (1990b). *The doctor of philosophy degree.* Washington, DC: Author.

Council of Graduate Schools. (1990c). *Organization and administration of graduate education.* Washington, DC: Author.

Council of Graduate Schools. (1991a). *International graduate students.* Washington, DC: Author.

Council of Graduate Schools. (1991b). *The role and nature of the doctoral dissertation.* Washington, DC: Author.

Cowley, W. H., and Williams, D. (1991). *International and historical roots of American higher education.* New York: Garland.

Cronbach, L. J. (1982). *Designing evaluations of educational and social programs.* San Francisco: Jossey-Bass.

Cronbach, L. J., and Suppes, P. (Eds.). (1969). *Research for tomorrow's schools: A disciplined inquiry for education.* New York: MacMillan.

Davis, C. R., and David, C. R. (1975). The Buckley regulations: Rights and restraints. *Educational Researcher, 4,* 11–13.

Davis, G. B. (1979). *Writing the doctoral dissertation: A systematic approach.* Woodbury, NY: Barron's Educational Series.

Day, R. A. (1979). *How to write and publish a scientific paper.* Philadelphia: Institute for Scientific Information Press.

Dearing, B., and Lederer, G. P. (1968). Trends in graduate education. *American Education, 4,* 6–7.

Declaration of Helsinki: Recommendations Guiding Doctors in Clinical Research. (1964). Adopted by the 18th World Medical Assembly, Helsinki, Finland, 1964. Cited in *World Medical Journal, 11,* 28.

Dillman, D. A. (1978). *The mail and telephone survey: The total design method.* New York: Wiley-Interscience.

Dressel, P. L., and Mayhew, L. B. (1974). *Higher education as a field of study.* San Francisco: Jossey-Bass.

Ducanis, A. J., and Golin, A. K. (1979). *The interdisciplinary health care team.* Rockville, MD: Aspen.

Dunne, P. F. (1969). *Dissertations by Mr. Dooley.* Upper Saddle River, NJ: Literature House.

Ebbitt, W. R., and Ebbitt, D. R. (1982). *Writer's guide and index to English* (7th ed.). Glenview, IL: Scott, Foresman.

Educational Testing Service. (1974). *Flexibility for the future.* Princeton, NJ: Author.

Edwards, M. (1974). *Studies in American graduate education.* New York: The Carnegie Foundation for the Advancement of Teaching.

Eichelberger, R. T. (1989). *Disciplined inquiry: Understanding and doing educational research.* New York: Longman.

Eisenhart, C. (1968). Expression of the uncertainties of results. *Science*, *160*(3833), 1201–1204.

Eisner, E. W., and Peskkin, A. (Eds.) (1990). *Qualitative inquiry in education: The continuing debate.* New York: Teachers College Press.

ERIC Clearinghouse on Educational Management. (1974). *Newsletter*, *7*, 3.

Etzold, T. H. (1976). Writing for publication: The art of the article. *Phi Delta Kappan*, *57*, 614–615.

Evans, B., and Evans, C. (1957). *A dictionary of contemporary American usage.* New York: Random House.

Fenner, P., and Armstrong, M. C. (1981). *A practical guide to finding information.* Los Altos, CA: William Kaufman.

Flexner, S. B. (Ed.). (1987). *The Random House dictionary of the English language* (2nd ed.). New York: Random House.

Follett, W. (1979). *Modern American usage: A guide.* New York: Hill and Wang.

Fowler, H. W. (1965). *A dictionary of modern English usage* (2nd ed.). Oxford, England: Clarendon Press.

Furniss, W. T. (1980). In spite of every sage: The value of a degree. *Educational Record*, *61*, 3642.

Gallagher, J. J. (1985). *Teaching the gifted child* (3rd ed.). Boston: Allyn and Bacon.

Gardner, D. C., and Beatty, G. J. (1980). *Dissertation proposal guidebook: How to prepare a research proposal and get it accepted.* Springfield, IL: Charles C. Thomas.

Gardner, J. W. (1978). *Excellence.* New York: Harper and Row.

Garfield, S., and Bergin, A. E. (1978). *Handbook of psychotherapy and behavior change: An empirical analysis* (2nd ed.). New York: Wiley.

Gay, L. R. (1992). *Educational research competencies for analysis and application* (4th Ed.). New York: Merrill.

Germeroth, D. (1990, November). *Lonely days and lonely nights: Completing the doctoral dissertation.* Paper presented at the annual meeting of the Speech Communication Association, Chicago, IL.

Gibaldi, J., and Achtert, W. S. (1988). *MLA handbook for writers of research papers* (2nd ed.). New York: Modern Language Association of America.

Glass, G. V. (1977). Integrating findings: The meta-analysis of research. In L. S. Shulman (Ed.). *Review of Research in Education.* Itasca, IL: F. E. Peacock.

Glazer, J. S. (1986). *The master's degree: Tradition, diversity, innovation.* ASHE/ERIC Higher Education Report. Washington, DC: Association for the Study of Higher Education.

Golin, A. K., and Ducanis, A. J. (1981). *The interdisciplinary team.* Rockville, MD: Aspen, 1981.

Good, C. V. (Ed.). (1973). *Dictionary of education* (3rd ed.). New York: McGraw-Hill.

Gorman, R. A. (1987). Copyright and the professorate: A primer and some recent developments. *Academe, 73,* 29-33.

Gorn, J. L. (1973). *Style guide for writers of term papers, masters' theses, and doctoral dissertations.* New York: Simon and Schuster.

Greenberg, B. (1987). *Using microcomputer and mainframes for data analysis in the social sciences.* Columbus, OH: Merrill.

Guba, E. G. (1967). *Educational improvement and the role of educational research.* Bloomington, IN: The National Center for the Study of Educational Change.

Halstead, D. K. (Ed.). (1981). *Higher education: A bibliographic handbook* (2 vols.). Washington, DC: U.S. Government Printing Office.

Hanson, D. P., and Penrod, D. A. (1980). *A desk reference of legal terms for school psychologists and special educators.* Springfield, IL: Charles C. Thomas.

Harvey, J. (1972). *The student in graduate school.* Washington, DC: American Association for Higher Education.

Haskins, C. H. (1957). *The rise of universities.* London: Cornell University Press.

Heinrich, K. T. Loving partnerships: dealing with sexual attraction and power in doctoral advisement relationships. *Journal of Higher Education,* 62:5 (September-October 1991) 514–538.

Hodges, L. V. (1986). Issues on meta-analysis. In E. Z. Rothkopf (Ed.). *Review of research in education.* Washington, DC: American Educational Research Association.

Honor in science. (1991). Research Triangle Park, NC: Sigma Xi, The Scientific Research Society.

Hudson, H. C. (Ed.). (1982). *Classifying social data: New applications of analytic methods for social science research.* San Francisco: Jossey-Bass.

In brief. (1992). News and notes from higher education. *Academe,* p. 5.

Ingelfinger, F. J. (1972). Informed (but uneducated) consent. *New England Journal of Medicine, 287,* 465–466.

Institute of International Education. (1990). *Open Doors.* New York: Author.

Isaac, P. D., Koenigsknecht, R. A., Malaney, G. D., and Karras, J. E. (1989). Factors related to doctoral dissertation topic selection. *Research in Higher Education, 30,* 357–373.

Issac, S., and Michaels, W. B. (1971). *Handbook in research and evaluation.* San Diego, CA: Robert R. Knapp.

Jackson, E. P. (1986). *Meta-analysis of school-based consultation outcome research.* Unpublished doctoral dissertation, University of Pittsburgh.

James, P. E. (1960). The dissertation requirement. *School and Society, 88,* pp. 147–148.

Jencks, C., and Riesman, D. (1968). *The academic revolution.* Garden City, NY: Doubleday.

Johnson, H. W. (1984). *How to use the business library, with sources of business information* (5th ed.). Cincinnati, OH: South-Western.

Johnston, J. M., and Pennypacker, H. S. (1980). *Strategies and tactics of human behavioral research.* Hillsdale, NJ: Lawrence Erlbaum Associates.

Jones, J. H. (1981). *Bad blood: The Tuskeegee syphilis experiment.* New York: Free Press.

Jordan, L. (Ed.). (1976). *The New York Times manual of style and usage.* New York: The New York Times Co.

Kerlinger, F. N. (1979). *Behavioral research: A conceptual approach.* New York: Holt, Rinehart and Winston.

Kerlinger, F. N. (1986). *Foundations of behavioral research* (3rd ed.). New York: Holt, Rinehart and Winston.

Kerr, C. (1963). *The uses of the university.* Cambridge, MA: Harvard University Press.

King, L. S. (1978). *Why not say it clearly? A guide to scientific writing.* Boston: Little, Brown.

Krathwohl, D. R. (1988). *How to prepare a research proposal* (3rd ed.). Syracuse, NY: Syracuse University Press.

Labovitz, S., and Hagedon, R. (1981). *Introduction to social research* (3rd ed.). New York: McGraw-Hill.

Lancy, D. (1993). *Qualitative research in education: An introduction to the major traditions.* New York: Longman.

LaPidus, J. B. (1990). *Research student and supervisor.* Washington, DC: Council of Graduate Schools.

Lee, M. E., Abd-Ella, M., and Burks, L. (1981). *Needs of foreign students from developing nations at U.S. colleges and universities.* Washington, DC: National Association for Foreign Student Affairs.

Leedy, P. D. (1985). *Practical research: Planning and design* (3rd ed.). New York: Macmillan.

Leinhardt, G., and Leinhardt, S. (1980). Exploratory data analysis: New tools for the analysis of empirical data. In D. C. Berliner (Ed.), *Review of research in education.* Washington, DC: American Educational Research Association.

Leinhardt, S. (Ed.). (1982). *Sociological methodology 1982*. San Francisco: Jossey Bass.

Lester, J. D. (1984). *Writing research papers* (4th ed.). Glenview, IL: Scott Foresman.

Lindvall, C. M. (1959). The review of related research. *Phi Delta Kappan*, *40*, 179–180.

Long, T. J., Convey, J. J., and Chwalek, A. R. (1985). *Completing dissertations in the behavioral sciences and education*. San Francisco: Jossey-Bass.

Lowman, R. P., Holt, V. E., and O'Bryant, C. (1982). *Guide to research support*. Washington, DC: American Psychological Association.

MacKinnon, D. W. (1962). The nature and nurture of creative talent. *American Psychologist*, *17*, 484–495.

Madsen, D. (1983). *Successful dissertations and theses*. San Francisco: Jossey-Bass.

Malden, H. (1935). *On the origin of universities and academical degrees*. London, England: J. Taylor.

Mallinkrodt, B., and Leong, F. (1992) International graduate students, stress, and social support. *Journal of College Student Development*, *33*, 71.

Manheimer, M. L. (1973). *Style manual: A guide for the preparation of reports and dissertation*. New York; Marcel Dekker.

Martin, R. (1980). *Writing and defending a thesis or dissertation in psychology and education*. Springfield, IL: Charles C. Thomas.

Mauch, J., and Spaulding, S. (1992). The internationalization of higher education: Who should be taught what and how? *Journal of General Education*, *41*, 111–129.

McConkie, G. (1977). Learning from test. In L. S. Shulman (Ed.). *Review of research in education*. Itasca, IL: F. E. Peacock.

Mecklenburger, J. A. (1972). "Merely journalism" as educational research. *Phi Delta Kappan*, *53*, 202.

Merriam, S. B. (1988). *Case study research in education: A qualitative approach.* San Francisco, CA: Jossey-Bass.

Merrill, G. E. (1992). The Ph.D., upholding the sciences. *Academe,* 78(5), 24–25.

Michaels, J. (1979). *An investigation of the prevailing practices of selected school districts and municipalities in the United States with regard to continuous residence requirements for public school employees.* Unpublished doctoral dissertation proposal. Pittsburgh: University of Pittsburgh.

Miles, M. B., and Huberman, A. M. (1984). *Qualitative data analysis: A sourcebook of new methods.* Newbury Park, CA: Sage Publications.

Milgram, S. (1973). Behavioral study of obedience. *Journal of Abnormal and Social Psychology, 67,* 371–378.

Miller, D. C. (1985). *Handbook of research design and social measurement* (4th ed.). New York: McKay.

Millman, J., and Gowin, D. B. (Eds.). (1974). *Appraising educational research: A case study approach.* Englewood Cliffs, NJ: Prentice-Hall.

Monaghan, P. (1989a, December 6). Psychologist specializes in counseling, graduate students who seem unable to finish their doctoral dissertations. *The Chronicle of Higher Education,* pp. A13–A16.

Monaghan, P. (1989b, March 29). Some fields are reassessing the value of the traditional doctoral dissertation. *The Chronicle of Higher Education,* p. A8.

Morris, W., and Morris, M. (1985). *Harper dictionary of contemporary usage* (2nd ed.). New York: Harper and Row.

Myers, R. A. (1993). The 1992 Leona Tyler Award Address. *The Counseling Psychologist, 21,* 326–337.

National Academy of Sciences. (1989). *On being a scientist.* Washington, DC: National Academy Press.

National Center for Educational Statistics. (1985). *The condition of education.* Washington, DC: U.S. Government Printing Office.

Neusner, J. (1977), May 31). The scholar's apprentice. *The Chronicle of Higher Education*, 40.

Newman, E. (1974). *Strictly speaking*. Indianapolis: Bobbs-Merill.

Norusis, M. J. (1982). *SPSS introductory guide: Basic statistics and operations*. Chicago, SPSS, Inc.

Norusis, M. J. (1983). *SPSS X introductory guide*. Chicago, SPSS, Inc.

Nuremberg Code cited in: *Trials of war criminals before the Nuremberg military tribunals under control council law*, (No. 10). Washington, DC: U.S. Government Printing Office. (n.d.).

Onions, C. T. (1964). *The shorter Oxford English dictionary on historical principles* (3rd ed.). London: Oxford University Press.

On line. (1992, March 11). *The Chronicle of Higher Education*, A18.

Osterlind, S. J., Udinsky, B. F., and Lynch, S. W. (1981). *Implementing the evaluation: A handbook for catering, analyzing and reporting data*. San Diego, CA: Edits Publishers.

Oxford English Dictionary, 13 Vols. (1933). Oxford, England: Clarendon Press.

Parker, F. (1986). *American dissertations on foreign education: A bibliography with abstracts*. Troy, NY: Whitston Pub. Co.

Parr, G., Bradley, L., and Bingin, R. (1992). Concerns and feelings of international graduate students. *Journal of College Student Development, 33*, 20.

Parsons, T. (1969). Research with human subjects and the professional complex. *Daedalus, 98*, 325–360.

Passow, A. H. (1979). *The gifted and the talented: Their education and development* (*78th NSSE Yearbook*). Chicago: University of Chicago Press.

Pederson, P. B. (1991). Counseling international students. *The Counseling Psychologist, 19*, 10–49.

Perrin, P. G. (1972). *Writer's guide and index to English* (5th ed.). Glenview, IL: Scott, Foresman.

Peters, D. P., and Ceci, S. J. (1980). A manuscript masquerade. *The Sciences, 20,* 16-19; 35.

Plimpton, G. (Ed.). (1976). *Writers at work: The Paris review interviews, seventh series.* New York: Viking.

Pool, R. (1990). Who will do science in the 1990's? *Science, 248,* 433-435.

Porter, A. L., and Wolfle, D. (1975). Study of the doctoral dissertation. *American Psychologist, 30,* 428-436.

Pournelle, J., and Banks, M. (1982). *PC communications bible.* Redmond, WA: Microsoft Press.

Pulling, B. S. (1992). The D. A., Alive in Idaho. *Academe, 78* (5), 23.

Quay, R. H. (1985). *Research in higher education: A guide to source bibliographies* (2nd ed.). Phoenix, AZ: Oryx Press.

Reynolds, J. Master's candidates' research skills. *Research Strategies, 5:*2 Spring, 1987, pp. 78-89.

Rice, J. (1989). Managing bibliographic information with person desktop technology. *Academe, 75*(4), 18-25.

Robertson, N., and Sistler, J. K. (1971). The doctorate in education. *Phi Delta Kappan.*

Root-Bernstein, R. S. (1989). Breaking faith. *The Sciences, 29,* 8-11.

Rothstein, L. F. (1991, March 11). Campuses and the disabled. *The Chronicle of Higher Education,* B3, B10.

Rutman, L. (Ed.). (1984). *Evaluation research methods: A basic guide* (2nd ed.). Beverly Hills, CA: Sage Publications.

Saalbach, R. C. (1955). The doctor of education degree. *Journal of Higher Education, 26,* 37-41.

Sadler, D. R. (1980). Conveying the findings of evaluative inquiry. *Educational Evaluation and Policy Analysis, 2,* 53-57.

Sanaff, A. P. (1980). Reaffirming intellectual standards. *Educational Record, 61,* 11-14.

Sax, G. (1968). *Empirical foundations of educational research.* Englewood Cliffs, NJ: Prentice-Hall.

Schein, E. H. (1972). *Professional education.* New York: McGraw-Hill.

Schuckman, H. (1987). Ph.D. recipients in psychology and biology. *American Psychologist, 42,* 987–992.

Scriven, M. (1980). Self referent research. *Educational Researcher, 9,* 11–30.

Seeman, J. (1973). On supervising student research. *American Psychologist, 28,* 900–906.

Sellin, D. F., and Birch, J. W. (1980). *Educating gifted and talented learners.* Rockville, MD: Aspen Systems Corporation.

Sellin, D. F., and Birch, J. W. (1981). *Psychoeducational developments of gifted and talented learners.* Rockville, MD: Aspen Systems Corporation.

Sellitz, C., Wrightsman, L. S., and Cook, S. W. (1976). *Research methods in social relations* (3rd ed.). New York: Holt, Rinehart and Winston.

Slavin, R. E. (1992). *Research methods in education.* Needham Heights, MA: Allyn & Bacon.

Smith, W. (1980). *Getting grants.* New York: Harper and Row.

Spring, M. B. (1991). *Electronic printing and publishing: The document processing revolution.* New York: Marcel Dekker.

Steggna, R. (1972). What is a university not? *Intellectual Digest, 2,* 55.

Sternberg, D. (1981). *How to complete and survive a doctoral dissertation.* New York: St. Martin's Press.

Struening, E. L., and Guttentag, M. (Eds.). (1975). *Handbook of evaluation research* (Vol. 1). Beverly Hills, CA: Sage Publications.

Strunk, W., Jr., and White, E. B. (1979). *The elements of style* (3rd ed.). New York: Macmillan.

Stuart, E. B. (1979). *A manual for preparation of theses and dissertations for the school of engineering* (4th ed.). Pittsburgh: The University of Pittsburgh (mimeo).

Taylor, M., and Powell, R. R. (1985). *Basic reference sources* (3rd ed.). Metuchen, NJ: Scarecrow.

Terman, L. (1954). The discovery and encouragement of exceptional talent. *American Psychologist, 9*, 221–223.

Thompson, B. (1980). Validity of an evaluator typology. *Educational Evaluation Policy Analysis, 2*, 59–65.

Travers, R. M. W. (1978). *An introduction to educational research* (4th ed.). New York: Macmillan.

Tufte, E. R. (1983). *The visual display of quantitative information.* Cheshire, CT: Graphics Press.

Tufte, E. R. (1990). *Envisioning information.* Cheshire, CT: Graphics Press.

Turabian, K. L. (1987). *A manual for writers of term papers, thesis, and dissertations,* (5th ed.). Chicago: University of Chicago Press.

U.S. Department of Health, Education and Welfare. (1974a). Protection of human subjects. *Federal Register, 39*(165), 30648–30657.

U.S. Department of Health, Education and Welfare. (1974b). Protection of human subjects. *Federal Register, 39*(208), 37993.

U.S. Department of Health and Human Services. Protection of human subjects. (1981). *Federal Register, 46*(16), 8366–8391.

U.S. Government Printing Office. (1984). *Style manual.* Washington, DC: Author.

University of Chicago. (1969). *A manual of style.* Chicago: University of Chicago Press.

University honors college. (1992). Pittsburgh: University of Pittsburgh.

University of Pittsburgh. (1974). *Office of Measurement and Evaluation.* Pittsburgh: Author (mimeo).

University of Pittsburgh, School of Education. (1981). *Style manual.* Pittsburgh: Author

van Leunen, M. C. (1979). *A handbook for scholars.* New York, NY: Knopf.

Van Til, W. (1986). *Writing for professional publication* (2nd ed.). Boston: Allyn and Bacon.

Vartuli, S. (Ed.) *The Ph.D. experience: a woman's point of view.* New York: Praeger Publishers, 1982.

Watson, G. (1987). *Writing a thesis: A guide to long essays and dissertations.* New York: Longman.

Webb, E. T. (1981). *Nonreactive measures in the social sciences* (2nd ed.). Boston: Houghton Mifflin.

White, P. *The Idea Factory: Learning to Think at MIT.* New York: Dutton, 1991.

Whitehead, A. N. (1953). *Science and the modern world.* New York: Macmillan.

White-Stevens, L. (1981). *Guidelines for writing and printing manuals.* Upper Montclaire, NJ: I.E.M. Innovative Educational Materials.

Wiersma, W. (1969). *Research methods in education.* Philadelphia: Lippincott.

Wilson, V. L. (1980). Research techniques in AERJ articles: 1969-1978. *Educational Research, 9,* 5-10.

Wittrock, M. C. (Ed.). (1986). *Handbook of research on teaching* (3rd ed.). New York: Macmillan.

Wolins, I. (1980). Secondary analysis in published research in the behavioral sciences. *New Directions for Higher Education, 4,* 45-56.

Woodbury, M. (1982). *A guide to sources of educational information* (2nd ed.). Arlington, VA: Information Resources Press.

York, C. C., Sobel, L., Gratch, B., and Pursel, J. (1988). Computerized reference sources: One stop shopping or part of a search strategy? *Research Strategies, 6*(1), 8-17.

Zinsser, W. (1980). *On writing well, an informal guide to writing nonfiction* (2nd ed.). New York: Harper and Row.

Ziolkowski, T. (1990). The Ph. D. Squid. *The American Scholar, 59,* 175-195.

Zuber-Skerritt, O. Helping postgraduate research students learn. *Higher Education 16*, pp. 75–94.

Zuber-Skerritt, O., and Knight, N. (1986). Problem definition and thesis writing. *Higher Education, 15,* 89–103.

Zusman, J., and Wurster, C. R. (Eds.). (1975). *Program evaluation: Alcohol drug abuse, and mental health services.* Lexington, MA: Lexington Books.

Author Index

Subject Index

Academic discipline, 10–16,
  26–27
Advice (*see also* Advisor)
  from committee members,
    129–130, 234
  defined, 231–232
  from students, 232–233
  technical, 232–235
  from typists, 234–235
Advisor
  advocacy, 34–36
  background, 30–31
  change of, 56–58
  as committee chairperson,
    29, 240–242
  ethical behavior, 45–47
  for foreign students, 31
  functions, 29–30, 233–
    234
  as mentor/tutor, 37–38, 40
  as model, 38–39, 240–242
  as principal investigator,
    216–217
  research, 29–59

[Advisor]
  responsibilities, 26–27, 40,
    43–54, 171–182, 212
  role, 31–36, 58, 171–182
  selection, 29–30, 54–58
  student-advisor interaction,
    32–37, 63
Appendices, 125–126
Archivist (*see* Libraries)

Bibliographer (*see* Libraries)
Bibliography, 126–127, 195,
  200–201
Bit-Net, 51

Citation, 25 (*see also*
    Bibliography)
Clearinghouse (*see* Databases)
Committee
  communication among
    members, 50-51